A Journal of the American Civil War

Managing Editor:
Mark A. Snell

Director, George Tyler Moore Center for the Study of the Civil War
Shepherd College, Shepherdstown, West Virginia

D1566069

VOLUME SIX   NUMBER TWO

Published quarterly by Regimental Studies, Inc.

Subscription and General Information

Civil War Regiments is published quarterly by Regimental Studies, Inc., an affiliation of Savas Publishing Company, 1475 South Bascom Avenue, Suite 204, Campbell, CA 95008. Executive Editor Theodore P. Savas, 408.879.9073 (voice); 408.879.9327; (fax); MHBooks@aol.com (E-Mail). Managing Editor Mark A. Snell may be contacted at the George Tyler Moore Center for the Study of the Civil War, 136 W. German Street, Shepherdstown, WV 25443. 304.876.5429 (voice); 304.876.5079 (fax). All manuscript inquiries should be directed to this address.

Trade distribution and back issues are handled by Peter Rossi at Stackpole Books, 5067 Ritter Road, Mechanicsburg, PA 17055-6921. Voice: 1-800-732-3669; Fax: 1-717-976-0412.

SUBSCRIPTIONS: $29.95/year, ppd (four books). Civil War Regiments (Subscriptions), 1475 South Bascom, Suite 204, Campbell, CA 95008, or call 1-408-879-9073. Prepayment with check, money order, or MC/V is required. Institutions will be billed. Two hundred and fifty signed and numbered four-issue Collector's Sets for the premier volume were printed. Cost is $40.00ppd. Inquire as to availability. Back issues may be ordered from Stackpole Books (see address above). FOREIGN ORDERS: Subscriptions: $35.95/year, including surface delivery. Payment in United States currency only or MC/V. Allow eight to twelve weeks for delivery.

MANUSCRIPTS AND CORRESPONDENCE: We welcome manuscript inquiries. For author's guidelines, send a self-addressed, double-stamped business envelope to: Editor, *Civil War Regiments*, 136 W. German Street, Shepherdstown, WV 25443. Include a brief description of your proposed topic and the sources to be utilized. No unsolicited submissions will be returned without proper postage. Book review inquiries should be directed to Archie McDonald, Book Review Editor, Stephen F. Austin University, Department of History, P.O. Box 6223, SFA Station, Nacogdoches, Texas 75962-6223. (409) 468-2407. Enclose a SASE if requesting a reply.

Regimental Studies, Inc., and Savas Publishing Company, expressly disclaims all responsibility for statements, whether of opinions or fact, contained herein. We are not responsible for journals lost in the mail because of failure to provide, in writing, timely notice of a change of address.

Thanks to your support, *Civil War Regiments* has been able to make a number of donations to Civil War-related preservation organizations. Some of the recipients of these donations are listed below:

(LIFE MEMBER) ASSOCIATION FOR THE PRESERVATION OF CIVIL WAR SITES

RICHARD B. GARNETT MEMORIAL, HOLLYWOOD CEMETERY

HERITAGEPAC / CIVIL WAR ROUND TABLE ASSOCIATES

SAVE HISTORIC ANTIETAM FOUNDATION / TURNER ASHBY HOUSE,
PORT REPUBLIC, VA

THE COKER HOUSE RESTORATION PROJECT, JACKSON, MS CWRT

AMERICAN BLUE & GRAY ASSOCIATION

APCWS 1993 MALVERN HILL/GLENDALE CAMPAIGN

SOUTH BAY CIVIL WAR ROUND TABLE PRESERVATION DRIVE

Cover Illustration:
"Federal Artillery at the Battle of Shepherdstown"
Antietam National Battlefield

Civil War Regiments: A Journal of the American Civil War, Vol. 6, No.2, Copyright 1998
by Regimental Studies, Inc., an affiliation of Savas Publishing Company
ISBN 1-882810-56-2

CONTRIBUTORS:

John Howard is the Superintendent, Antietam National Battlefield. He is a career park ranger who formerly served as the site manager of Monocacy National Battlefield.

Anders Henriksson chairs the Department of History at Shepherd College. He received his Ph.D. from the University of Toronto, and his specialty is Russian history. This is Dr. Henriksson's first published article on the American Civil War.

Helen Trimpi received her A.B. at Stanford and her Ph.D. in English at Harvard. She has taught English and American Literature at Stanford, Michigan State, College of Notre Dame, and University of Alberta. Her many publications include a historical study, *Melville's Confidence Men and American Politics in the 1850s* (1987). She currently is researching the role of Harvard alumni in Confederate service. Ms. Trimpi, a member of three Civil War Round Tables, makes her home in Palo Alto, California.

Terry A. Johnston, Jr. graduated from Tufts University and also hold an M.A. in history from Clemson. A free-lance associate editor with Savas Publishing Company, Terry is the editor of *"Him on one side and Me on the Other": The Civil War Letters of Alexander Campbell, 79th New York Infantry Regiment, and James Campbell, 1st South Carolina Battalion* (Columbia, 1998). He currently is studying for his doctorate at the University of Delaware.

B. Keith Toney is a free-lance historian and a Gettysburg Battlefield licensed guide. Keith writes frequently for various Civil War publications. He resides in Winchester, Virginia.

Mark A. Snell is the director of the George Tyler Moore Center for the Study of the Civil War at Shepherd College in Shepherdstown, West Virginia, where he also teaches American History and Civil War courses. Mark is the managing editor of *Civil War Regiments*. He makes his home in Gettysburg, Pennsylvania.

Ted Alexander is park historian at Antietam National Battlefield. He is the co-author of *When War This Way Passed* (1982), and numerous other articles and book reviews.

Scott Sherlock is an attorney with the United States Environmental Protection Agency. He received an A.B. in history from Franklin and Marshall College, and a J.D. from the University of Baltimore School of Law.

Table of Contents

INTRODUCTION

John Howard

Superintendent, Antietam National Battlefield

It is a great pleasure to introduce to the growing readership of this publication "The Maryland Campaign of 1862 and its Aftermath," the second Antietam issue of *Civil War Regiments: A Journal of the American Civil War*. The earlier publication, "Antietam: The Maryland Campaign of 1862" (Vol. 5, no. 3), focused on events leading up to the battle and the morning phase of the fighting. While the current issue also covers some of the preliminary maneuvering and fighting, it primarily includes aspects of battle's afternoon phase as well as events that occurred in the wake of this epic struggle, such as the fight at Shepherdstown and the Battle of Antietam's impact on the civilians of Sharpsburg.

Since the publication of the two Antietam studies, James Murfin's *The Gleam of Bayonets* (1965) and Stephen W. Sears' *Landscape Turned Red* (1983), historians have taken a more critical look at Antietam and the other military and political events of the Fall of 1862. Indeed, many scholars now view that period of Civil War history as the "first turning point" of the war with the September 17 battle as the pivotal event. Confederate armies not only threatened Maryland, but Kentucky and Union-held western Tennessee as well. All of these incursions were stopped. The bloodiest repulse of course, was along the banks of a muddy little stream near Sharpsburg, Maryland.

The essays in this and the earlier Antietam issue are among the most insightful studies of that bloody day since the seminal works of Murfin and Sears. We are pleased to open this issue with "The Narrative of Friedrich Meyer: A German *Freiwilliger* (Volunteer) in the Army of the Potomac," edited by Anders Henriksson. More than 233,000 Germans came to the United States between 1861-1865. This made them the principal immigrant group to arrive on the American shore, rivaled only by the Irish. Tens of thousands of Germans served in the Union army, many in ethnic regiments. One of these units, the 20th New York Infantry, was one of the few VI Corps regiments to see action in the battle. We are very fortunate to have the language skills of Dr. Henriksson, who translated the piece from the original German and edited this moving account of the campaign and battle. In addition, Henriksson's contribution includes Friedrich Meyer's experiences before Antietam, including a fascinating account of his service during the Seven Days' Battles, his capture, and subsequent exchange.

Another rare primary source in this volume is "Lafayette McLaws' Aide-de-camp: The Maryland Campaign Diary of Captain Henry Lord Page King." Editor Helen Trimpi, a former professor at Stanford University, has made available to us a gold mine of information and insight into the daily routine of some of the Confederate high command during the campaign. The diary includes a vivid account of the action in the West Woods, where more than 2,000 Federals fell in less than twenty minutes. King, a native of Georgia and graduate of Harvard Law School (1855), was an astute observer of his fellow comrades, and his account of the invasion of Maryland will be welcomed by students of this campaign.

From matters relating to Confederate divisional affairs, we next turn to issues surrounding another Federal ethnic regiment in Terry A. Johnston, Jr.'s "From Fox's Gap to the Sherrick Farm: The 79th New York Highlanders in the Maryland Campaign." A veteran author and chronicler of the 79th, Terry has written an engaging and scholarly piece on this overlooked regiment which fought in many of the major campaigns across several theaters of war. The Highlanders were one of several regiments that glimpsed ultimate victory on the outskirts of Sharpsburg before questionable generalship and A. P. Hill's charging veterans ended Ambrose Burnside's near-fatal stab into General Lee's right rear.

Complimenting Johnston's contribution is "'Dying as Brave Men Should Die': The Attack and Defense of Burnside's Bridge," by B. Keith Toney. Burnside's Bridge, a three-arch stone structure, is rivaled only by Concord Bridge as the most famous span in American military history. Toney, a well known Gettysburg battlefield guide and author, has penned an insightful study of this often overlooked phase of the battle. His analysis of this action incorporates the principles of war and how each side used them to their advantage (or loss).

It is appropriate that "Baptism of Fire: The 118th (Corn Exchange) Pennsylvania Regiment at the Battle of Shepherdstown," is written by Mark A. Snell, the managing editor of *Civil War Regiments* and Director of the George Tyler

Moore Center for the Study of the Civil War at Shepherd College. Snell is perhaps the leading authority on this little known action. Fought three days after the Battle of Antietam, it is a story of military incompetence on both sides, resulting in unnecessary loss of life. Interestingly enough, the battle was the result of the only sizable pursuit by the Federals of Lee's beaten army, and it was the bloodiest Civil War engagement on West Virginia soil.

What happens to families whose farms are caught in the middle of two warring armies? That question is fully explored and answered in "Destruction, Disease, and Death: The Battle of Antietam and the Sharpsburg Civilians." Antietam National Battlefield Park Historian Ted Alexander has provided us with the first scholarly study of the impact of this momentous clash on the local population. As he points out, Sharpsburg was the first American town of any size to suffer so extensively from a battle. The author's exhaustive research provides us with a fascinating view of a community torn asunder by combat.

Critics have sometimes carped that everything we need to know about the Civil War has already been written. Scott Sherlock, in "The Lost Order and the Press," has proved them wrong with his discovery of two newspaper articles that appeared at least two days before the Battle of Antietam. Both of these news items mention the discovery of the famous "Lost Order." The postscript to this volume certainly raises more questions than it answers, particularly regarding the effectiveness of Confederate intelligence.

We hope this issue of *Civil War Regiments* inspires a better understanding and appreciation for the sacrifices made by Americans on both sides during the Maryland Campaign and the Battle of Antietam. May it also inspire our readers to visit one of this country's best preserved Civil War battlefields.

"A disgusting stench putrefied the air
and the screams of wounded men. . .tore at our ears."

THE NARRATIVE OF FRIEDRICH MEYER

A German *Freiwilliger* (Volunteer)
in the Army of the Potomac

translated & edited by Anders Henriksson

C ivil War armies mirrored the kaleidoscope of peoples, languages, and cultures that was mid-nineteenth century America. Ethnicity was the organizing principle for various units on both sides of the conflict, and many immigrant soldiers marched to commands barked in German, Hungarian, Swedish, and other languages. The Union army, which was able to recruit from a large pool of immigrants, included significantly more ethnic units than its Confederate adversary.

The three decades preceding the Civil War were the peak years of German immigration to America, and Germans represented the largest and most concentrated minority presence in the Union forces.[1] Volunteer militias, among them German and other ethnic units, had been a feature of American life long before the 1860s. With the outbreak of the Civil War, German-American leaders threw themselves into the task of raising new and larger ethnic military formations. Their motives were a complex blend of passionate idealism, crass opportunism, ethnic pride, and the desire to display loyalty to their adopted country.[2] New York's large and vibrant German community contributed ten regiments and five artillery batteries of volunteers to the Union forces.[3] Among these was the 20th New York Volunteer Infantry, which was organized in New York City on May 6, 1861. Also known as the United Turner Rifles, the regiment was the creation of the city's Turner societies (*Turnvereine*). The Turner movement traced its origins to early nineteenth-century Germany, where it promoted civic education, national consciousness, and physical fitness. The liberal, nationalist Turners played a major role in the 1848 German revolution, and the movement's establishment in the United States was largely the work of revolutionary *emigres* who involved themselves in various reform movements, among them the anti-slavery cause.

Friedrich Meyer enlisted as a private in the 20th New York when the regiment was first organized, and in January 1862 was promoted to corporal.[4] Born in 1838, he had spent his childhood in Russia, which rivaled the United States and Latin America as a destination for Germans seeking economic opportunity. His father, Eduard Meyer, was a teacher at a German-language high school in Tallinn (now capital of Estonia).[5] The family eventually returned to Germany, where Eduard Meyer, unable to find a new position, died in poverty. Sons Friedrich and Rudolf emigrated to America shortly before the Civil War. The family's Russian connections, however, apparently remained intact. Meyer's Civil War narrative originally formed part of a letter which he sent to Germany in October 1862. It subsequently appeared in the *Baltische Monat-schrift*, then Russia's leading German-language periodical, in February 1863.[6]

Meyer does not reveal himself as a man fighting for a cause. His perception of his Confederate foes, whom he came to know as a prisoner of war, is remarkably detached. His strong sense of ethnic identity surfaces repeatedly in the narrative, which portrays the Germans as a group set apart from "Americans" and distinguished by superior skills as soldiers. His story is above all, however, a window into the experience of the common soldier.

On June 13, 1861, Meyer's regiment departed New York for duty at Fort Monroe, Virginia. The *New York Times*, lauding the Turners' physical prowess, boasted that the German soldiers could "climb like cats, bound like deer, fight like men, and run a-foot like Indians."[7] Assigned to Fort Monroe and Camp Hamilton, the regiment received its baptism of fire in August 1861 during the Union capture of Fort Hatteras, North Carolina. On June 9, 1862, it was reassigned to the Army of the Potomac as part of Davidson's brigade in Smith's division of Franklin's VI Corps. Meyer's personal account begins with the Seven Days' Battles on the Virginia Peninsula, and ends shortly after Antietam. (When Meyer's narrative was translated, several new paragraph breaks were added in order to give the text greater clarity. On occasion, Meyer used English phrases for emphasis; these appear in italics in his narrative.)

From America. The Experiences of a Volunteer in the 1862 Campaign[8]

The position of the Army of the Potomac before Richmond became untenable when its right wing, under Gen. Fitz John Porter, was outflanked by Stonewall Jackson, the ablest of the rebel generals. Hence it was decided to move the
base of operations to the banks of the James River, where our much feared
gunboats could give us adequate protection. The main body of the army de-
camped on June 28; but our division, which was assigned to cover the retreat,
advanced in order to mask this movement. At first light the 20th Regiment took
up a position opposite an enemy battery and was greeted by a heavy rain of shot
and shell. Only four men suffered wounds and one of our batteries soon silenced
our adversaries; but we still had to stand to arms for twenty four hours, and many
of us, among them, unfortunately, myself, still had to work hard strengthening
our fortifications.[9]

At 2:00 a.m. the next morning our supply column pulled out; and the remainder of our stores, including vast amounts of provisions, weapons, tools,
articles of clothing and many sutler goods, were burned. We then left our positions, but not before enemy bullets wounded some of the men in our rear guard.
Our retreat was in very good order, but extremely arduous. After daybreak the hot
sun scorched our necks. There was little food and hardly time to eat. We had
nothing to drink but foul marsh water. Our only rest came when, five or six times,
we were ordered to form a line of battle at potential danger spots in order to buy
time for the rest of the army to complete its retreat. Afterwards, though, we had
to march *double quick*; and this more than made up for the short time we had
spent standing still.[10]

Around sunset our division was relieved. A murderous battle broke out at
Savage Station between the pursuing enemy and the division which had replaced
us at the rear of our army. Our colonel wanted to lead our regiment into the battle,
but was forbidden to do so by the general, as we were too tired to perform
effectively. The colonel nevertheless ordered us to move double quick back toward the fighting. We were of course unaware of the general's order, and we
followed our colonel. When we neared the battlefield he announced that we
would fall on the enemy's flank and led us away from the road through a thick
woods. It was pitch dark and we could not even see our hands in front of our
faces. We soon fell out of order and lost our way. After blundering around for
three hours, we moved in the direction of the cries and shouts made by the

wounded near Savage Station. When we finally emerged from the woods and found the road, the battle was already long over.[11] Thanks to this clever maneuver we had managed to lose not only our brigade, but also our division. The rear guard informed us that we had better march as quickly as possible to White Oak Swamp, because the bridge over it was to be burned by sunrise. Meanwhile, it began to rain. The road became so muddy and boggy that our feet constantly got stuck. It was impossible to march in proper order. We came upon many broken or abandoned wagons; and the road was littered with discarded packs and other equipment. Soon three regiments—the 20th Indiana, the 20th Illinois and the 20th New York—became mixed together. Repeated calls of "*here twentieth, here twentieth*" only added to the confusion and made the disorder worse.[12] Finally, perhaps a half hour before dawn, about 150 of us reached White Oak Swamp. About 300-400 had arrived earlier, while the rest had collapsed from exhaustion along the road. Without further ado every one of us simply lay down in the mud for an all too brief sleep.

By 8:00 a.m. all of the stragglers had been collected and our division, which again served as the rear guard, was formed into a line of battle.[13] Our position lay between two hills. Our left wing ended in a wooded area and another woods stood not far from our right. The other regiments in our division, which also were deployed on low ground, were not visible from our positions. Only a single battery sat on the hill behind us, and I am convinced that most of our people believed that our regiment had been left to face the enemy alone. We stayed there for perhaps three hours, during which time (as I later heard), an artillery captain named Mott reported to Davidson, our brigadier, that enemy batteries had been placed on several hills on the other side of the swamp. Mott was abruptly told to "mind his own business." Suddenly, though, we came under a frightful bombardment. I hope never again to experience such a hail of shells.[14] The colonel and most of the officers immediately fled the field without giving any indication of what the men should do. The colonel even abandoned his horse. Most of the regiment, in the wildest disorder, followed their example.[15]

My brother and I, Captain Hoym, our company commander, and about 10 men on the left wing of our company remained in the line. We had been given no orders to leave. As we thought about our situation, it became clear that we were in no greater danger from bullets than were those who were fleeing. Our division commander, General Smith, and his adjutant also bolted from the field. When he passed near us we asked him for some kind of order to tell us what to do (should we remain there? should we retreat?), but he was in such a rush that he did not answer us.[16]

Captain Hoym was then wounded in the foot, and we dragged him into the woods on our left, washed his wound, and tried to bandage it as best we could. Not long after this we saw enemy cavalry ride down the nearest hill and through the position we had just abandoned. I went with another man from my company in the opposite direction, deeper into the woods–partly to fetch more water and partly to see if there was any way to escape, as the cavalry had already cut us off from the rest of our army. Before I had a chance to see very much we were surrounded by the enemy and taken prisoner.[17]

We were led back over the ruins of the still smoldering bridge. Our path was exposed not only to enemy bullets, but also to fire from our own batteries, whose shells were whistling by our ears. In front of us was a rider clad like a farmer. He had the pleasing appearance of someone trustworthy. I already had demanded to see an officer, because I wanted to make sure that Hoym, who must also be a prisoner, received medical attention. The rider summoned me, asked what I wanted, and promised to have the captain treated as soon as the action was over.[18] Then he asked me about our losses and inquired after McClellan's whereabouts. Naturally, I could not answer these questions. Heedless of the shells which crashed around him, he kept peering through a telescope and telling his artillery where to aim. After we were led away our guard said that the man who had spoken with me was "feared more than the devil" and asked if I knew who it was. I learned that this fearsome personality was *Old Stonewall Jackson himself.*"

In the meantime, more prisoners joined us. There were eight Germans from our regiment and perhaps 10 or 12 Yankees from various down east states regiments. We found a young artillery sergeant from a Rhode Island battery lying by the road. Shot in both legs, he had been left by the wayside during the retreat. He was in terrible pain and begged to be taken with us. None of his fellow Americans showed any interest in helping the poor man; but we Germans took turns carrying him. With this burden on our shoulders we passed by the entire pursuing Southern army, which, in comparison with ours, appeared ragged and hungry. They did not, though, carry heavy packs. This made marching easier for them than us, because we always dragged heavy packs even through the most scorching heat. We were treated very decently. Our guards, who were at least as exhausted as we were, regularly brought us water. We spent the night at a farm which had been transformed into a hospital, where a surgeon, left behind by our army to care for the wounded, treated our Rhode Islander's legs with a poultice.

The next morning the number of prisoners grew by approximately 100. We were moved to Savage Station; and once again we had to carry our Rhode Islander. Even among this crowd there was no one else who would help us with him. The battlefield through which they led us was strewn with corpses, mostly with faces turned black and blue. There were also many wounded still about, covered with flies and whimpering from pain. The station itself had become a huge hospital. More than 3,000 wounded lay there.[19]

A disgusting stench putrefied the air and the screams of wounded men undergoing amputations without chloroform tore at our ears. After we had arrived and rested for a couple of hours we were told that all able bodied men would be put to work. Naturally nobody wanted to admit that they were able bodied, although at least 70 or 80 men were as fit as I was. We were told that, "You men from the 20th who carried an invalid this far can certainly work!" Utterly exhausted, and accompanied only by five men from the 5th Wisconsin and two Irishmen, we went to work digging graves, dragging the dead and wounded from the field, and holding down men during amputations. Initially I found this last task to be terrible work, but eventually my exhaustion prevailed and I became numb to it. Once we were sent to retrieve a corpse only to discover the man still alive and asking for water; but a surgeon's assistant told us, "never mind, wait a moment, he will die soon." Ten minutes later we buried him.

By 3:00 p.m. we had buried 30 dead and brought in many wounded. Ten men were picked to remain for hospital work. I felt lucky not to be among them. The rest of us (approximately 300) were then assembled for escort to Richmond. During the journey our captors treated us with great courtesy. To our shame, I must say that they treated us much better than we treat our prisoners. They behaved very well toward us the whole way, making a considerable effort to provide us with drinking water in an area where it was hard to come by. On the whole, the rebel army appears to display a better spirit than ours. They bear their far greater privations with less grumbling, endure but half as much petty formality, and, from what I have seen, are quicker to obey their officers. On average, their officers are better than ours and nowhere near as stiff-necked and arrogant. We encountered, for example, a general and his staff. The general recognized a man in our escort, dismounted, and kept his staff waiting while he shook the man's hand and asked him if he needed anything at home. Later I asked the man if the general was a close friend. I learned that the general merely had a farm in the same county where the man's parents lived and that a few years earlier the man had worked for the general. During our march through Jackson's army I also saw a lieutenant fetch water from a creek not only for himself, but also for several soldiers. Such would not happen in our army.

When we marched through our old positions at Camp Lincoln I was astounded at the huge amount of military equipment which we had abandoned. The rebels had already stacked up whole mountains of weapons, some of them never used. Thousands of barrels of meat lay about. Except for some ruined tents, the whole camp remained standing. Between Camp Lincoln and Richmond we passed through four lines of fortifications. The first three were of shallow construction. The fourth was about a mile from the city. Defended by great ships' guns from the Norfolk Navy Yard, it was quite formidable. After this we marched through the camp of the Home Guards, who lacked both uniforms and discipline. They hurled insults at us and had to be constantly shoved aside by our guards. One of these hooligans, bragging that he would rather be in a field regiment than the Home Guards, mocked us for always aiming too high. The sergeant of our guard shouted back, *"You had better step out in the front rank when the battle is raging. Then you will be able to judge whether they shoot low enough. I wish every miscreant like you had been killed by their deadly aim rather than the thousands of brave and gallant fellows we lost in the late battles."*

Late that night we reached our prison, a large, three-storied tobacco factory which housed perhaps 800 prisoners. They registered our names, searched us, and confiscated our packs. Then they allowed us to find a place in the building to sleep—no easy task in that severely overcrowded space. Eventually we found space under a pair of workbenches between the tobacco presses. We flung ourselves down and fell into a long and deep sleep.

The first day began on a positive note. My brother, whom I feared I might not see ever again, had entered the prison several days earlier. He had been transported directly from White Oak Swamp to Richmond without stopping at Savage Station. Soon enough, however, we came to know the hardships of prison life. The lack of fresh air in those stuffy, crowded rooms was a real hardship. We also suffered from a water shortage and had to fight our way through the crowd to the one water spigot in the building where we could wash ourselves. The whole building crawled with vermin of every kind. In the long run, though, the worst thing was the constant hunger. Twice a day we received a little piece of bread without a trace of salt; and. once a day they gave us either a small bit of meat–hardly more than a mouthful–or a half teacup of completely unsalted soup. Even this was irregular. Sometimes breakfast was served at seven in the evening and then we would go 36 hours with nothing to eat. Once we went 10 days without meat. At every meal we feared that we might not be fed again for a long time; and this robbed us of any pleasure we might derive from eating what little we had. Fortunately, the jail still contained a few barrels of tobacco, which we greedily plundered. Thus we could at least fortify ourselves by smoking.

After 14 days of this torment the whole body of prisoners from several tobacco factory buildings (4,000-5,000 men) was ordered out onto the street, marched through Richmond and Manchester, which lays on the other bank of the James, and then some three miles upriver to Belle Isle. Here there was a camp that appeared to have been around for a long time. There were many guards on the perimeter, but we could move around freely within the camp. We could even bathe in groups of six. This was a popular activity, and eager bathers stood in long lines in the hot sun to await their turn. Conditions on Belle Isle were much better than in the tobacco factory. It was a pretty place. The views were magnificent—high romantic riverbanks, upstream a small waterfall, downstream the seven hills of Richmond adorned with the capitol, steeples and cupolas. The guards were not as friendly as the soldiers of the [Confederate] field army, but, on the whole, they treated us quite well. The only brutalities I saw were provoked by the insolence of the rowdies among us. One young hooligan from Vermont, for example, not only refused to obey the orders of a sentry, but also taunted him and spit in his face. He was bayonetted in the chest for this. If I had been in the position of that sentry, who was only trying to do his duty, I believe that I would have done the same thing. The guards were under the strictest orders not to allow prisoners to break the camp regulations.

The mortality rate on the island began to rise. Every day we buried from one to six dead. With regard to the hunger problem, I should note that the soldiers of the Confederacy fared no better than we. They too received small rations, and these were just as monotonous as ours. They had no more tea or coffee than we. Therefore, I believe that our hunger was due to rebel poverty and not to malice.

After five weeks imprisonment our hour of liberation finally arrived. The orders came on the evening of 5 August. Three thousand of us were to be ready to march on the next morning. We were told that anyone too weak to march 25 miles should report this to the authorities. Many interpreted this to mean that the sick and wounded would be evacuated first. Naturally, many men wanted to pass themselves off as sick; and some of the strongest, healthiest people crowded into a fenced area reserved for the sick. A Lieutenant Shin had been in charge of us during our entire time [in prison]. He was a friendly, forthright man whom we had come to call "our lieutenant." When he noticed what was happening, he saw to it that these shameless malingerers were the very last men to leave the island. All through that night they made lists. We were counted and then counted again. They took down our names. There was no thought of rest. On the morning of the sixth there were no rations. From 5:00 a.m. we stood in endlessly long lines impatiently awaiting the order to march, which did not come until mid day.

We marched back through Manchester, over the James bridge, and through Richmond. We were nearly perishing from heat and dust, and the kindly inhabitants of Richmond opened their doors and came out to give us water. I cannot remember ever experiencing such heat. I think that I can bear heat and fatigue as well as anyone, but that day I collapsed more than once. After Richmond there were twenty more miles more to go to Aikens Landing, which we reached at 11:00 p.m. Our empty bellies had slowed us even further.

Towards evening we met prisoners returning from the North, men who had been exchanged for us.[20] All of them seemed fresh, well fed and clad in good clothing. They compared favorably even with our ragged, half starved, scrawny guards. They received friendly greetings from the Southern officers and men there to receive them. Then, free and without supervision, they then marched on to Richmond, where they could rest until summoned back to duty by notices in the press.

At Aikens Landing we camped in a somewhat swampy field of clover. I was so cold, wet and overwrought, that, despite my exhaustion, I could not sleep. On August 7 we boarded the steamer *Knickerbocker* and sailed down the James to the Union army camp at Harrison's Landing. On the ship they gave us as much as we wanted to eat; and we realized what a blessing it is to have enough food. We felt human again. Toward evening we disembarked and thought that we would be able to move about freely again. How wrong we were! What a difference from the manner in which the rebel prisoners had been received by their side the day before! We were ordered to line up. Mounted provost guards encircled us. Anyone who moved or tried to sit down received a harsh "Get back there" or "Get up there!" We were greeted not by friendly words, but by scornful looks and remarks. After standing for hours we were mustered by division, brigade, and regiment. We were then sent off to rejoin our units.

It was late at night before we found our regiment. The regiment had undergone many changes—mostly for the better—during our absence. Our miserable Colonel Weiss, among others, had either resigned or been reassigned.[21] Better men took their places. That stupid bungler, our lieutenant colonel, was, to be sure, still commanding the regiment; but Baron Ernst von Vegesack, a Swedish officer who had formerly served as aide-de-camp to General Wool, had been named as

Colonel Ernst von Vegesack

Following the Greek Cross

our colonel. He arrived two days later. We could not have wished for a better commander. In many ways he even surpassed the much admired Max Weber.[22] Although he could not understand German, he knew our wishes and needs better than any other officer. Unlike his predecessors, he did not spend all his time writing reports, but went out among the men to find out what needed to be done. He was very strict, but equally so with officers and men. On the march he was everywhere, now in the rear, then at the head of the column. He had a friendly or instructive word for everyone. He roused those who were tired, joked with us, and did everything possible to see that his people had enough rest as they could get. Everyone who had witnessed his behavior at the battle of Fair Oaks spoke of his ability and courage (he had remained in his saddle for 48 hours, dismounting only when his horse was shot from under him).[23]

At Harrison's Landing I was happy to get news from the homeland. There was a whole stack of letters for me. Since we had received marching orders for the next morning, I had no time to reply; and in any case I didn't have enough money to buy paper. Unfortunately, for the first time during this campaign I was separated from my brother. He had fallen ill in Richmond and was now so sick that he had to be sent to the hospital at Fort Monroe.

On August 13 the great column set off, skirting the unhealthy, marshy area called Chickahominy Swamp, which had cost the Union more people than all the battles on the Peninsula. Once again, we were detailed to cover the rear, and we watched as regiment after regiment passed by until we moved out during the evening. The march was peaceful and orderly. In order to lighten the army's burden, the soldiers' packs were taken and transported separately. This really did make the men march more easily, although no one had the least protection from rain or from the cold and plentiful dew, which froze us at night. None of this mattered, of course, for those of us who had returned from Richmond. We had lost everything there and had not been re-outfitted. It took us six days to march through Charles City Court House, Williamsburg, Yorktown, Big Bethel and Hampton to Fort Monroe, where we rested for 18 hours. Here I was able to visit my brother in the hospital. He was still very weak, but the doctors assured me that he was not fatally ill.[24] I was astounded at the cleanliness and order which prevailed here. I had not expected to see this in an army hospital which housed thirty thousand casualties.

We boarded the *Empire City*, a smart looking steamship, for the 24-hour trip to Alexandria. We disembarked and pitched camp (without tents) near Fort Ellsworth. They paid us here, and I was able to buy an India-rubber blanket and an old overcoat so that I would not freeze so much at night. Our high hopes that we would be able to rest were, however, soon dashed. Hardly a couple of days had passed when we received new marching orders. We were to hurry to the aid of the hard-pressed Army of Virginia under generals Pope and Sigel.[25] We hurried through Fairfax Court House and Centreville to Manassas; but unfortunately we arrived too late to influence the outcome of the second battle of Bull Run. Sigel's two divisions (composed mostly of German regiments) had fought bravely enough, holding the onrushing Rebel hordes in check for 24 hours with a relatively small force.[26] When reinforcements under McDowell and Porter arrived, however, the senior command lost its coherence and its clear vision. Despite the fact that our army was then twice as large as the day before, the lack of unity among the generals and the indisputable perfidy of McDowell led to a decisive defeat on the second day of the battle.[27]

Yet again we covered the retreat. This had become routine business for us. We took up positions not far from Centreville and watched as a huge number of wounded men marched or were carried past us. Anyone who could manage to walk had to slog through rain and deep mud. Among those passing by were many good friends from the various German regiments of Sigel's corps. Many others would never be coming back. Then came the troops of generals Heintzelmann, Porter, and vile McDowell. Last to pass through were the brave, but frightfully decimated German regiments who had covered themselves with new glory under Sigel. Late Sunday evening (the battle had ended Saturday afternoon), after all of our troops had marched by us and only the enemy remained to our front, we too marched off in a driving rain. The roads had deteriorated into a sticky mud which captured many pairs of boots, leaving their unfortunate owners to march back to

Alexandria barefoot or in their socks. Toward morning we reached Fairfax Court House. An enemy attack was expected, and we were deployed in a battle line at the edge of a woods. The attack never came, and at 3:00 p.m. we received marching orders. We were relieved by General Sumner's corps and reached our old camp near Alexandria on the following morning. We hoped that we could enjoy some rest and receive some badly needed changes of clothing. This, however, was not to be. Only the men who had lost their boots in the mud were re-supplied.

On the evening of our second day in camp we were ordered to march out once again. I had just finished washing my shirt, which I had to put on wet. We marched along the right bank of the Potomac and then crossed the river on the splendid Long Bridge. We had to hustle *double quick* in the dark through the streets of Washington and Georgetown. Unfortunately, we could make out little of what was there. By morning, when we had already put the boundary line of the District of Columbia behind us, we were given a chance to rest a bit on Maryland soil. This unreasonable hurrying is, I believe, the chief mistake which our generals make. They would be able to make far longer marches if only they did not force their troops to move at such an unreasonable pace and if they gave the troops more rest and water. They would never tell us ahead of time if we were to have a chance to rest, so that, when the leading brigade would halt, we never knew if this was just for a moment or for a longer rest. At the same time, the places chosen for rest stops always seem to be at some distance from the nearest source of water. If a man leaves his unit to fetch water and the column pulls out before he returns, he will be unable to catch up to them until the next rest stop. Sometimes we have to march across a bridge that is too narrow to accommodate the full width of the column. When the first ranks cross the bridge, they do not wait for their compatriots, but march quickly on, forcing the rest of the column to push themselves until they are winded in an effort to catch up.

We marched for about 14 days in Maryland (in this gypsy life one loses track of time) through a bountiful region. Friendly little towns like Rockville, Barnesville, Poolesville, Buckeystown, Monocacy, Jefferson and others, alternated with beautiful forests and fertile fields. The rolling countryside gradually gave way to mountainous terrain. We were treated to beautiful scenery; but as the landscape became more picturesque, the march became more strenuous. At night we usually camped in the forests. The glow of campfires, around which we ate our sparse supper—often our only meal of the day—made a magnificent sight. On Sunday, September 14, we first came under fire at the storming of

Middletown Heights. In the face of heavy enemy cannon fire, which did us remarkably little damage, we took the town of Burkittsville. We then marched right over the Heights, from which the Vermont Brigade had already driven the enemy. We spent the night on the battlefield, expecting the fight to be renewed the next day. The enemy, however, had pulled back from this sector of the battlefield, leaving behind two or three thousand prisoners and some weaponry.[28] The fight had moved elsewhere.

Reveille sounded very early, at 2:00 a.m. on September 17. Without any breakfast, we moved at top speed toward the battle at Antietam Creek. Around 9:00 a.m. we marched through the very pro-Union town of Lorrisville [Rohrersville], whose inhabitants cheered us and gave us water and apples. But we could not stop here, and continued forward across the rocky ground. We waded across Antietam Creek, which was swift and up to our bellies. On the other bank we encountered many wounded men, who had dragged themselves to the rear. As we advanced further the ground became more and more thickly littered with corpses. We formed into a line of battle at the edge of a woods. Shouting 'hurrah," we advanced in close formation over the dead and wounded, through fields and past the still glowing remains of burned buildings.[29] We climbed over three fences. As we scaled the second of these our company commander was killed by a sharpshooter's bullet in the chest. Our second lieutenant, a young and recently promoted man (Albert Ritz from Braunschweig), took command. He carried out his duties with an intelligence and coolness which surprised me.

Meanwhile, we encountered the Rebels at close quarters in a cornfield. We charged and threw them back over some high ground. No sooner had we gained this high ground, though, than we came under murderous fire from enemy batteries, which cut a swath of death and destruction through our ranks. We were ordered to lie down, so that our artillery could return the fire. Just as I threw myself down, a bullet struck the thick overcoat which I carried rolled over my chest. More than once I had thought to discard it on the march, because it was tight around my chest. Now it saved my life. The bullet, which had enough force to knock me over, penetrated the overcoat and struck me on the arm. It felt as though I had received a hefty blow from a club, and the arm was very sore for several days.

Our capture of this high ground was important to the outcome of the battle, and we had to hold it at any cost. We were deployed in a skirmish line to keep the enemy in check. We held this position at the extreme front of our line for 24 hours before we were relieved.[30] Our regiment began the day with 600 men (400 others lay sick in various hospitals). We lost 38 killed and 110 wounded in the

The 20th New York Infantry Monument, located behind the Antietam National Battlefield Visitor Center. It sits on the "high ground" that Meyer said his regiment "had to hold it at any cost."

Antietam National Battlefield

battle. Of our 10 officers, five were killed, two mortally wounded, and two very seriously wounded. I mention here only severe wounds. No one paid much attention to lesser wounds, like the one to my arm, which did not put one out of the fight.[31]

After we were relieved, we went into the nearest woods, where bullets were still whistling overhead. Fatigued from our efforts, we fell asleep. During the middle of that day the enemy sent over a flag of truce to request a cease-fire for a few hours in order to bury the dead. For some unfathomable reason the cease-fire was granted. Without even burying their own dead, the enemy used the cease-fire to slip away under the cover of night. Early on the morning of the nineteenth we set out in pursuit. We marched across the frightful looking, very foul smelling battlefield into the town of Sharpsburg, which was much shot up by bullets, and then further toward the Potomac, near which we camped for the evening. Since then we have been moving around the area between Sharpsburg, Hagerstown, and Williamsport. We have camped in several places, often quite near Sharpsburg. Most of our time has been spent on patrol duty.

Our colonel distinguished himself highly during the battle. His coolness, good humor, and concern for our wounded has earned him even more popularity

Stylized contemporary illustration of Colonel von Vegesack at Antietam

Antietam National Battlefield

among the men than he enjoyed before. Unfortunately, he is now sick in the hospital; and we are again entrusted to the command of our bungler, who is incapable of protecting us from the intrusive behavior of American officers. I will offer one example of this problem. A general sees several soldiers picking fruit from an apple tree. He orders that all soldiers found outside their camps be arrested; but no one is ever told that they are forbidden to leave camp. In fact, we had to leave our camp even to fetch water. The provost guard, a disgraceful lancer regiment, picks up every man they can find outside camp.[32] I was one of about 15 men from our regiment apprehended for the terrible crime of fetching water. Together with about 100 men from Irish and Yankee regiments, we were driven like criminals to General Franklin's headquarters. Along the way we encountered a wagon carrying fresh bread, a rare delicacy here. A lancer captain, who was in charge, allowed us to buy bread and waited as we paid for it. At that moment Franklin's guard regiment, the 7th Maine, approached us. The bread was taken from us (in the captain's presence), and we had to watch while the officers of the 7th Maine and the lancers ate it. When we complained, we were told that we stole it anyway. Without any hearing, we were placed under guard for 24 hours in the camp of the 7th Maine. With neither overcoats nor campfire, we froze during the night. I suffered particularly, because I had washed my clothes that morning and had gone to fetch water wearing only a thin jacket (no shirt) and my torn unmentionables.

Another 20th New York Infantry monument, this one in Antietam National Cemetery.

Antietam National Battlefield

The next morning we were sent under guard back to our regiments. Our lieutenant colonel and temporary commander, the bungling Schnepf, refused to listen to our demands for an inquiry and instead condemned us to march around in a circle (a punishment devised by him) for 24 hours as a penalty for our 24-hour absence without permission. For the crime of fetching water I lost the bread I had purchased (I paid 75 cents, the equivalent of a Prussian Thaler), was arrested for 24 hours—during which time I had nothing to eat, and then forced to march in circles like a carousel for another 24 hours. Water supply has a special place in the history of this army. After a long, tiring march we would camp for the night, perhaps near several farms with water pumps. At one pump we would normally find a guard placed there to keep us away. It would be reserved for General Smith and his staff. The next pump would belong to General Franklin, the next to some other general, until one was happy to find a creek or a ditch with water that we could use to brew coffee.

Despite these petty nuisances, I prefer this gypsy life to garrison duty, even though we rarely eat our fill and suffer from heat on the march and cold at night. Since August 6, I have not slept in a tent, let alone under a real roof that would shelter me from rain and dew. So far I have still managed pretty well; but it cannot continue this way much longer. Nights are colder and winter approaches with every day. By the time that you across the ocean read this, I hope to be in a camp that provides us with tents. President Lincoln is here and is conducting a grand review of his troops. I am lucky to be excused from this, as I have sentry duty. The review signifies the beginning of another troop movement. I do not know how soon our marching orders will arrive, and so I hurry to finish these lines.

F. Meyer,

Camp near Sharpsburg, Maryland[,] October 3, 1862

Ambrose Burnside succeeded McClellan as commander of the Army of the Potomac after the latter failed to pursue his advantage gained at Antietam. Burnside's attempt to drive a wedge between Richmond and the main Confederate army under Lee ended in bloody disaster at Fredericksburg in December 1862. President Lincoln replaced Burnside with Gen. Joseph Hooker early the following year. Hooker, however, had a similar lack of success at Chancellorsville that May. Still assigned to VI Corps, the 20th New York was present at both battles. The regiment saw little action at Fredericksburg but fought at Marye's Heights (Second Fredericksburg) during the Chancellorsville Campaign.[33] Meyer was captured a second time on May 4, 1863, but was paroled on May 15 at City Point, Virginia.[34]

As the war progressed, various reorganizations of the army led to the dissolution of many of the ethnic units raised at the beginning of hostilities. The 20th New York was mustered out of service on June 1, 1863. Meyer, whose term of enlistment had expired, was present on that day, but subsequently disappears from American records.[35] He may, like many immigrants, have returned to his homeland. Beyond that, his fate is unknown.

Notes

1. Most immigrants were artisans or small farmers seeking escape from the economic dislocations caused by the advent of the industrial revolution in central Europe. Others, a droplet of a few thousand in a tide of more than a million and a half, were bourgeois political refugees fleeing the repressive aftermath of the abortive German revolution of 1848. Though few in number, these "forty-eighters" formed an educated, activist elite within the German-American community. See Theodore Hamerow, *Restoration, Revolution, and Reaction: Economics and Politics in Germany*, 1815-1871 (Princeton, 1958), pp. 81-4; and La Vern Rippley, *The German-Americans*, (Boston, 1976), pp. 44-52.

Figures compiled in 1869 by the U.S. Sanitary Commission show that 176,817 German-born men served in the Union military. These records, however, are incomplete, and the actual German total has been estimated at 216,000. Wilhelm Kaufmann, *Die Deutschen im Amerikanischen Bürgerkrieg*. Munich, 1911, pp. 118-23.

2. William L. Burton, *Melting Pot Soldiers: The Union's Ethnic Regiments*. (Ames, IA, 1988), pp. 48-50.

3. Still other New York units had a high proportion of Germans. Kaufmann, *Die Deutschen im Amerikanischen Bürgerkrieg*, pp. 184-6.

4. U.S. National Archives. Military Service Record of Frederick Meyer, Co. H, 20th N.Y. Vol. Inf., Company Muster Roll January-February, 1862, card 4318284.

5. The first Russian census, taken in 1897, revealed a German minority of 1.42 million. The Baltic provinces (contemporary Estonia and Latvia) were home to one of Russia's principal concentrations of Germans. *Tsentral'nyi statisticheskii komitet. Per-*

vaia vseobshchaia perepis' naseleniia Rossiiskoi Imperii, 1897 (St. Petersburg, 1905), vol. 2, pp. 1-19.

6. *The Baltische Monatschrift (Baltic Monthly)* was published in Riga, the largest city in the Baltic provinces, from 1859 until 1914.

7. "Departure of Col. Max Weber's Regiment," *New York Times,* June 14, 1861; see also Burton, *Melting Pot Soldiers,* pp. 177-178.

8. Originally published as "Aus Amerika. Erlebnisse eines Freiwilligen im Feldzug von 1862," *Baltische Monatschrift,* 7 (February, 1863), pp. 167-84.

9. The Seven Days' Battles began on June 25, 1862, with inconclusive fighting at Oak Grove. The next day Confederate armies defending Richmond went on the offensive against the Army of the Potomac, whose right flank was indeed vulnerable to Jackson's turning movement. On June 28, McClellan ordered a fighting withdrawal southward toward the James River. William F. Smith's division, including the 20th New York, covered the retreat as rear guard.

10. Meyer understood at least some English, and he sprinkled his text with English words and phrases. These are italicized in the translation.

11. Col. Franz Weiss commanded the 20th New York during the Seven Days' Battles. A bookkeeper in an insurance company before the war, he had served as the regiment's second-in-command until his promotion to colonel at the end of April, 1862.

The Battle of Savage Station, on June 29, pitted units of McClellan's rear guard against attacking Confederates under John B. Magruder. Smith's report indicates that the 20th New York was ordered back toward Savage Station, but reached its destination after the battle was over. "Report of Brig. Gen.William F. Smith, U.S Army, commanding Second Division, of actions at Garnett's and Golding's Farms, Battle of Savage Station, and engagement at White Oak Swamp Bridge." U.S. War Department, *The War of the Rebellion: The Official Records of the Union and Confederate Armies,* 128 vols. (Washington, 1890-1901), series I, vol. 11, pt. 2, p. 463. Herinafter cited as *OR.* All references are to series I unless otherwise noted. Meyer's claim that Weiss disobeyed orders may reflect hostility within the regiment toward the highly unpopular Weiss, who abandoned his men under fire the next day.

12. The 20th Indiana (in Phil Kearney's division of III Corps) passed that night between Savage Station and White Oak Swamp. There was no 20th Illinois in the Army of the Potomac; the 20th Massachusetts (in Sedgwick's division of II Corps), however, was engaged at Savage Station and departed for White Oak Swamp on the heels of the main body of Smith's division. Meyer probably confused the regiments. Frank Welcher, *The Union Army, 1861-1865. Organization and Operations,* 2 vols.(Bloomington IN, 1989), vol. 1, pp. 822-825.

13. Meyer is describing the engagement at White Oak Swamp Bridge. White Oak Swamp ran parallel to the James. When the last of McClellan's forces had crossed it in the small hours of 30 June, the bridge was burned. Smith's division joined units from the II and IV Corps in a defensive alignment on the south bank. Davidson's brigade was positioned astride the road immediately south of the burned-out bridge.

14. Captain Thaddeus Mott commanded the 3rd Battery, New York Light Artillery, attached to Smith's Division. The fire mentioned by Meyer was from Jackson's artillery, positioned north of White Oak Swamp. Others present agree that the German troops came under particularly intense fire. Major Thomas Hyde of the adjacent 7th Maine remembered that Meyer's regiment, "drew a perfect blizzard from Jackson's smoking guns." Thomas Hyde, *Following the Greek Cross; Or Memories of the Sixth Army Corps.* (Boston, 1894), p. 73. See also C. E. Miller and Forrest Steinlage, *Der Turner Soldat. A Turner Soldier in the Civil War* (Louisville, 1988), p. 89.

15. Davidson's report cryptically noted that the 20th New York "lost their formation" and were eventually rallied by the intervention of a brigade staff officer. "Report of Brig. Gen John W. Davidson, U.S. Army, commanding Third Brigade, of the action at Garnett's and Golding's Farms, battle of Savage Station, and engagement at White Oak Swamp Bridge," *OR* 11, pt. 2, p. 481. Other witnesses are more graphic. Research in the papers of Erhard Futterer, another soldier in the 20th New York, describes a panic that set in when most of the officers disappeared, and Hyde excoriates Weiss, whom he claims "certainly led the wild flight several lengths." Miller and Steinlage, *Der Turner Soldat* pp. 89-90; Hyde, *Following the Greek Cross*, p. 74.

16. Friedrich and Rudolf Meyer had enlisted together and served in the same company since 1861. U.S. National Archives. Military Service Record of Rudolf Meyer, Co. H, 20th N.Y. Vol. Inf., Company Muster-in Roll, May 6, 1861, card 4318286.

General Smith was in the area of Davidson's brigade during the battle, but no other source corroborates Meyer on this issue. The Futterer research sketches a scene of confused and frightened soldiers looking for officers to take charge. If some of the Germans did approach Smith, the language barrier and the terrific noise of the cannonade may have rendered meaningful communication impossible. Miller and Steinlage, *Der Turner Soldat,* p. 89. Mark Snell, dissertation ms., p. 192.

17. Confederate cavalry forded the swamp shortly after the artillery barrage ended. Jackson, however, did not advance in force; the Union army, notwithstanding the rout of the 20th New York, retired in good order.

18. Captain Otto Hoym, who had managed the German Theater in New York City before the war, was also taken prisoner. He was released in August 1862 as part of a prisoner exchange, but his wound rendered him unfit for further military service. U.S. National Archives. Military Service Record of Otto Hoym, Co. H, 20th N.Y. Vol. Inf. Company Muster Rolls May-June, 1862, card 4318908 and July-August, 1862, card 4319008; letter of Otto Hoym to Col. Ernst von Vegesack September 25, 1862.

19. Retreating Union forces had purposely left large numbers of wounded and medical personnel at Savage Station. For more information on this and an in-depth account by a Federal surgeon, see William Miller, ed., "To Alleviate Their Sufferings: A Report of Medical Personnel and Activity at Savage's Station During and After the Seven Days' Battles," by Dr. Swinburne, in William J. Miller, series editor, *The Penin-*

sula Campaign of 1862: Yorktown to the Seven Days, 3 vols. (Savas 1998), 3, pp. 143-175.

20. Meyer was the beneficiary of a prisoner exchange cartel arranged on July 22, 1862.

21. On July 4, 1862, Weiss resigned his commission "for reasons well known to the commanding general of the brigade." U.S. National Archives. Military Service Record of Francis Weiss, 20th N.Y. Vol. Inf. Letter of Francis Weiss to General Davidson, July 2, 1862; Field and Staff Muster Roll, July-August, 1862, card 4307719. Weiss would later claim that he resigned for health reasons (rheumatism). He also had harsh words for the regiment, which he described as "a very overbearing, turbulent, socialistic body of men, who lacked discipline." Pension Record of Francis Weiss, Certicate No. 801872, Letter of Francis Weiss to the Hon. Green Raum, Commissioner of Pensions, September 23, 1892.

22. Lt. Col. Engelbert Schnepf had served with the regiment since its formation. Colonel Max Weber had commanded the regiment from its incorporation until his promotion to brigadier general in April, 1862. He was a "forty-eighter" who had once been a career army officer in the Grand Duchy of Baden. After his arrival in New York City, he operated a hotel which served as a gathering place for German political *émigres*. Kaufmann, *Die Deutschen im Amerikanischen Bürgerkrieg*, pp. 561-2.

23. The aristocratic von Vegesack was one of many European officers who sought professional experience in the American Civil War. A captain in the Swedish army, he arrived in Washington in 1861 to win appointment at the rank of major to Wool's staff at Fort Monroe, only to resign his commission to serve as a private in the battles of Yorktown and Williamsburg. Breveted back to major and placed on McClellan's staff, he won the Medal of Honor for his actions during the Seven Days' Battles. The Futterer materials agree with Meyer's assessment of von Vegesack. According to Hyde, "Of all the foreign officers I knew, and there were scores of them with us, he was the best." Hyde, *Following the Greek Cross*, p. 89. See also Miller and Steinlage, *Der Turner Soldat*, p. 80; and Ella Lonn, *Foreigners in the Union Army and Navy* (Baton Rouge, 1951), p. 287.

24. Rudolf Meyer recovered and rejoined the regiment in January 1863. Mil. Serv. Rec. of Rudolf Meyer. Company Muster Roll January-February, 1863, card 4319435.

25. John Pope commanded the Army of Virginia, and Franz Sigel, who had served with Max Weber in the Baden army during the 1848 revolution, commanded its I Corps. See Stephen Engle, *Yankee Dutchman. The Life of Franz Sigel* (Fayetteville, 1993).

26. Sigel's Corps contained mostly German troops, and all but two of its division and brigade commanders were foreign born. Lonn, *Foreigners in the Union Army and Navy*, p. 115.

27. Irvin McDowell was relieved of his command of the III Corps of the Army of Virginia after Second Bull Run. He was subsequently cleared of any wrongdoing.

28. The Battle of Crampton's Gap (part of South Mountain), which Meyer describes here, resulted in the capture of numerous Confederate prisoners. "Reports of Maj.Gen. William F. Smith, U.S. Army, commanding Second Division, of the battles of Crampton's Pass and Antietam," *OR* 19, pt. 1, p. 401.

29. Smith's Division spent September 15-16 in Pleasant Valley. "Lorrisville" is a corruption of Rohrersville. See Welcher, *The Union Army*, pp. 778-9. The burning buildings to which Meyer refers were on the Mumma farm.

30. Around 10:00 a.m. on September 17, the 20th New York and other units of Smith's division's 3rd Brigade, now commanded by Col. William Irwin, attacked the Confederate left. Irwin's Brigade drove its foes back toward the Hagerstown Pike, occupying high ground near the Dunker Church and held it under fire of varying intensity for 24 hours. Irwin lauded the 20th New York, which was "exposed to the heaviest fire in line, which it bore with unyielding courage. The firmness of this regiment deserves very great praise." "Report of Col. William H. Irwin, Forty Ninth Pennsylvania Infantry, commanding Third Brigade, of the battles of Crampton's Pass and Antietam," *OR* 19, pt. 1, p. 411.

31. The 20th New York lost 38 killed, 96 wounded, and 11 missing at Antietam. Five of its officers were killed outright and two more mortally wounded. "Return of Casualties in the Union Forces at the Battle of Antietam, Md.," *OR* 19, pt. 1, p. 196.

32. Elements of the 6th Pennsylvania Cavalry, known as Rush's Lancers, were attached to General Franklin's headquarters.

33. This action cost the regiment nine wounded and 89 killed. Frederick Phisterer, *New York in the War of the Rebellion*, 5 vols. (Albany, 1912), vol. 3, p. 1959.

34. Mil. Serv. Rec. of Frederick Meyer, National Archives.

35. The service record of Rudolf Meyer also ends with his mustering out in June, 1863. More complete information is available for the regiment's senior officers. Brig. Gen. Weber commanded a brigade in Sumner's corps at Antietam, where he lost his right arm. In 1864, Weber was posted as commandant of the Harpers Ferry garrison. He later served as an American diplomat in France and then as a Federal tax collector in New York City, where he died in 1901. Baron von Vegesack (1820-1903) commanded the regiment until it was dissolved, and then returned to the Swedish army, where he eventually attained the rank of major general. Franz Weiss (1821-1915) worked briefly as a New York City policeman and then as a legal clerk. Engelbert Schnepf was a saloon-keeper in Brooklyn until his death in 1880. U.S. National Archives, Pension Record of Francis Weiss. Sworn Statement of Francis Weiss, Troy, NY, April 26, 1884; Pension Record of Englebert Schnepf. Death Certificate, issued by the Brooklyn Dept. of Health, October 22, 1890.

"The longest, saddest day."

LAFAYETTE MCLAWS' AIDE-DE-CAMP

The Maryland Campaign Diary of Captain Henry Lord Page King

edited by Helen Trimpi

The following account of the experiences of Capt. Henry Lord Page King, an aide-de-camp to Maj. Gen. Lafayette McLaws at Maryland Heights and Sharpsburg, is a transcript of pages for September 4 through September 21, 1862, cut or torn from a daily war diary the young officer kept throughout most of his period of service. He mailed the transcribed pages to his sister Florence Barclay King (1834-1912) in Georgia: one section on September 21—four days after the battle on Antietam Creek—and another on September 26 from near Martinsburg immediately after the campaign ended. Both sections were accompanied by notes assuring her that he was well "after a most severe campaign." Though not written in an intimate tone—as Civil War diaries seldom were—and probably intended to be read aloud to family and friends at home, the diary is a remarkably engaging reflection of the day-to-day happenings at division level command in the Army of Northern Virginia. It also reveals some personal characteristics of the staff officer and former lawyer.[1]

Captain King was born into a family with distinguished ancestry on both the Northern and Southern sides of the war. His father was Thomas Butler King (1800-1864), a lawyer born in Palmer, Massachusetts, whose father, Daniel King, had fought in the Revolution. Young King's mother, Anna Matilda Page, was the only child of Maj. William Page (1764-1827), who served in the Revolution with the "Swamp Fox," Francis Marion. After marrying and settling in Georgia in 1824, the elder King enjoyed a career as a legislator in state government and in

Captain Henry Lord Page King
(1860, New York City)

Southern Historical Collection

Washington as a Whig congressman from 1839-1843, where he promoted the founding of the National Observatory and the appointment of Matthew Fontaine Maury as director. During his long absences, his wife skillfully managed their extensive plantation "Retreat," located on the southern end of St. Simons Island. Under her care "Retreat" was famous for the beauty of its plantings and for horticultural experiments.

In politics, the elder King helped President Zachary Taylor see to it that California entered the Union as a free state. For his services Millard Fillmore appointed him first Collector of the Port of San Francisco. He ran in 1851 for senator from California, but lost narrowly and returned to Georgia. Like many Southerners, King opposed secession as a delegate to the Democratic convention in 1860. When it came, however, he followed his state, as did his four living sons. Continuing in public service, he was sent to Europe by Governor Joseph Brown as a commissioner to gain recognition for Georgia.[2]

Lord (or Lordy, as he was called) King was born April 25, 1831, the third of ten children. Educated at home, he attended college in New Haven and graduated from Yale in 1852. Thereafter he studied at Harvard Law School in 1853 and 1854, where he received an LL.B in 1855. During the Civil War, Lord King fought on several battlefields where his Harvard Law School contemporaries (on both sides) were killed. He was one of 68 Harvard Confederates who died in the war.[3]

Returning to St. Simons from Cambridge, King assisted in running the family estate, especially after his older brother, Thomas Butler King, Jr., and his mother, died in 1859. In January 1860, Lord traveled north once again to New York City, where until late December he read law in the firm of a family friend. While there he kept a diary which discloses a routine of reading law for the New York bar examination in his office every week-day and socializing (for example, hearing Adelina Patti sing at the opera and attending art exhibitions) evenings and weekends——including church on Sunday. At home again on December 30, 1959, Lord wrote that he was "for immediate secession & separate state action & a Southern Confederacy after."[4]

When war became imminent, King was commissioned on March 16, 1861, as a first lieutenant in the 10th Georgia Infantry. The regiment's colonel was fellow Georgian Lafayette McLaws. He reported at Fort Pulaski, in Savannah, on April 18, and four days later was assigned duty in the Ordnance Department, District of Savannah, under Capt. William G. Gill, Chief of Ordnance. By June 10, Lord King was in Company K (Pulaski Guards) of the 10th Georgia, an artillery unit commanded by Capt. John P. W. Read of Savannah. Captain Read may already have been a friend of King's (he is frequently mentioned in the diary).[5] Read's Battery would play a significant role at Sharpsburg and again at Fredericksburg. By September 25, King was serving as an aide on McLaws' staff.[6]

If he had been on duty with McLaws on April 16, 1862, King would have witnessed his first action of the war when Gen. George McClellan broke the relative quiet of the siege of Yorktown by assaulting Dam No. 1 at Lee's Mill. This fortified position was the center of Maj. Gen. John Bankhead Magruder's cleverly-constructed defensive line of dammed water, redoubts, and earthworks along the Warwick River on the peninsula between the York and James rivers. In his report of the Confederate repulse of one of McClellan's first strikes at Joseph E. Johnston, McLaws mentions several of his aides (who later appear in King's diary), although King's name was conspicuously absent.

The young aide was very active, however, in the Confederate rearguard action at Williamsburg on May 4. While retiring toward Richmond with the rest of Johnston's army, McLaws, who was in command of Brig. Gen. Paul Semmes' and Brig. Gen. Joseph Kershaw's brigades, was obliged to turn back and occupy a line of redoubts adjacent to Fort Magruder. There, he helped fend off Maj. Gen. Edwin V. Sumner's advance troops on the afternoon preceding the larger engagement at Fort Magruder (Williamsburg) the following day. In his report of the sharp engagement, McLaws noted that Lieutenant King was "active and useful in placing troops in position and bringing them forward from the rear."[7] He mentions as well several other officers and aides who figure largely in King's diary: Maj. James M. Goggin, Maj. A. H. McLaws (McLaws' brother), Capt. Thomas Spaulding McIntosh, and Captain Read. Like Read, Captain McIntosh was either already a good friend of King's from previous acquaintance at home in Georgia, or he became so in their service together.[8]

By mid-1862, King's three brothers and a brother-in-law were in Confederate service—all but one of whom are mentioned in the surviving diary. Captain Mallory (or Mallery) Page King (or "Mall," as Lord King called him), served as assistant adjutant general in 1862 on the staff of Brig. Gen. William Duncan Smith in South Carolina and Georgia.[9] General Smith was married in 1861 to their sister, Georgia Page King.[10] Lord King refers several times to General Smith in his diary, expressing anxiety about his health. His concern was well-founded, for after participating in the Confederate victory at Secessionville in June 1862, Smith fell ill that summer and died of typhoid fever in Georgia on October 4.

Another brother, John Floyd King, who in June 1862 visited Lord at the Richmond front as an observer of the opening of the Battle of Mechanicsville, had a long career as an artillery officer in several commands in southwestern and western Virginia, in Jubal Early's Army of the Valley in 1864, and finally in the Richmond defenses.[11] In 1864, the youngest King brother, Richard Cuyler, commanded the 1st Georgia Battalion Sharpshooters in Henry Rootes Jackson's Brigade, Benjamin Cheatham's Corps, Army of Tennessee.[12]

The earliest surviving part of King's diary covers the period June 4, 1862, to June 27, while he was waiting for promotion to captain. During this time he served with McLaws in the part of the Richmond defensive line established by General Magruder astride the Nine Mile Road and along the New Bridge Road between the Richmond and York River Railroad and the Chickahominy River. Later, the division was moved slightly south to rest entirely on the right of the Nine Mile Road. During this tense period, just after Gen. Robert E. Lee had taken command of what would thereafter be known as the Army of Northern Virginia and leading up to the fight at Mechanicsville, King engaged in a variety of staff duties, including the repositioning of troops and observation of enemy activity. He also made social calls in Richmond, including visits to Mrs. Joseph E. Johnston and Mrs. Jefferson Davis. He records meeting both President Davis and General Lee a number of times when they visited the front. On June 26, he met them again on the Mechanicsville Turnpike and spent the afternoon observing with considerable excitment from a height above the river the Confederate attack on Fitz John Porter's V Corps of McClellan's right wing. With him were his brother Floyd, apparently on leave from western Virginia, and two other staff officers, Maj. John F. Edwards and Maj. William M. Inge.[13] On the 27th he observed the unrolling "panorama" across the river, but the diary breaks off in mid-sentence just as Kershaw's Brigade is advancing to feel the enemy on his front.

King saw service in the Seven Days' Battles at Allen's Farm (Peach Orchard) and Savage Station on June 29, and again at Malvern Hill on July 1 (for which he was promoted to captain on July 7, 1862). In his report of the campaign, McLaws commended King's "gallant conduct," as well as that of another aide, Lt. Thomas S. B. Tucker.[14]

From the time the diary entries resume on August 6, 1862, until King's departure from the defenses of Richmond, he records both the division's general activities and some personal excursions as well. Most interesting, he reveals a penchant for scouting. For example, on August 17, he and another aide rode as far as the formerly Union-occupied Haxall property on the James River, where he encountered enemy videttes posted to cover McClellan's withdrawal. Reporting what he had seen, he wrote with some pleasure, "Campbell & I did all the scouting." He followed this up the next day with a 45-mile ride in the hot sun to Evelington Heights, where he found the abandoned Federal fortifications to be "Beautiful."

By August 19th and 20th, McLaws' Division was marching under orders to join the rest of the Army in Northern Virginia, confident that McClellan had evacuated Harrison's Landing and was heading north by water to Washington, D.C. On the 21st, King was busy sending farewell notes to friends in Richmond, including one to Varina Davis, who was impressed with the young officer from Georgia. After King's death, Mrs. Davis wrote a friend that "[h]e was the most lovely and remarkably attractive young man she had ever seen."[15]

While in the city King eagerly received his mail, in which he first learned of his brother-in-law's illness. That same evening, he directed the divisional troops and officers' horses onto a train of 80 cars, which carried them all to Hanover Junction in two hours. North of Richmond on August 23, temporarily headquartered at Anderson's Crossing, King found the opportunity to engage in additional scouting. With Brig. Gen. Wade Hampton, King rode to Mount Carmel Church, and the following day made a 40-mile reconnaissance ride up the Telegraph Road over the Mat and Ta Rivers nearly as far as Fredericksburg, looking for Union troops on his side of the Rappahannock River. Orders dated 10:00 p.m. on August 25 directed that McLaws' entire division, as well as Maj. Gen. Daniel Harvey Hill's Division and the Reserve Artillery, move toward Louisa Court House and Culpeper Court House. Marching, sometimes in the van and sometimes bringing up the rear, the division travelled over some "unfrequented" roads, often making 16 miles a day.

The column crossed the North Anna River on the 28th of August, the Rapidan on the 30th, and Hazel Run and the north fork of the Rappahannock on the 31st. The men marched into Warrenton and crossed Broad Run on September 1, and finally came to a "halting ground," near Gainesville, having just missed the victorious battle at Second Manassas. "A terrible storm of wind & rain drenched everyone," scribbled King in his diary on September 1, the same day the sharp fight at Chantilly took place. When he learned that his friend, Maj. Delaware Kemper, had been wounded there, King paid him a visit.[16] Although Kemper was badly wounded in the shoulder, King found him "cheerful." He left his wounded comrade and passed through the "recent battleground," [Second Manassas] noting "great numbers of dead Yankees," including "nearly a whole Regt. dead—shot by one of our La. Regts from the old R. R. excavation, and 95 bodies in one pit yet uncovered." That night they camped north of "Sudley's ford," after an eight-mile march. On the march again on the 3rd, they turned from the Centreville Road, traveled across to Little River Turnpike, and over to the Leesburg Road before camping "near Leesburg" that evening.

The night of September 3, after an evening spent "delightfully" in town with the Fadeley family and with Generals McLaws, Kershaw and Barksdale, King expected the division would receive orders to march in the morning "for 3 days." Although he did not yet know it, the army was about to cross the Potomac River and embark on a momentous campaign in Maryland.[17]

[Sept.] 4th [1862]

Wrote farewell notes to Father, Mall & Flora. No orders came to move, provisions have not [come] up. Costin & Tucker came back from town & I went in before dinner.[18] Dined at Fadeley's. Gen. Lee arrived in Leesburg & Divisions of Jackson, Ewell, Longstreet & A. P. Hill came up during the afternoon. Firing heard in the distance in various directions during the day. Col. Long of Gen. Lee's Staff told me the Enemy had retired to his works at Arlington & Alexandria. Thank God we are successful thus far! It seems as tho' the whole [army] was here. Gen. McLaws in town. Called on the Bentleys. Jolly people in Leesburg.

Came out to Camp about 9 1/2 or 10.

[Sept.] 5th [1862]

Gen. stayed in town last night. Firing heard in direction of Harper's Ferry. Gen. came out about 11 oclk.

Waggons move by road to Winchester. Baggage reduced, what can be thrown away? Rumor that the Yankee Govt. has left Washington!

D. H. Hill has moved to Point of Rocks. Gen. Hampton rode up. Finally Gen. McLaws gave us the order—We are to cross White's Ford into Maryland in the morning moving at daylight. Hurrah! We go indeed at last to Maryland! Gen. & Staff rode into town. The whole army is to go into Maryland, it seems.

Gen. Lee is certainly pushing everything with vigor. McIntosh returned—heard Gen. Smith was better.[19] I took tea at Fadeley's.

Came out to Camp & to bed.

[Sept.] 6th [1862]

Up and ready at daylight. Our Division marched early. Breakfasted at Fadeley's and kept on towards the Potomac. Met Whiting's, Longstreet's, and R. H. Anderson's Divisions. D. H. Hill crossed yesterday. The whole Country crowded with troops.

Reached the river at White's Ford with the Gen. about 10 oclk some 7 miles from Leesburg. Jones' Division crossing the river. Gen. Lee has gone over. Glorious to know that at last we are to cross the Potomac. Met Gens. Wilcox and Pryor on the way. Pryor escaped from capture in the recent battle by killing one & wounding another Yankee.[20] Gen. R. H. Anderson came with us to the river bank. Such a large column crossing that we were ordered by Gen. Lee to cross elsewhere so we marched across the country to another road and reached the river again at Cheek's ford some three miles above and the Division crossed before dark. At 4 1/2 P.M. I bid adieu to Virginia and crossed the Potomac. Horse fell over a rock and I got a ducking.

Met canal men from Georgetown who left there this morning—report great alarm in Washington. In fact it is said Lincoln has left the City. Heard that Yankee pickets were 14 miles above us at Point of Rocks, a trooper was fired on this afternoon. Gen. Jackson said to be in Frederick. Gen. Jackson has been injured by a horse presented by some Marylanders. Camped near the river.

[Sept.] 7th [1862]

Marched early through Buckeyestown on the Junction—Monococy [sic]—Gen. McLaws sent me out to get information. Met Gen.Toombs comd'g 3 Brigades of D. R. Jones' command, passed on to D. H. Hill's H'd Qrs, met D. R. Jones—are still sending back information.

Passed the Junction to Gen. Lee's H'd Qrs. Gen. Lee referred me to Gen. Longstreet who sent back a Courier to Gen. McLaws.

Went 4 miles further to Frederick. Bought gloves & engaged coffee &. &. The whole army halted here to mass the troops for further action. Returned about dark some 5 miles to our H'd Qrs.

[Sept.] 8th [1862]

Soon after breakfast Campbell & I went into town calling at Gen. Lee's H'd Qrs.[21] Bought supplies—great crowd in town in spite of the guard. Returned on a borrowed horse. Glorious news! Gen. Lee issued a circular to the troops announcing that Maj. Gen. E. Kirby Smith had captured Gen. Nelson and his Army & everything they had near Richmond Kentucky. 3,000 prisoners—cannon &c. &c.

Washington said to be in mourning for the death of Gen. Buell!

[Sept.] 9th [1862]

Still remaining here and supplying the troops from Frederick. Troops moving during the day but don't know the object or plan. In Camp all day. Gen. McLaws went to see Gen. Lee & on his return it was announced that we march early in the morning with little or no baggage. 1 waggon to the Regt. on some rapid and important movement.

[Sept.] 10th [1862]

Up early. Gen. McL. sent me to Gen. Longstreet to learn the order of march and the direction. Found the way as far as I could see blocked with troops, artillery & waggons. Gen. Jackson moves first. 2nd Longstreet, consisting of D. R. Jones (2 Div.) Evans 1 & R. H. Anderson 1—then McLaws & D. H. Hill in rear. Div. moved out but had to halt. Hill's waggon train &c. Went up to the gate and back. Waited a long time. Horribly dusty. At last column moved. I had to bring up the rear with Semmes's Brigade. Eternal halts—passed through town about 4 1/2. Considerable demonstration of welcome from the young ladies &c. Told my acquaintances good bye. Took the road for Middletown over the Katoctan [sic] mountain. Most fatiguing march since Barhamsville. Thought we would never halt. Reached Middletown about 12, some 13 miles only. Saw all the Brigades into the fields and found H'd Qrs further on about 1 A.M. Gen. up—Union people—all women.

Supper & to bed at 2.

[Sept. 11th [1862]

Fatigued. Prepared to march. These people only <u>partly</u> Confederate. Reduced train again—as little as possible. About 9 took the road and diverging to the left marched towards Burkittsville. Lt. Campbell had gone on with two companies of cavalry before. About 2 miles from Burkittsville met 5 Yankee prisoners, cavalry, taken in the village. Various reports of the Yankee strength, at Harper's Ferry.

Kept on & met warm reception from some few people in the village & county.

Our Cavalry had captured these fellows and were halted by a force of Y. cavalry behind a stone wall. Campbell was going on 2 1/2 miles over the mountain with a citizen of the country belonging to a Texas Regt. to get a map. Asked permission to go—granted. Cavalry had gone wrong road so I led with C.[,] a Courier and a volunteer across the Mt.— At the top met tracks since the rain (20 mts.) & saw three videttes below. Met a citizen and he corroborated all. Passed down the Mt. the Yankee cavalry retreating before us. Gen. Kershaw was in our rear & the Cavalry expected. Reached Brownsville about 4 P.M. seeing

Yankee pickets retreat. Dubious reception, but some information. Enemy strong on opposite Mt. below and seen directly opposite. Cavalry arrived 30 minutes after we did. Kershaw arrived with Brigade. Enemy seen opposite on the Mt. —two shots from Read's Battery scattered them (Cavalry). Stopped at Mr. Boteler's to wait for the Gen.—Beautiful valley.[22] The parson asked us to spare it from devastation. A Union man I suppose. Gen. & Staff invited to stop at Boteler's. They arrived—great excitement among people. Received with great hospitality. House crowded, over 100 persons entertained.

[Sept.] 12th [1862]

Gen. McLaws now in command of a Corps—his own & R. H. Anderson's Divisions. I go with Gen. Kershaw with his & Barksdale's Brigades up the mountain (Elk Ridge.)—Gen. Cobb by the lower road. Semmes in reserve. Marched at 8 1/2 A.M. Reached top of Mt. at 10—two shots from cavalry videttes. Advanced at 10 1/2 over the top of Mt—two roads—Capt. Cuthhert with 3 cos. of skirmishers the right & Maj. Bradley the left.[23] Cuthbert had skirmish at 10 3/4—Bradley at 12 3/4—driving in pickets—Cuthbert lost the way by fault of the guide. We took the ridge and lost Maj. Bradley by reason of a high stone ridge running on top the mountain. We kept on sending messages to Gen. McLaws by Signals. Almost impassable woods rocks—no road—blind path & no path. Maj. B. came up at last about 6 P.M. & found the enemy beyond an abattis. Attacked them quite late by the skirmishers but Gen. K. concluded to wait till morning for main attack. Night dark at first—Men had had no water since morning, almost famished—little to eat and no fires allowed. Horses destitute. Laid down on the ground and slept, surrounded by troops & hearing groans of wounded men. Wakeful—water came!—2 1/2 miles distant had to be brought.

[Sept.] 13th [1862]

All up early—sent horses to the valley as no one can ride here. Enemy still in same place. At 7 A.M. the long roll was beat— At 7.50 attack made by Col. Aiken 7th S.C. and after 15 mts. rapid firing he drove the enemy, his men crossing the abattis & pursuing them running through the woods to a 2nd. & larger abattis beyond, near the point of the Mt. which was also protected to [sic] entrenchments.[24] Lost several. Enemy reported advancing from Harper's Ferry. Messages to & from Gen. McLaws at 8 3/4. Col. Henagan 8th. S.C. passed to the right & could not get in.[25] Gen. Barksdale on the left below the ridge. Enemy in strong force beyond abattis. As Barksdale could not mount the ridge Gen. Kershaw sent Aiken in again at 9 3/4. Then began a terrible engagement of small arms. Aiken held his position, losing many men, but could not take the entrenchments beyond the abattis. He could not withdraw but accepted that Nance's Regt. should advance over him.[26] We were under a terrible fire. Nance went forward and a most terrific fight ensued and Henagan was heard on the right. Barksdale sent word that if Kershaw would cease firing he could now flank on the left, as some of the 17th. Miss. were being fired into from the front. Order given after one of the most hotly contested affairs I have seen. It was terrible to hear the cries and groans of the wounded and dying, but splendid to see the gallantry of the troops.

After a little preparation by throwing forward a Miss. Regt. we proceeded through the old lodges to the "Signal Station" on the highest point of the celebrated Maryland heights. 12 oclk they began shelling us smartly with their immense guns on Bolivar Heights, but of course overshot us, having to elevate so much. Our army in view below in Pleasant Valley. Enemy shelling both valleys. (1 P.M.)—Gen. Kershaw then sent Barksdale to scour the lower & last point of the Mt.—Capt. Holmes A.A.G. to Kershaw led them.[27] They soon met rear skirmishers of enemy—a few shots—enemy in the woods. More troops sent in. Constant shelling at both valleys and the heights coming very near us at the Signal Station.

3 1/2—Holmes & I concluded to go to the extreme point of the Mt. if possible and be sure that we possessed the whole of it. Met Gen. B's messenger saying we had it. Went on & found the skirmishers still a mile from it. The Mt. descends very much to the brink. Kept on occasionally getting a single shot at them. Finally reached it. Harper's Ferry at our feet—troops in view & battle going on in the distance. Took two prisoners and presently had a skirmish with rear stragglers—as we were in front we came near having trouble. Saw the Yankees hurrying into Harper's Ferry—Maryland Heights are certainly ours. Sent despatch at 4 1/2 P.M.

Returned to Gen. Kershaw—saw battle again & heard it was Jackson fighting the enemy having driven them from Martinsburg. Came down the Mt. to H'd Qrs. almost directly with three prisoners. Horrible walk—been on my feet over that stony precipitous mountain since yesterday, fighting, running, & walking many miles till almost tired out, no water and little else. Great reports. Jackson crossed at Wmsport & was attacking Harper's Ferry from the West. Gen. Walker has possession of Loundon [sic] Heights, Gen. Longstreet has the Hagerstown road & we have the Heights and Gap! How can they get away? Gen. Pryor brought some men from Washington—report enemy advancing and skirmishing up the river and by way of Frederick. D. H. Hill is in their way and we also, let them come.

Made my report verbally. I feel quite satisfied with my two days tho' they have been so fatiguing.

———————

Captain King experienced more significant personal action on Elk Ridge than at any earlier time in the war, as his satisfaction, despite his fatigue, reveals. Being detached as a special aide with General Kershaw in the arduous ascent of the heights and the driving of the Union infantry and guns from the ridge obviously tested him—perhaps as he had been wishing to be tested.[28] After Kershaw's South Carolinians, led by Colonels Aiken, Henagan and Nance, aided by some of Barksdale's men in Col. John C. Fiser's 17th Mississippi, had taken the heights, his friend Major Read, and Capt. Henry H. Carlton's Troup (Georgia) Battery, on the next day dragged four Parrott guns up an improvised road to the crest of the heights overlooking Harper's Ferry.[29] Read would later report serious damage to one of his guns from this effort.[30]

Of the entire operation McLaws reported afterward—in part from King's verbal report—that they were "laboriously employed for two days and one night, along the summit of Elk Ridge, constantly working their way, under fire, during the day, and at night resting in position, all this time without water, as none could be obtained but from the valley beneath, over a mile down the mountain." He commended Captain King, "who accompanied General Kershaw during the whole of the operation on the heights," for "aid and active assistance."[31]

At Sharpsburg on September 17, where his service entailed far greater hazard as McLaws' staff officer, King performed as well or better than on Elk Ridge. In the thickest of the fighting he would lose two personal friends.[32] McLaws' Division, which had arrived at the field about 4:30 or 5:00, was sent into action about 9:00 A. M. to help repulse Maj. Gen. John Sedgwick's attack on Lee's center through the West Woods in the third phase of the long day's action.

Of the Confederate success during this part of the day, Stephen Sears writes that Lee, by throwing in McLaws' reserve division to aid Jackson, "succeeded, narrowly, in blunting the main thrust of the Federal effort to turn the Army of Northern Virginia's flank" and "played on General McClellan's worst fear."[33] McLaws, crowing somewhat, would report afterward that he had nothing to gain by a further advance and that he felt that he could claim the battle of Sharpsburg "as one of the greatest successes, if not the greatest success, of the war, when the enormous disparity between our forces and those of the Yankees are considered." And, as in earlier battles, he would commend Captain King for "zeal and activity. . .gallantry. . .in performance of his duties."[34]

As this section opens on September 14, King has returned to McLaws' headquarters at the foot of Elk Ridge in Pleasant Valley. There they are waiting for General Jackson to open his attack on Harper's Ferry, at which point Read's and Carlton's guns will throw shells into the town while Brig. Gen. John G. Walker's artillery on Loudoun Heights join in from across the Shenandoah. Unexpectedly they learn that owing to the Federal penetration of South Mountain at Crampton's Gap and at Turner's Gap to the north they are, in King's words, "here between two fires"—that is, in between the Union forces at Harpers Ferry, not yet surrendered, and McClellan's forces, who have the South Mountain passes open to them.

[Sept.] 14th [1862]

Cannonading heard over towards Harper's Ferry—nothing new of importance. 9 1/2—Gen. Wright has some rifle pieces on Blue Ridge & we send 4 [rifle pieces] this morning up the Maryland Heights. Rapid firing heard towards Boonsboro or Burkittsville, probably battle between enemy and Hill or Longstreet. Cavalry fighting been going on in our rear for several days. Maj. Gen. R. H. Anderson & Gen. Pryor called. Cobb's Brigade ordered to upper pass & Semmes to the lower of Blue Ridge.[35] About 1, firing heard again beyond Harper's Ferry. Read's guns in position on Maryland Heights. Signaled to know if he should begin firing on Harper's Ferry. Gen. McLaws absent with Gen. Anderson, gone to the Heights. Maj. Gen. J. E. B. Stewart [sic] came up & said yes. Soon, just before 3 P.M. Read opened & the firing was very rapid. Despatch from Gen. Jackson beyond Harper's Ferry on the subject of the attack, ordered simultaneous attack, non-combatants out of the way, & to destroy the town if necessary.

I, as A. A. A. G. read & sent it on to Gen. McLaws—the work begun. 5 P.M. Presently came despatch from Semmes that enemy were pressing towards the Pass at Rohrersville and asking for reinforcements—sent it on.[36] Then pressing demand for help. Gen. McLaws returned and ordered Maj. Gen. Stewart forward with his cavalry.

The Gen. went on himself & I following found him at Maj. Gen. Anderson's H'd Qrs. Cobb had gone to the Pass and we could not believe that the enemy were so pressing. After expecting a battle, it being too late, the Gen. sent me back to H'd Qrs. After tea the startling news came by McIntosh that the enemy had carried the Pass & were in the valley! Lt. Tucker who had been sent by the Gen. to Gen. Lee for "reinforcements or he would abandon the Heights" with Boteler & a courier had been halted by the enemy, they pretended to do so, turned their horses & put spurs—were shot at and the courier fell but they escaped, it was now quite dark. Very sad news for us in the valley, but Gen. Stewart had sent previously similar information. Gen. McLaws & Gen. Stewart returned about 10 P.M. The news is too true. So we are here between two fires. The troops must have done badly tho' many good men have fallen. Tomorrow will doubtless bring a heavy & perhaps decisive battle. A very anxious predicament. Troops ordered up—Gen. Kershaw sent for and came, anxious feeling in all our bosoms—sat up late consulting. All feel that tomorrow will be a bloody day.

[Sept.] 15th [1862]

Gens. Wright & Pryor & Semmes came about 3 oclk A.M. to get instructions. All up about 3 1/2 A. M.—Before six heard Jackson open a terrible fire on Harper's Ferry. I pray to God that he may take the place and thus give us a fair fight with the enemy in our present front.

Gen. & Staff go to the front, line of battle at Brick Church this side Brownsville, thereby abandoning the lower Pass. Enemy's pickets in sight—hear from Col. Munford so our connection is not broken on the left.[37] Surprise that the enemy do not attack—thought they were trying to follow to the Mt.

Returned to H'd Qrs 10 A.M. Glorious! Report from Maryland Hts. that Harper's Ferry has surrendered!! Thank God! Whatever the result of our battle we are not cut in two. Gen. Featherstone [sic] on the river ordered to advance his pickets towards the Ferry until fired into to ascertain the exact state of the case. Gen. refused me permission to go to the Ferry. At last about 1 oclk the Gen. went forward to find Gen. Jackson (McIntosh had reported the surrender as correct) and we crossed the pontoon bridge about 2 P.M. Gens. Jackson & McLaws had a long interview. The town crowded with Yankee Marylander "Home Guards." Disgusting. Went to Bolivar Heights to see the prisoners. Magnificent! (if I may use such a term) to see 12,000 prisoners with all their beautiful new arms stacked, 47 pieces of Artillery and 600 horses all our capture! Battle going on up the country in Maryland, supposed to be Longstreet & enemy. Returned to the town and crossed the river again with the Gen. Sent on a tedious ride to ascertain the positions & give directions to the Divisions of our

Corps. (Letters from home, i.e. the South, for I have no home.[38] Smith better. Letters from Georgia, Florence, Mall & Floyd.)

Gen. Kershaw in com'd of our Div.—We took a nap on the floor of a little house at the foot of the Mt. till the way was clear over the Pontoon Bridge. Up at 1 1/2 A.M. & crossed again at the head of this column, glad that the enemy had not molested our rear. Tedious waiting, so many Yankee paroled prisoners, had to guard the Bridge.

[Sept.] 16th [1862]

Finally started out of town about 3 1/2 oclk towards Charlestown. Heard that the battle of yesterday made for our defence was a success! Thank God! for smiling upon our cause.

Rode until after sun rise and reached Chastown [sic]. Hospitably received and breakfasted—very much needed considering our hard service.

Cincinnati "reported as captured & believed [sic]." Returned to Halltown to dine (miserable!).

A. P. Hill's Division marched this morning towards Shepherdstown & came back. What is "en tapis" "quien sabe?" Marched in afternoon towards Shepherdstown and halted after dark. H'd Qrs at Dr. Lucas'. Met Chas. Y. Kerr.

Before going to sleep orders came thro' Mason A. A. G. to Gen. Lee that the enemy were drawn up in line of battle before him with his entire force and there must be a battle in the morning.[39] That we must move over during the night &c. Orders issued to march in an hour or two. McIntosh & Holmes busy writing them.

Laid down on a sofa for an hour or two & waked at 1 A.M. to go to the front, and to prevent confusion in the positions of the Divisions, ours first, Anderson's 2nd. So tired and chilled. Marched in the dark,

[Sept.] 17th! [1862]

and crossed the Potomac again at the ford below Shepherdstown—about 2 1/2 or 3.

Reached near Sharpsburg about 4 1/2 or 5—the battle begun as soon as light enough. Anderson's Div. partly with Longstreet. We at first as reserve. Witnessed the battle from a hill—extended firing over a long semicircular line around Sharpsburg. Rode around to Hospitals—wounded coming in. Met Gen. Ripley wounded. Orders came to move to the front & left to Jackson! Marched nearly a mile. Met Gen. Jackson & he & Gen. McLaws had a conference. Shell fell at our feet, wounding one of Gen's couriers—did not explode or it would have killed both Gens.

Samuel Breck Parkman
(Harvard College, 1857)

Harvard University Archives

Severe battle going on—our forces contending for a wood in our front. Moved forward—referred to Gen. Hood for knowledge of the ground, order on the left from centre,—D. H. Hill, Hood, Early, Stewart—We to take Hood's position. Hood said his men had taken the wood and had been driven from it & the enemy were now advancing through it in large force. The Division came up in fine stile, and formed line of battle beautifully. Momentous hour! (It was before 8 A. M.) Gen. McLaws made his dispositions speedily & was in every direction, giving requisite orders—other troops extended the line to the left. Officers com'dg Brigades and Regts. spoke a few words of fire to their men, and onward moved the line without a waver. In less than five minutes the dropping fire of skirmishers turned into the roar of musketry and our men drove the enemy through the wood gallantly

Read's Battery was ordered to the open field on the right and occupying the most exposed position opened a most rapid fire—acting splendidly. Gen. McLaws & Staff dashing about wherever needed directing the attack. I cannot recount all the orders I carried but was constantly engaged at half speed under heavy fire. Tucker's horse shot in the leg when we were all together. Frequent interviews with Gens. Jackson and Hood. Our Division took the wood, and advanced near to the Enemy's batteries on the right, but being unsupported had to fall back. Trying moment, seeing our men returning. Rallied the S. C. troops & some of the Miss Brig. behind a stone fence. Met Col. Kennedy shot in the foot, had been within 100 yards of the batteries.[40] Terrific artillery fire going on all the time. The Battle of Malvern Hill was less severe in Artillery & no musketry of war equaled it.

The enemy again in the wood! Up came reinforcements and again the same death dealing fire and again we drove them out—again our men breaking across the open field from which Read's Battery had been ordered to retire, the place was almost impossible to hold.[41] Again reinforcements came up. Gen. McLaws had positively demanded them of Gen. Jackson. I was sent for another Battery—found Macon in position on a hill as second line—went on—met Read's Battery—poor Breck Parkman lying dead on a caisson, shot through the heart from shoulder to side![42]

Found Carleton's [sic] Battery & brought it forward.[43] But before I had been sent to order in a Regt. of Walker's Division and in doing so near the wood under heavy fire met Spaulding McIntosh riding up and down the line—exchanged a few words—the last I ever heard him speak.

Brought in Carleton's Battery and Gen. & Staff went into the wood, immediately again the deafening roar of Artillery & musketry. We were in the hottest fire of the battle & remained a long time. We had lost several Gens. killed & wounded up to this time. Gens. Armistead & Ransom with us part of the time. Carleton's Battery driven out in 25 minutes. The longest, saddest day. It was now only 12 oclk! Of how the fight raged to right and left I had no time to enquire. Several of our horses were struck, but thank God! none of us, tho' the shot & shell & rifle balls fell all around us.

After a while Gen. McLaws went to the left with Gen. Fitz Hugh Lee & we saw the position of the enemy, in that direction. Returned to the wood which we held. Gen. Kershaw came back with his Brig. reformed, what there was left of it & Gen. Barksdale who had driven the enemy far beyond our line. Message came from Gen. Longstreet that he was holding the right without a cartridge! We could not advance but could hold our own—The day wore on but the afternoon was occupied principally with the artillery and a most terrific artillery fire it was—four times did our Batteries drive back the enemy. To add to the scene several houses were set on fire and burned to the ground & some caissons were blown up .

McIntosh did not return. Finally night closed upon the strife and gradually the fire ceased—we occupying the ground right, left & centre, upon which the main battle was fought, a battle surpassing all others of the war in the numbers engaged and its intensity.

The day had closed, but what a scene presented itself to our view! The dead lay in every direction—in numerous places piled on each other, but gladly did I mark that the enemy were 10 to 1 of ours. We occupied the entire wood for which we had been contending all day, and about dark the men rested. I & Capt. Costin left the Gen. to look for McIntosh as one of our couriers reported his horse taken by a wounded Col. who found him hitched near the barn & hay-stacks near which I had left him. Too dark to see faces on the ground & kept on to Hospitals—found nothing—took a mouthful with Maj. Goggin near the river & returned through Sharpsburg to the wood & slept on the ground surrounded by the dead & wounded crying and groaning with agony without taking saddles off our horses.

[Sept.] 18th [1862]

Up before daylight expecting a renewal of the battle but everything quiet. Sent by Gen. McLaws to place batteries in position to protect our right as the enemy reported to have advanced batteries 400 yards during the night.

Found Gen. Longstreet, who took the matter in charge. Returned, & Flag of truce reported from the enemy to arrange for the wounded.

Sent by Gen. McLaws to Gen. Jackson for a reply. Met Gen. Stewart there. Sent back to learn the exact proposition—Found that it was only Surgeon's flag. About giving up the matter of flags when Gen. Ransom galloped up & said a veritable flag had been sent. I went out to meet it & found Maj. Rogers [sic] of Maj. Gen. Slocom's [sic] Staff—Franklin's Corps—A. A. G. proposing to exchange the wounded at any intermediate point agreed upon.[44] Returned to Gen. Jackson to deliver message. Met him & Gen. Lee. Gen. Lee replied in Jackson's name that no partial or informal proposition could be entertained, but if the Commander of the Army on the other side made a general proposition it would be referred to Gen. Lee for consideration.

Again I went to the flag of truce and delivered the reply to Maj. Rogers who said if he could find Gen. McClellan & succeed in making the arrangement he would do so and meet me again with a flag as soon as possible. Skirmishing going on in the meantime. So McClellan in person commanded the enemy. Rogers said Franklin commanded opposite us—when I mentioned Jackson commanding on our left, there was a very significant look exchanged between the three Yankee officers.

I reported to Gen. Jackson. The wood was filled with dead Yankees—but it made me sad to see so many of our dead in the fields up to the enemy's lines when I went to meet the flag. McClellan never sent the proposition but, tho' skirmishers were ordered to fire on every one, yet many bodies were recovered by both sides within range without molestation.

Found poor McIntosh's body near where I left him in the battle by the straw stacks—shot through the heart, he had a pleasant expression of countenance not in the least disfigured. He had been shamefully robbed, but I got his keys & some papers for his family. Maj. Goggin had him buried nearby at the foot of a tree on some rocky ground & I wrote his name &c on his headboard—poor fellow "requiescat in pace!"

The rest of the day spent in line of battle with the enemy right before us and the sharpshooters picking at each other.

Sent to Gen. Jackson on the subject of Qr. Mrs. of Div. to report &c.—

Back to our place in the woods. A great many stragglers &c. came up so we had a larger force than when we went into action. As night came on a move of importance became evident & I thought we were going to attack the enemy, in the dark. Slept a little and then silently ordered to horse—the troops marched out of the wood, the Gen. keeping me with him to show him the way or sending me off to bring up stragglers. I then learned that we were going to recross the

Potomac. It was dark & foggy—We left four Cos. to picket the front. I then took the Gen. to report to Gen. Jackson that we were on the road marching silently.

We all joined the Division after some trouble in the dark, and amid such an immense mass of troops and waggons of all descriptions.

After great difficulty we got to the river and upon crossing I found Gen. Lee in person superintending the crossing of the Army with Gen. Kemper as a Provost Marshall[.] I missed Gen. McLaws in the river and after waiting from 12 1/2 to 2 1/2 for him I joined the head of the column with Gen. Kershaw and marched till daylight nearly, when we halted by a haystack and slept a short time.

[Sept.] 19th [1862]

At sun rise I mounted again and went into Shepherdstown some 2 1/2 miles. Breakfasted, saw Cols. Aiken & Kennedy wounded. Skirmishing then began across the river & several shells fell about me as I went back to find the General. Found them (Gen. & Staff) and we marched to Kearneysville & hearing that he—the Gen.—had gone towards Martinsburg when I stopped to change horses I followed after dressing at the waggons [sic] (the first time in five days.)

I took the road towards Martinsburg and found Gen. Kershaw & Brigade near there on the Opequon. Kept on & learned that neither Gen. McLaws nor Gen. Jackson were in M'sburg—however I stayed the night there, & was glad of the rest!

[Sept.] 20th [1862]

Returned to find the command gone—followed back to Kearnestown [sic] & found the Army in line of battle & enemy reported on this side the river. Found Gen. & Staff.

In afternoon the whole of our Corps (Longstreet's) marched by a side road towards Martinsburg & halted on the bank of the Opequon.

[Sept.] 21st [1862]

The Corps crossed the Opequon and halted on the other side. Firing heard but turned out to be nothing. Gen. Jackson gave the enemy a severe repulse, killing & capturing or running into the river a part of their forces which had crossed. We lost some 4 pieces of Artillery however taken from Gen. Pendleton's Reserve Corps by the enemy.

I went into town but being Sunday everything was shut up or the people are Yankees.

General William Duncan Smith

Massachusetts Commandery, Military Order of the Loyal Legion and USAMHI

When the Sharpsburg Campaign ended, King and the rest of Lee's army went into autumn camp. King camped first at Martinsburg, and later at Winchester (September 27 to October 31). On October 11, he heard of the death of General Smith a week earlier in Georgia. King commented that the "Spell is broken"; of four brothers and one brother-in-law, none had yet been injured in battle. Also during this period, King wrote a brief descriptive sketch—the only one of its kind in the surviving diary—of Stonewall Jackson, just after visiting him in camp above Martinsburg on October 19 and 20. King found Jackson and his staff in four small tents "without flies," and he described "Old Jack" as "much more gentle in manner than on the Battlefield, in fact quite urbane, and [I] thought him very good looking indeed—a pretty mouth, good nose and handsome eyes,—the same faded uniform and old slouch hat."

On October 31, McLaws' Division left its bivouac and marched through a variety of weather via the Valley Turnpike, Front Royal, Chester Gap and Sperryville to Culpeper. On November 7, snow fell on the tramping troops. In Culpeper, from November 7 until the diary ends on November 16, King was occupied mainly in inspecting brigades, which he found very "tiresome."

When word was received of a Federal advance toward Falmouth on the Rappahannock in mid-November, Lee moved quickly to meet the enemy at Fredericksburg. Longstreet's Corps arrived there by November 21, and he took up a strong position behind and above the city. Opposite him was Edwin Sumner's Grand (Federal) Division, camped at Falmouth and on Stafford Heights, awaiting pontoon bridges to cross the river. Henry J. Hunt's Federal artillery, in one of its strongest concentrations of the war, overlooked the river and the historic town. Longstreet stationed McLaws' Division, when it arrived on the 25th, on Willis' Hill and Marye's Hill, together commonly called Marye's Heights.

King reached Fredericksburg with the division. McLaws kept him occupied directing the "minute and careful preparation" which the conspicuously conscientious general made to "defeat any attempt to cross the river" in his front. Rifle pits were dug close to the bank to command the shores on both sides, with zig-zags to enable the men to get in and out under cover. Cellars of the houses in town were prepared for riflemen. On the night of December 10, Brig. Gen. William Barksdale, who had occupied the town and rifle pits with his Mississippi Brigade, reported that he believed the Federals were laying pontoon bridges in the dark. About 4:30 a.m. on December 11, McLaws ordered Major Read's Battery, posted on the high point of the hills on the main road leading into the city, to give the two-gun signal to Barksdale's riflemen, which alerted them to open fire on the enemy bridge-builders working in their front.[45]

King's whereabouts and duties on the 11th are only roughly understood. He was probably occupied with the same tasks he had undertaken at Sharpsburg. This would have included carrying messages between McLaws and his superior officers (Longstreet and Lee), or between McLaws and Barksdale, who was directing the vigorous delaying action, first on the river banks from 5:00 a.m. until 4:30 p.m., and then in the heavy street fighting in the town, from about 5:00 p.m. to 7:00 p.m.. King may have guided two regiments (the 16th Georgia and 15th South Carolina) down to the river bank below the town, where Lt. Col. William H. Luse of the 18th Mississippi required their support. (Luse is mentioned often in King's diary as a social friend.) At day's end, King may well have carried the orders McLaws sent to his several units to withdraw from their positions: Barksdale to a position behind the stone wall on Telegraph Road, and Luse's men to the river road, where they remained until daylight.[46]

On December 12, "heavy fog hung over the valley concealing the town and the river bank from view until late in the day." When McLaws expressed anxiety for news from his pickets, Captain King volunteered to "go to the river and collect information by personal observation." McLaws wrote more than 20 years later, "I consented to his going but did not send him." King rode off and was gone two hours. On his return, he told McLaws he had "ridden down Deep Run as far as he could go in safety on horseback." He then dismounted and hid his horse, and went on down the run to its mouth on the Rappahannock. There, he "watched the enemy crossing the river on 2 bridges." He saw from there one or two hundred yards further down from the mouth "Large bodies of infantry, artillery and some cavalry had crossed, while heavy forces on the opposite side were waiting their turn to cross." On his way back up again he had "gone into a two-story wooden dwelling on the banks of the river" and had viewed the "whole surroundings," which confirmed what he had seen from the mouth of Deep Run. "This was a daring reconnoissance," wrote McLaws, "as, at the time, none of our troops were within a mile of him." It was also valuable, claimed McLaws, because "the enemy had not shown us any very large body of troops, either in Fredericksburg, on the opposite side, or below."[47]

Whether this account is entirely accurate in detail or not, written so many years after the events had transpired, King's offer to scout the enemy in an independent action is consistent with his actions earlier in July, when he rode out over the apparently evacuated ground near Harrison's Landing, and again in August, when he scouted toward Fredericksburg with General Hampton. He preferred this kind of duty to the "tiresome" inspection of brigades and hanging around camp headquarters. Whatever his reason for volunteering for this individual reconnaissance, it was the last one he made.

The next day, December 13, dawned misty and cloudy. Later in the day the fog burned off and exposed the Federal preparations for an attack against Lee's lines. The first strike was launched against the right-front of the line, which was held by Jackson's Corps. The subsequent attack on the left against Longstreet's front, part of which fell upon McLaws' carefully placed and prepared lines—lines which King had assisted in laying out—did not begin until just after 11:00 a.m., according to McLaws. King's role during the main battle is largely unknown. In the successive assaults—as many as eight or nine were counted—it may be imagined that King carried orders, as at Sharpsburg, "under heavy fire," that he had "frequent interviews" with Longstreet and perhaps R. H. Anderson and others. Perhaps he also witnessed the death of dear friends, as he had seen Spaulding McIntosh and Breck Parkman on the field at Sharpsburg.

As McLaws remembered it, the story of King's last service came after 1:00 p.m., at a critical moment in the early afternoon engagement. In response to an urgent message from Brig. Gen. Thomas R. R. Cobb, McLaws' sent his staff officer with a written order: "General: Hold your position, with no fear of your flank, it will be protected." McLaws told King to carry it to General Cobb and "to inform him that both ammunition and reinforcements were on the way." This was, he wrote, the last he saw of Captain King until his body was found after the battle. According to notes taken by Brig. Gen. Robert Ransom, a division commander at Fredericksburg, Captain King "was killed on the front slope of the hill near Marye's house." Artilleriest E. Porter Alexander in 1882 wrote that King was killed by Federal sharpshooters, who were discharging during the whole day "a murderous fire" on the slope of the hill leading to Marye's house. "Invulnerable sharpshooters kept up a fusillade more deadly than a line of battle," he claimed, adding that King's body received "five balls."[48]

King's body was discovered on the field by his servant, Neptune Small, while the battle was still raging across the landscape. King had grown up with Small, who had accompanied him throughout his wartime service. Small dutifully carried the remains home to Georgia, probably to "Refuge" in Ware County, where the family had traveled to get away from the Federal-occupied coast. Even though he was offered the chance to remain home, Small preferred to travel back to the front and join Maj. Cuyler King, with whom he served to the end of the war. When "Retreat" was reoccupied by the King family after

Reconstruction, Small returned there with them. When he died, he was buried on St. Simons.

After the war, Captain King's body was moved to St. Simons and interred in Christ Episcopal Church cemetery in Frederica, near the graves of his father, mother, and the two brothers who had died earlier. His grave-marker reads: "Capt. Henry Lord Page King, C. S. A., third son of Thos. B. and Anna M. King, Died at Fredericksburg, Dec. 13, 1862. Advancing gallantly in the storm of battle on Marye's Hill, he fell pierced by five balls. Aged 31 years. Dulce et decorum est pro patria mori."[49]

Notes

1. War Diary of Henry L. P. King, in Thomas Butler King Papers no. 1252, series 6, vol. 11, in Southern Historical Collection, University of North Carolina Library, Chapel Hill, North Carolina. Published by courtesy of the University of North Carolina Library. The excerpt (September 4-21, 1862) published here is taken from the library's typed transcript of the original manuscript diary, and was checked against a microcopy of the original. It has been in some small instances corrected. Quotations from the parts of the diary not published here are also from the typed transcript. The letter of Captain King quoted to Florence King (September 26, 1862) is in the same collection. The author wishes to thank Robert K. Krick, Chief Historian of the Fredericksburg and Spotsylvania National Military Park, for drawing her attention to King's diary.

2. *Dictionary of American Biography*, ed. Allen Johnson, 20 vols. (New York, 1929), 5, 403; Burnette Vanstory, *Georgia's Land of the Golden Isles* (Athens, 1956), pp. 132-139; Margaret Davis Cate, *Our Todays and Yesterdays* (Brunswick, Ga., 1930), pp. 124-130. In 1863, the ubiquitous British officer, Lt. Col. Arthur J. L. Fremantle, recorded meeting Butler King in Richmond. It was, he wrote, "surprising to hear the extraordinary equanimity with which he and hundreds of fellow-sufferers talk of their entire ruin and the total destruction of their property." King's equanimity was no doubt feigned for the benefit of a sympathetic foreigner, for Vanstory writes that when the war came, it shattered the foundations of the older King's life, when he endured the conflict between the government to which he had given a lifetime of service, and the Georgia land where he had reared his children. Arthur J. L. Fremantle, *Three Months in the Southern States: April-June, 1863* (Bison rpt. Lincoln, 1991), pp. 216, 219; Vanstory, *Georgia's Land* p. 136. For a portrait of Anna King see Elizabeth Fox-Genovese, *Within the Plantation Household: Black and White Women of the Old South* (Chapel Hill, 1988), p. 126.

3. Henry N. Blake, "Harvard Confederates Who Fell in the Civil War," *Harvard Graduates' Magazine* (December 1912), pp. 429-430; Charles Warren, *History of the Harvard Law School and of Early Legal Conditions in America*, 3 vols. (New York,

1908), 3, 70. On the field at Sharpsburg, Lt. Jesse Reed, 6th Georgia Infantry, a fellow Law School alumnus (1859) of King, was mortally wounded when his regiment, in Colquitt's Brigade, D. H. Hill's Division, was decimated in the Cornfield. He died September 21. Lieutenant Reed was of very different background from King. After his death his father, Daniel Reed, of Cobb County, signed for his son's army pay with an "X." Service Record of Jesse Reed, National Archives, Washington, D. C.

4. Manuscript Diary (1860) of Henry L. P. King, in Thomas Butler King Papers #1252, series 6, vol. 10, Southern Historical Collection, University of North Carolina Library. Microcopy of the manuscript diary, courtesy of the University of North Carolina Library. There is a possibility that Lord King may have practiced law in Savannah during some or all of this time; the record is unclear.

5. Captain John Postell Williamson Read (1829-1884), third son of Jacob Read (1794-1830) and Ann Williamson (1807-1830), was born in Savannah April 21, 1829. He was the grandson of John Postell Williamson (1778-1843), one of the richest planters and landowners in Savannah in the first half of the nineteenth century. His paternal grandfather, Jacob Read (1751-1816) of South Carolina, was a colonel in the Revolutionary army, delegate to the Continental Congress and United States Senator. Read became captain of the Pulaski Guards, Company K, 10th Regiment Georgia Volunteers on May 18, 1861. Later his company was attached as Company L to the 1st Regiment Virginia Artillery. In March 1863, after King's death, Read's Company transferred to the light artillery arm of service and became Captain Read's Battery Georgia Light Artillery (38th Battalion Virginia Light Artillery). This unit was later called Fraser's Battery, commanded by John Couper Fraser, who was also a friend of King's and a relation through the marriage of his oldest sister, Hannah King, to William Audley Couper (1817-1888). Read became a major March 2, 1863, and lieutenant colonel October 27, 1864. He lost an arm at Gettysburg. After the war he lived in Alabama and Virginia and is buried in Savannah. Robert Manson Myers, ed., *The Children of Pride: A True Story of Georgia and the Civil War*, 3 vols. (New York, 1972), 3, 1655.

6. Service Record of Henry Lord Page King, National Archives,Washington, D. C. A letter of McLaws (June 26, 1862) states that King had served as aide since McLaws' appointment as brigadier general September 25, 1861.

7. United States War Department, *War of the Rebellion: A Compilation of the Official Records of the Union and Confederate Armies*, 128 vols. (Washington, D. C., 1890-1901), series I, vol. 11, pt. 1, p. 443. Herinafter cited as *OR*. All references are to series I unless otherwise stated.

8. James Monroe Goggin (1820-1901) was born in Virginia and attended the United States Military Academy, class of 1842, although he did not graduate. After travel in Texas and California, he went into business as a cotton broker in Memphis. He first served as major in the 32nd Virginia Infantry on the Peninsula under Magruder. Then on McLaws' staff as A. A. G. and on Kershaw's staff, he went through all the campaigns of the I Corps. At Cedar Creek in 1864 he commanded Gen. James Conner's Brigade and was appointed brigadier general December 4, 1864. However, he returned

to staff duty with Kershaw. He was captured at Saylor's Creek. Ezra J. Warner, *Generals in Gray: Lives of the Confederate Commanders* (Baton Rouge, 1959), pp. 108-109; See also Jubal A. Early, "Winchester, Fisher's Hill, and Cedar Creek," in *Battles and Leaders of the Civil War*, eds. Robert U. Johnson and Clarence C. Buel, 4 vols (Castle rpt: Secaucus, N. J., n.d.), 4, p. 528. Major A. H. McLaws served his brother as Chief Quartermaster. Joseph H. Crute, *Confederate Staff Officers: 1861-1865* (Powhatan, Va., 1982), p. 140. In his diary, while in the Richmond defensive lines, Captain King refers to an obscure "disagreeable difficulty" with Major McLaws. This problem made King feel for a time that he might have to sacrifice his staff position. Major Thomas Spaulding McIntosh was A. A. G. as a captain (October 19, 1861) and major (May 23, 1862) on McLaws' staff. Crute, *Confederate Staff Officers*, p. 140. Born in 1837 in McIntosh County on the Georgia coast just north of King's home on St. Simons, McIntosh probably had been a friend before the war. His father, William Jackson McIntosh (1782-1863), was a former United States naval officer, who at age 79 volunteered his service to Commodore Josiah Tatnall, when Savannah was threatened by the Federal fleet. A graduate of Georgia Military Institute, young McIntosh read law and practiced in Savannah. Before his staff appointment in 1861, he briefly served as second lieutenant in Company F, 1st Regiment Georgia Regulars. He was married in 1861 to Maria B. Morris. After his death at Sharpsburg, McIntosh was buried on the field, as King sadly describes in the diary, but his remains were removed and reinterred in Laurel Grove Cemetery in Savannah in 1867. Myers, *Children of Pride*, 3, 1608-1609. McLaws wrote of McIntosh that "he exhibited that self-possession under fire and disposition to be under fire so characteristic of his name, his relations in the Old Army of the United States and our own." *OR* 11, pt. 2, p. 717. McIntosh was related to both Gen. James McQueen McIntosh, formerly of the U. S. Army, who was killed commanding Confederate cavalry at Pea Ridge, and to his brother, Gen. John Baillie McIntosh, who commanded Union cavalry throughout the war. Their father was James Simmons McIntosh, a United States officer killed in the Mexican War.

9. Captain Mallory Page King served with General Smith at Secessionville on James Island on June 16, 1862, and then on the staff of Brig. Gen. States Rights Gist as A. A. G. in 1863-1864. General Gist commended him for gallantly carrying an order under heavy fire at Chickamauga. *OR* 30, pt. 2, p. 246. He joined McLaws' staff as A. A. G. in July 1864, becoming his A. I. G. in December. *OR* 40, pt. 3, p. 765; *OR* 44, p. 952. As late as March 1865, he was serving with McLaws at Bentonville. *OR* 47, pt. 1, p. 1110. After the war and Reconstruction, he and his wife Eugenia Grant King of Glynn Country, returned to "Retreat," but finding it impossible to revive planting there, moved elsewhere. Vanstory, *Georgia's Land*, pp. 136-138.

10. Brigadier General William Duncan Smith (1826-1862) was a graduate of the United States Military Academy in 1846. Born in Georgia, he served in the Mexican War, where he was severely wounded at Molino del Rey. After garrison duty in the West, he resigned his commission as captain in the Second Dragoons in 1861 and was commissioned colonel of the 20th Georgia Infantry. By March 1862, he was a brigadier general

and serving under Maj. Gen. John C. Pemberton in South Carolina and Georgia. Myers, *Children of Pride*, 3, 1681; Warner, *Generals in Gray*, pp. 285-286. In June, while Lord King was near Richmond, General Smith was in command of the District of South Carolina, headquartered in Charleston. His role at Secessionville on June 16 is unclear because of the confusion in command there. In his diary on June 22, King refers to receiving a letter from Georgia saying that Smith had been "arrested by Gen. Pemberton & released to fight on James Island. . .at Secessionville," and that Smith "protested & was arrested, released & fought without 'adequate results'—losing 55." For more information on this action, see Pat Brennan, *Secessionville: Assault on Charleston* (Savas Publishing Co., 1997). Many years after General Smith's death his widow Georgia King Smith married J. J. Wilder of Savannah. Vanstory, *Georgia's Land*, pp. 136-138.

11. Lieutenant Colonel John Floyd King was born in Monticello, Georgia, April 20, 1842, and graduated from University of Virginia. Commissioned lieutenant in Company M, 1st Georgia Regulars on March 28, 1861, he transferred to Company L and Company A. Robert K. Krick, *Lee's Colonels: A Biographical Register of the Field Officers of the Army of Northern Virginia* (Dayton, 1991), p. 233. King served under Generals Henry Heth, William W. Loring, Samuel Jones, John S. Williams, Robert Ransom, and John C. Breckinridge in southwestern and western Virginia, and in eastern Tennessee from 1862 to June 1864. As an elected major and appointed lieutenant colonel, he commanded the battalion called King's Battalion or the 13th Virginia Light Artillery. It consisted usually of four Virginia batteries: Otey's (Capt. George Gaston Otey and Capt. David Norvall Walker), Ringgold's (Capt. Crispin Dickenson), Davidson's (Capt. George S. Davidson) and Lowry's (Capt. William M. Lowry). *OR* 12, pt. 1, pp. 492-493; *OR* 19, pt. 1, pp. 1076-1078; *OR* 25, pt. 2, p. 824; *OR* 29, pt. 2, pp. 812-813; pp. 857, 908-909; Crute, *Confederate Staff Officers*, p. 125. In June 1864, at Breckinridge's request, King commanded a different battalion, called McLaughlin's, in Lt. Gen. Jubal Early's Army of the Valley, with whom he served in battles at Monocacy, Third Winchester, Fisher's Hill, and Cedar Creek. In the last months of the war when Brig. Gen. William Pendleton was reorganizing the artillery of the Army of Northern Virginia, King was assigned his "preference," a command of stationary guns in the Richmond defenses consisting of his two former batteries, Otey's under Captain Walker, and Ringgold's under Captain Dickenson. They were surrendered at Appomattox as the 13th Virginia Light Artillery, under Walker's command. Whether King was present is uncertain. *OR* 30, pt. 2, pp. 640, 645; *OR* 36, pt. 2, p. 959; pt. 1, pp. 1051, 1053; *OR* 51, pt. 2, p. 1000; *OR* 37, pt. 2, pp. 594, 596; *OR* 42, pt. 1, p. 861-863; *OR* 43, pt. 1, p. 567; *OR* 46, pt. 2, p. 1184; *OR* 46, pt. 3, pp. 1322-1323, 1327, 1329, 1333; *OR* 46, pt. 1, p. 1279; Jubal Early, *Narrative of the War Between the States* (New York, 1989), pp. 381, 388, 427. After the war Floyd King became a planter and lawyer in Louisiana. He served, as had his father, in the United States Congress from 1875 to 1887, and died May 8, 1915 in Washington, D.C., where he is buried in Arlington Cemetery. Krick, *Lee's Colonels*, p. 223.

12. Lieutenant Richard Cuyler King is the Lt. R. C. King who served with the 1st Georgia Battalion Sharpshooters in Henry Rootes Jackson's Brigade, since family letters in the Thomas Butler King Collection are written from near Chattanooga, Chickamauga, Missionary Ridge, and Marietta in 1863, and from Atlanta and Dalton areas in 1864—all places where he would have seen action with the Army of Tennessee. *OR* 45, pt. 1, p. 668. Although the surviving portions of Lord King's diary often mention his father, sisters Flora (Florence), Georgia, and Appy (Virginia), and Floyd, Mallory, and General Smith, it does not mention Richard Cuyler. Later in her life Florence King became the second wife of General Jackson. Myers, *Children of Pride*, III, 1561.

13. Major John F. Edwards was chief of subsistence for McLaws October to December 1862 and chief commissary December 1862. At this time he may have been on Kershaw's staff. Crute, *Confederate Staff Officers*, pp. 109, 139. Major William M. Inge served first as captain on the staff of Brig. Gen. Richard Griffith of Mississippi in 1861, and as major with Brig. Gen. Charles Clark of Mississippi in April 1862. He was on Col. William Barksdale's staff as A. A. G. in June 1862 when King had contact with him. Crute, *Confederate Staff Officers*, pp. 10, 37, 76. Magruder commended him for his "dauntless and dashing manner" on June 29 at Allen's Farm and Savage Station. *OR* 11, pt. 2, p. 666.

14. *OR* 11, pt. 2, pp. 717, 681 (McLaws' report). Lieutenant Thomas S. B. Tucker was A. D. C. to McLaws in 1861 and was still on his staff from May 23, 1862. He resigned July 1864. Crute, *Confederate Staff Officers*, p. 140. He appears in King's diary most conspicuously in the account of September 14, when he was sent by McLaws to inform General Lee that he had been forced by the unexpected Federal breakthrough at Crampton's Gap to form a line of battle, and that he was guarding three positions at once. Tucker was nearly captured. He survived unscathed through Sharpsburg as the diary evidences, but was badly wounded at Fredericksburg while carrying a message on Marye's Hill on December 13. He does not appear later on McLaws' staff. *OR* 19, p. 582; *OR* 11, pt. 2, pp. 717, 681.

15. After King's death at Fredericksburg, Varina Davis wrote her husband, "My poor young friend Lord King is dead, as is also Tom Cobb—Does not Col. K. who dined with us wish he had said less and that little more kindly." *The Papers of Jefferson Davis*, eds. Lynda L. Crist, Mary S. Dix and Kenneth Williams (Baton Rouge, 1995), vol. 8, pp. 553-554.

16. Major Delaware Kemper (1833-1899), a Virginian, was captain of the Alexandria Light Artillery, which he commanded at First Manassas under Brig. Gen. Milledge L. Bonham. After skirmishes at Fairfax Court House on July 17 and Mitchell's Ford on July 18, Kemper's battery took part in the pursuit of Maj. Gen. Irvin McDowell's retreating troops near the Stone Bridge. Near Cub Creek Bridge, Kemper permitted the "venerable" Edmund Ruffin to fire one of his guns upon the enemy's column. *OR* 2, pp. 458-459, 535-536; William C. Davis, *Battle at Bull Run* (Mechanicsburg, 1977), pp. 107, 224. Kemper was promoted to major by June 25, 1862, and served on the Peninsula in the Seven Days' Battles. He was attached to Joseph Kershaw's Brigade in the same

actions as King. Just prior to Second Manassas, his battery became part of Stephen Lee's Battalion and in that unit's action on August 30, from a commanding ridge near the Brawner Farm on Longstreet's left, did considerable damage to the enemy. E. Porter Alexander wrote of Lee's Battalion on that day as "conspicuous for its brilliant service." Edward Porter Alexander, *Fighting for the Confederacy: The Personal Recollections of General Edward Porter Alexander*, ed. by Gary W. Gallagher (Chapel Hill, 1989), p. 134. Colonel Lee reported Kemper's "right arm shattered by a Minie ball." *OR* 12, pt. 2, p. 578; pt. 3, p. 933; John J. Hennessey, *Return to Bull Run: The Campaign and Battle of Second Manassas* (New York, 1993), pp. 315-316. Kemper served the remainder of the war in the Department of South Carolina, Georgia and Florida. Krick, *Lee's Colonels*, pp. 220-221.

17. In order that the reader may not be unduly distracted by footnotes, they have been confined to identifying only the less well-known officers. Civilians are not identified.

18. Major Ellison L. Costin first served Brig. Gen. Richard Griffith as A. D. C. in 1861-1862. As captain, he was A. D. C. for Brig. Gen. Paul J. Semmes. He served as an A. D. C. on McLaws' staff, and became a major (October 20, 1862), and served as both A. I. G. and D. I. for him. He later served on Kershaw's staff as A. I. G. in 1864. Crute, *Confederate Staff Officers*, pp. 76, 109, 139, 173. Costin was McLaws' signal officer. He served at Fredericksburg, Chancellorsville, and in October 1864 with Kershaw in the Shenandoah Valley Campaign. *OR* 21, p. 582; *OR* 25, pt. 1, pp. 827, 830; *OR* 43, pt. 1, p. 595. For Lt. Thomas S. B. Tucker, see above, n. 14.

19. For Maj. Thomas Spaulding McIntosh, see above, n. 8.

20. Brigadier General Roger A. Pryor alludes to this "misfortune" in his report of the battle at Manassas in explaining how he came to be separated from his command. He was looking for two of his regiments and "advanced unconsciously" into enemy lines and "was detained in [an] embarassing position." *OR* 12, pt. 2, p. 602. He does not mention shooting the two Yankees.

21. Earlier in the diary (August 17, 1862), King had mentioned scouting with "Campbell," who was probably Lt. Duncan G. Campbell, an engineering officer who served either on the staff of Brig. Gen. David Rumph Jones or on McLaws'. From King's allusion on September 8, he was evidently serving McLaws at least that early and went through the Maryland Campaign with him. King and he scouted together for McLaws' Division along the road over South Mountain at Brownsville Gap on September 11. After Sharpsburg McLaws commends Lieutenant Campbell for "zeal and activity" in "reconnoitering the positions of the enemy." *OR* 19, pt. 1, pp. 857, 860. At Fredericksburg he mentions "Campbell of the engineers who had been engaged day and night (frequently all night) in strengthening the different positions," as part of McLaws' meticulous preparations for the Federal attack on Marye's Heights. *OR* 21, p. 582. Crute lists Lt. Duncan G. Campbell as an engineering officer for Maj. Gen. Gustavus Smith in February 1862, and as a captain on Smith's staff again in March 1864. In between, he lists a Lieutenant Campbell on Jones' staff in June 1862, and on McLaws' staff from

October to December 1862. Crute, *Confederate Staff Officers*, pp. 105, 139, 178-179. I assume here that the references are to the same man and that he was King's congenial fellow staff officer.

22. McLaws' Division, preceded by Captain King and Lieutenant Campbell, has just passed through Brownsville Gap into Pleasant Valley. McLaws' report does not name it Brownsville, but writes "the gap the troops had passed over into the valley (the one next south of Crampton's)." *OR* 19, pt. 1, p. 853. It is uncertain which Mr. Boteler hosted McLaws' and his staff. Alexander Robinson Boteler (1815-1892), former U. S. Congressman and Confederate Congressman, lived at Fountain Rock in Shepherdstown across the Potomac in (West) Virginia, but he may have owned property in Maryland; or, this Boteler may have been a relative. King does not refer to Boteler as colonel, at which rank Alexander Boteler had served on General Jackson's staff and on that of J. E. B. Stuart. *Encyclopedia of the Confederacy*, ed. Richard N. Current, 4 vols. (New York, 1993), 1, 197-198. Mr. Boteler reappears again in the diary as a guide on September 14.

23. Captain George B. Cuthbert, 2nd South Carolina Infantry, Kershaw's Brigade. When they reached Solomon's Gap on Elk Ridge, Cuthbert ordered the skirmishers "thrown well down the mountain to [his] right, while the column filed to the left along the ridge." *OR* 19, pt. 1, pp. 862-863 (Kershaw's report). Major John M. Bradley, 13th Mississippi Infantry, Barksdale's Brigade, commanding skirmishers on the left along the rocky ridge, found abatis, some picket resistance, crags and other "natural obstacles," much as King describes them. *OR* 19, pt. 1, pp. 862-863. Major Bradley was wounded at Sharpsburg, again at Gettysburg, and died July 28, 1863. Krick, *Lee's Colonels*, p. 65.

24. Colonel David Wyatt Aiken, 7th South Carolina Infantry, Kershaw's Brigade, did not submit a report, probably because he was wounded at Sharpsburg. Born in South Carolina in 1828, he was a teacher and planter. After commanding a post in Macon, Georgia, he resigned as disabled in July 1864. Krick, *Lee's Colonels*, pp. 30-31. Kershaw singled out Aiken and his men—as well as Major Bradley—"who bore the brunt of the battle and suffered the greatest loss" on Maryland Heights. *OR* 19, pt. 1, p. 864.

25. Colonel John Williford Henagan, 8th South Carolina Infantry, Kershaw's Brigade, was born in 1822 and served in the state legislature and as sheriff of Marlboro, South Carolina. He may have received a wound at Maryland Heights, since his regiment was commanded at Sharpsburg by Lt. Col. Axalla J. Hoole. *OR* 19, pt. 1, pp. 803, 865. Later in the war he was taken prisoner near Winchester on September 13, 1864, and died on Johnson's Island April 26, 1865. Krick, *Lee's Colonels*, p. 189.

26. Colonel James Drayton Nance, 3rd South Carolina, Kershaw's Brigade. Nance's report supplements Kershaw's account. *OR* 19, pt. 1, pp. 867-868. Nance was born in 1837 and graduated from South Carolina Military Academy. He rose from captain to colonel by May 14, 1862. He was killed in the Wilderness. Krick, *Lee's Colonels*, p. 287.

27. Captain Charles Rutledge Holmes was appointed A. A. G. to Kershaw's staff on March 22, 1862, and was still serving in November 1864. Crute, *Confederate Staff Officers*, p. 109. Kershaw commended him for "intelligent and efficient assistance in

carrying orders to all parts of the field at both Maryland Heights and Sharpsburg." *OR* 19, pt. 1, pp. 864, 866.

28. While Lord King had been marching through Maryland over Brownsville Gap and climbing Elk Ridge, his brother Floyd, now chief of artillery in Brig. Gen. John S. Williams' command in the Army of Western Virginia, was fighting in the Kanawha Valley. On September 10, he directed four batteries in an engagement at Fayetteville, pursued the enemy to Charleston, and fought again there on September 13. *OR* 19, pt. 1, pp. 1076-1078.

29. Lieutenant Colonel John Calvin Fiser (or Fizer), 17th Mississippi, is mentioned in parts of King's diary as a friend, although not in the portion printed here. Born in Tennessee in 1838, he rose from lieutenant to lieutenant colonel by April 1862, and colonel by February 1864. Barksdale commended him for "coolness and gallantry" in leading his regiment at Sharpsburg. *OR* 19, pt. 1, p. 884. He played a very important role at Fredericksburg in defending the town on December 11. *OR* 21, pp. 601-603. Wounded at Gettysburg and having lost an arm at Knoxville, he retired as disabled in June 1864. Krick, *Lee's Colonels*, p. 141.

30. *OR* 19, pt. 1, p. 867 (Read's report).

31. *OR* 19, pt. 1, pp. 856-857 (McLaws' report). For a classic account of the entire operation, see Douglas Southall Freeman, *Lee's Lieutenants: A Study in Command*, 3 vols. (New York, 1944), 2, pp. 184-192.

32. In addition and probably unknown to him, two of King's classmates at Harvard Law School were killed at Antietam on the Union side. Like King, Maj. William Dwight Sedgwick (Harvard L.L.B., 1855), formerly of the 2nd Massachusetts Infantry, served as a divisional staff officer for Maj. Gen. John Sedgwick. William, the general's cousin, was mortally wounded in Sedgwick's attack in the West Woods and died at Keedysville on September 29. A second classmate, Lt. Col. Wilder Dwight (Harvard LL.B., 1855) of the 2nd Massachusetts, Gordon's brigade, had been killed earlier in the day during the advance of Alpheus Williams' division, XII Corps, probably before McLaws' Division went into action. *Harvard Memorial Biographies*, ed. Thomas Wentworth Higginson, 3 vols. (Cambridge, 1866), 2, 179-189, 271-293.

33. Stephen W. Sears, *Landscape Turned Red: The Battle of Antietam* (New York, 1983), p. 234.

34. *OR* pt. 1, p. 860 (McLaws' report).

35. The "upper pass" would be Crampton's Gap, which emerged at Rohrersville. The "lower" or Brownsville Gap, which was also called Burkittsville Gap, was located less than two miles south of Crampton's and emerged at Brownsville. The latter is the one over which McLaws had marched on the 11th. Brigadier General Semmes posted a picket guard consisting of most of his brigade in the pass, which he calls Burkittsville Gap in his report. *OR* 19, pt. 1, pp. 872-873. It is now a jeep trail. Jay Luvaas and Harold W. Nelson, eds., *U. S. Army War College Guide to the Battle of Antietam: The Maryland Campaign of 1862* (Carlisle, 1987), pp. 75-76. See also James V. Murfin, *The*

Gleam of Bayonets: The Battle of Antietam and the Maryland Campaign of 1862 (Baton Rouge, 1965), pp. 140, 182; Sears, *Landscape Turned Red*, Map, p. 138.

36. The "Pass" referenced here is Crampton's. Rohrersville was in Pleasant Valley about a mile and a half north of the western foot of the pass. Semmes had been alerted to Howell Cobb's difficulties at Crampton's and attempted to aid him. *OR* 19, pt. 1, pp. 872-873. Although both passes were defended, it was mainly at Crampton's that men of Cobb's Brigade, of Semmes' 10th Georgia Infantry Regiment, and of William Mahone's Brigade, under command of Col. William A. Parham, engaged the Federal troops of William B. Franklin's VI Corps. By the end of the day the Confederate were, as McLaws reported, "badly crippled" and forced to yield their ground. *OR* 19, pt. 1, p. 857.

37. Colonel Thomas Taylor Munford, 2nd Virginia Cavalry, commanding Robertson's Brigade, Stuart's Cavalry Corps, had held Crampton's Gap on September 14, delaying for three hours the advance of Henry Slocum's division of Franklin's corps. *OR* 19, pt. 1, p. 826 (Munford's report).

38. "Retreat" and the other plantations on St. Simons belonging to King's neighbors, the James Hamilton Couper family at Cannon's Point and the Pierce Butler family at Hampton, had been evacuated earlier in the war at the approach of Union navy gunboats and later of Union troops. The King sisters moved to "Refuge" in Ware County. Vanstory, *Georgia's Land*, p. 136. Two Union officers who were fellow Harvard alumni viewed King's home in 1863: Col. Thomas Wentworth Higginson (A.B. 1841) and Col. Robert Gould Shaw (Class of 1860). Of "Retreat" in January 1863 Higginson wrote that it had "the loveliest gardens, though tangled and desolate," which he had ever seen in the South. He added that he could not "waste much sentiment over it, for it had belonged to a Northern renegade, Thomas Butler King." However, he felt "heartsickness at this desecration of a homestead," especially when looking out from a bare upper window of the empty house "upon a range of broad, flat, sunny roofs, such as children love to play on," and how it "might have been loved by yet innocent hearts." Thomas Wentworth Higginson, *Army Life in a Black Regiment* (New York, 1984), p. 82. For another poignant description of the deserted and vandalized buildings and gardens on the island, and of the burning of Darien on the Altamaha River, which was the King family's local post office and village in June 1863, see *Blue-Eyed Child of Fortune: The Civil War Letters of Colonel Robert Gould Shaw*, ed. Russell Duncan (Athens, 1992), pp. 341-350.

39. Lieutenant Colonel A. P. Mason was appointed A. A. G. on Lee's staff August 1862 and was still with him March 6, 1863. Earlier he had served on Joseph E. Johnston's staff in March and was with him again in December 1862. Crute, *Confederate Staff Officers*, pp. 104, 116. Longstreet mentions Mason as assisting him, among others of Lee's staff, at Sharpsburg. *OR* 19, pt. 1, p. 842. In a later part of the diary King characterizes Mason as a "stick."

40. Colonel John Doby Kennedy, 2nd South Carolina, in Kershaw's Brigade. He recovered to command his regiment at Fredericksburg in support of T. R. R. Cobb's men at the stone wall on Marye's Heights. *OR* 21, p. 592. Earlier in the war, Kennedy had been wounded at First Manassas and had suffered fever during the Seven Days, but

recovered to serve with Kershaw until Cedar Creek in 1864. After Kershaw's promotion, Kennedy commanded the brigade, was promoted to brigadier general on December 22, 1864, and served under Gen. Joseph Johnston in the Carolinas. As a lawyer, who had studied at South Carolina College, he returned to his profession after the war and took part in Democratic politics in South Carolina, where he served in the legislature and as lieutenant governor. He died in 1896 and is buried in Camden. Warner, *Generals in Gray*, pp. 170-171.

41. Joseph Mills Hanson's account of the artillery at Antietam states that of McLaws' five divisional batteries, "Read's went into such close action in the open on the right of the West Woods that it lost fourteen officers and men and sixteen horses in a quarter of an hour." Curt Johnson and Richard C. Anderson, Jr., *Artillery Hell: The Employment of Artillery at Antietam* (College Station, Texas, 1995), pp. 49. Read may have had four guns in action, one of which was commanded by Lt. Samuel Breck Parkman.

42. Macon's (Richmond "Fayette") Virginia Battery was commanded at Sharpsburg by Lt. William Izard Clopton while Capt. Miles C. Macon was on detached duty at Bolivar Heights. Johnson and Anderson, *Artillery Hell*, p. 86. Johnson and Anderson also assert that Lieutenant Clopton commanded Macon's Battery at Crampton's Gap, which does not appear to be accurate. General Semmes' report on that action and on the related one at Brownsville Gap claims that Captain Macon assisted him with three pieces of artillery in defense of Brownsville Gap and then, as senior artillery officer, shifted his guns to fire on Federal troops as they moved up into Crampton's Gap. Macon and Manly's Battery "did good service in breaking the enemy's lines, checking his advance, and inflicting loss on him" at "Burkittsville Gap." *OR* 19, pt. 1, p. 873. See also report of Col. E. B. Montague, 32nd Virginia Infantry, on Macon's assistance at "Brownsville Gap," *OR* 19, pt. 1, pp. 881-882. Lieutenant Samuel Breck Parkman, a fellow Harvard alumnus, was a friend of King's, probably from shared legal experience in Savannah, although they may have been acquainted earlier. Parkman was born November 1, 1836, near Augusta, Georgia. At less than two years old he lost both parents, three sisters and a brother, when the ship *Pulaski* burned at sea on June 14, 1838. His mother was from Westborough, Massachusetts. Raised by his aunt, Parkman attended military school in Sing Sing, New York, and John B. Felton's School. After graduating from Harvard College in 1857, where his friends included Robert Gould Shaw, he read law in Savannah and was admitted to practice. Parkman belonged to the Georgia Historical Society and a Savannah cavalry troop before the war. In 1860, he married Nannie Bierne of Virginia. Newspaper clipping in Report of the Class of 1857, Harvard University Archives. Parkman's war service began with an appointment May 18, 1861, as second lieutenant, then first lieutenant in Captain Read's (Pulaski) Georgia Light Artillery. Service Record of Samuel B. Parkman, National Archives; Blake, "Harvard's Confederates," p. 425. He served at Fort Walker under Thomas F. Drayton in defense of Port Royal in November 1861. On the Peninsula he was with Read as part of Cabell's First Regiment Virginia Artillery at Lee's Mill, Williamsburg, Garnett's Farm,

Savage Station, and Malvern Hill. He may have assisted Read on Maryland Heights. At Sharpsburg his performance and death, "in a position of great danger," on a "hill to the right of the wood" (West Woods), was mentioned by Kershaw. *OR* 19, pt. 1, p. 866. He was buried in the Bierne family vault in Richmond. News of Parkman's death in battle travelled quickly into Union lines, for Lieutenant Shaw, in the 2nd Massachusetts, wrote his family September 25, "Breck Parkman, of Savannah, was killed at Sharpsburg; on the other side of course," *Blue-Eyed Child*, pp. 247-248. Moxley Sorrel remembered both Parkman and Major McIntosh many years later: "Here fell my dear personal friends of school days, McIntosh and Parkman." Moxley Sorrel, *Recollections of a Confederate Staff Officer* (New York, 1994), p. 115.

43. Captain Henry H. Carlton commanded Carlton's (Troup) Georgia Battery. Two of his guns had earlier, on the 14th, been dragged up Maryland Heights with Captain Read's two pieces and had taken part in the firing on Harpers Ferry. Two others, while attached to Cobb's Brigade and commanded by Lt. Henry Jennings, had been engaged at Crampton's Gap, where one was lost. *OR* 19, pt. 1, pp. 854, 861 864, 871. Read's, Macon's and Carlton's batteries, with those of Manly and McCarthy, made up the artillery at McLaws' disposal. The batteries came into action when McLaws counter-attacked Sedgwick between 9:00 a.m. and noon. Carlton's was "nearly cut to pieces" while giving aid to McLaws' infantry. Johnson and Anderson, *Artillery Hell*, pp. 49, 58, 106; *OR* 19, pt. 1, pp. 858, 862.

44. Major H. C. Rodgers, A. A. G. on the staff of Maj. Gen. Henry W. Slocum. *OR* 19, pt. 1, p. 381. General Slocum's report does not include any mention of a proposal to exchange the wounded.

45. Lafayette McLaws, "The Confederate Left at Fredericksburg," *Battles and Leaders*, 3, 86-94.

46. *OR* 21, pp. 578-579 (McLaws' report).

47. McLaws, *Battles and Leaders*, 3, 89-90.

48. McLaws, *Battles and Leaders*, 3, 92; Robert Ransom, "Ransom's Division at Fredericksburg," *Battles and Leaders*, 3, 94; Porter Alexander, "The Battle of Fredericksburg," *Southern Historical Society Papers*, 10, pp. 453-454.

49. Vanstory, *Georgia's Land*, pp. 136-137; Cate, *Our Todays and Yesterdays*, pp. 155-156; 277.

"It was a terrible ordeal."

FROM FOX'S GAP TO THE SHERRICK FARM

The 79th New York Highlanders
in the Maryland Campaign

Terry A. Johnston, Jr.

I t was not until September 21, 1862, that Private Robert Davidson was able to find the time to put aside his duties as a Union soldier and resume his role as special correspondent to the New York City-based newspaper, the *Scottish-American Journal*. Davidson's job had been the same since the beginning of the war: to report to the interested readers of New York's Scottish community the goings-on of their pet regiment, the 79th New York "Highlanders." It was a task the thirty-one-year-old native of Forfarshire, Scotland, performed well; save for a period of several months in 1861 during which Davidson languished in Confederate prison, the readers of the *Scottish-American Journal* could look forward to his weekly reports on their beloved "Highlanders," his detailed and stunningly candid letters to the editor published for all to read. On this day in September, Davdison took pen in hand to relay his regiment's role in the recent battles of South Mountain and Antietam, the fourth and fifth major engagements in which the 79th New York Infantry had participated over the previous three months. No doubt the weary private wrote his opening line with a feeling of great relief, a sentiment surely shared by his anxious readers: "This portion of the army is having a little rest after a week's heavy work. . . ."[1]

At the time, it must have seemed to the men of the 79th New York that they had incurred little more than heavy work since their departure for the war back in June 1861. It might even be said that the Highlanders' first fight was before the war, during the final months of 1858, when some of New York City's leading Scottish citizens began to push for the acceptance of a Scottish militia regiment, what was to become the 79th New York State Militia, formed in the early months of 1859.[2]

Opposition to the formation of a "Highland" regiment in 1858 came from both military circles and the city's press corps. The problem: the proposed attire of the Scots—kilts, tartan trews, sporrans, glengarry caps, and other items worn by soldiers in contemporary British Highland regiments.[3] Though several similarly-clad Scottish volunteer militia companies had functioned successfully in New York City since the beginning of the century, a move to form a kilted regiment in the late 1850s ran counter to the more recent efforts of the leaders of the New York State Militia to create a uniformity of dress among the city's militia units.[4] Although the garb was a source of pride and ethnic identity to the Scottish militiamen, it was a "foreign ridiculous costume" to the proposed regiment's detractors. The kilt soon became the major sticking point: "If they like the bare leg. . .better than they like their adopted land," wrote the editors of the *New York Military Gazette*, "let it be so, and let us try to do without their aid."[5]

A compromise, however, was reached—the Scots could don tartan trews (a form of trousers), though not kilts—and the regiment was accepted into the Fourth Brigade, First Division, New York State Militia, where it served alongside the 69th N.Y.S.M. of eventual Irish Brigade fame. Scots and descendants of Scots filled the ranks of the new 250-man regiment, which was granted the numerical designation "79" after the famed British Highland regiment of the same number. The 79th N.Y.S.M. (also known as the Highland Guard and the Scotch Regiment) not only wore the tartan of the British 79th, but eventually the kilt, which the Highlanders went ahead and adopted in 1860 (probably unilaterally), much to the displeasure of the regiment's original opposers.[6] Regardless of their uniform, the 79th N.Y.S.M. quickly became one of the city's prized militia regiments.

In the wake of the firing on Fort Sumter and Lincoln's call for 75,000 militiamen to enter national service for three months, the officers and enlisted men of the 79th N.Y.S.M. voted to volunteer and be "ready to march at a moment's warning to defend the flag of the Union."[7] Though one of the first units so to vote, the 79th N.Y.S.M was "kept on the tip-toe of expectation" for the next four weeks until finally accepted for Federal service on May 13.[8] The delay had several causes, the primary being that the regiment was undersized; though it had grown to 300 men in six companies by 1861, the 79th N.Y.S.M. fell well short of the 1,000 men in ten companies required by Federal guidelines. The regiment vigorously recruited to meet the Federal standard, and men were admitted regardless of nationality. (In fact, though the 79th New York would remain in the minds of both soldiers and citizens as the "Highland" regiment for the entire war, Scots soon became outnumbered by Irish in the ranks.[9]) Although frustrating to many in the 79th, the delay had caused the Highlanders to miss the opportunity to enlist for the three-month term of Lincoln's first call; when the men of the regiment were sworn into Federal service, they did so under the terms of the president's second call for troops, meaning they would serve three-year terms. Once sufficiently sized, equipped, and sworn in, the 79th New York Volunteer Infantry departed on June 2, 1861, for Washington, D.C.

Luck and good fortune continued to elude the Highlanders during the first fifteen months of their participation in the war. As part of William T. Sherman's Brigade, Tyler's Division, at the First Battle of Bull Run, they were bloodied on the slope of Henry Hill, where they lost their colonel, James Cameron (brother of Secretary of War Simon Cameron), to a bullet through the chest, and suffered an additional 197 casualties (roughly 26% of their strength)—among the highest number of any Union regiment that day.[10]

The humiliating and costly Union defeat at Bull Run set the stage for what was arguably the darkest day of the 79th New York's history: the mutiny of the regiment. On August 14, 1861, all but two companies refused to obey orders to strike camp for a move to Maryland. The reasons behind the insubordination were manifold: sagging morale; increased incidence of illness; a shaky command structure due to the resignation of many homesick officers; the slight of not being allowed to elect their new colonel, Isaac Ingalls Stevens—a right the Highlanders believed was theirs as militiamen; too much whiskey; and, on the morning of August 14, the realization that their rumored and much anticipated return to New York City to recruit new men and visit with family and friends was not to be, as orders to head to Maryland were issued.[11]

The consequences of the regiment's disobedience of orders were swift and severe. Major General George B. McClellan ordered a detachment of regular infantry, cavalry and artillery to quell the mutinous Highlanders, who had quickly become "an infuriated mob." Surrounded by the detachment, the mutineers were suppressed, and thirty-five so-called "ring leaders" were placed under arrest. McClellan issued the humiliating Special Order No. 27, which was read aloud to the subdued men of the 79th. McClellan ordered the regiment's colors taken away, not to be returned "until its members have shown by their conduct in camp, that they have learned the first duty of soldiers—obedience—and have proven on the field of battle that they are not wanting in courage." Not until their colors were restored a month later for good conduct during a reconnaissance mission could the members of the 79th New York begin to put the events of August 14 behind them.[12]

In October 1861, the 79th New York was attached to Isaac Stevens' brigade of General Thomas W. Sherman's expeditionary force headed for Port Royal, South Carolina, a strategically important harbor situated between Charleston and Savannah. (Stevens, the 79th's new commander, recently had been elevated to command of the brigade.) The 79th eventually was positioned at Beaufort, South Carolina, where the men spent the first five months of 1862. The regiment's respite from heavy fighting came to an end when Gen. Henry Benham ordered two Federal divisions, including the 79th New York, to move upon James Island, push aside its Confederate defenders, and open a route to Charleston. The resulting Battle of Secessionville, fought on June 16, was a resounding Confederate victory. As at Bull Run, roughly one of every four Highlanders engaged became casualties.[13]

The soldiers of the 79th New York had little time to lick their wounds. Union forces were soon ordered from James Island, and the 79th was shipped back to Virginia where, on July 22, 1862, the Highlanders and other regiments of Gen. Isaac Stevens' division were joined with the returning soldiers of Gen. Ambrose Burnside's expedition to North Carolina to form the IX Corps, Army of the Potomac. In early August, the IX Corps received orders to proceed to Fredericksburg, Virginia, to reinforce Maj. Gen. John Pope's Army of Virginia. After playing a peripheral role in the disastrous Union defeat at the Battle of Second Bull Run on August 29-30, the 79th was heavily engaged in the rearguard action of September 1 at Chantilly, where two divisions of the IX Corps, led by former 79th New York colonel, Gen. Isaac Ingalls Stevens, were detached to protect the Federal retreat from General Thomas J. "Stonewall" Jackson's pursuing Confederates.[14]

Though the successful Federal stance at Chantilly checked Jackson's hopes of cutting off Pope's retreating columns, it was not without substantial cost. Generals Stevens and Philip Kearny were killed, the former falling at the head of the 79th New York, its standard clasped in his hands. Losses at Chantilly increased the 79th's casualties for Pope's Virginia Campaign to a total of 105 men—troops the regiment could ill afford to lose. A roll call taken on September 3 revealed that the Highlanders could muster only one field officer, seven line officers, and 200 enlisted men for duty, many of whom were in desperate need of new shoes and clothing, their uniforms literally worn down during the previous months' campaigning. "The Regt was in an awful plight when I rejoined it," observed Private George Ryerson of Company E, who returned from a well-timed leave from the regiment shortly after the fight at Chantilly. "Some had no shoes[,] some wanted clothing of all descriptions and they were the most ragged looking set of men I ever saw. . . .They. . .have been fighting and marching for three whole weeks without stopping long enough to wash their clothing and some have went for that length of time without even washing their face and hands because they had no time."[15]

Private Ryerson was not the only one to note the sorry condition of the 79th New York. "The Regiment has been in five large battles," lamented Captain William T. Lusk in a letter to his mother after Chantilly, "and. . .while adding on each occasion new luster to its own reputation, it has never taken part in a successful action. The proud body that started from the city over a thousand strong, are now a body of cripples." Or, as Color Sergeant Alexander Campbell, one of five Highlander color bearers to fall on September 1, observed: "The 79th has a poor show now."[16]

General Robert E. Lee's raid of the North was both quickly planned and bold. Just two days after the rearguard action at Chantilly, Lee put pen to paper and enumerated to Confederate President Jefferson Davis the reasons for such a move: 1) the Federals were again beaten and demoralized, and had withdrawn to the defenses of Washington; 2) to shift the war from the fields of Virginia to those of Maryland would relieve the pressure both on the Confederate capital at Richmond as well as the northern-Virginia farmers whose harvests were so vital to the sustenance of the Army of Northern Virginia; and 3) to provide relief and support to those loyal Maryland citizens who had known nothing but Federal occupation since the war's inception. Additionally, as Lee and Davis knew well, a decisive Confederate victory on Northern soil could be the undoing of the Lincoln administration, as upcoming national elections in the North were bound to be a referendum on the status of the Union war effort.[17]

As Lee's 50,000-man Army of Northern Virginia began crossing the Potomac River into Maryland on September 4, 1862, the men of the 79th New York found themselves bivouacked at Fort Worth, near Alexandria. Late that night, the Highlanders resumed their march toward the nation's capital. In an ironic moment that surely did not escape many of the weary and demoralized New Yorkers, the regiment crossed the Long Bridge into Washington in the early hours of September 5 and filed into their new camp on Meridian Hill, settling within fifty yards of the site of the previous year's mutiny of the regiment.[18] The Highlanders, like their comrades in the Army of the Potomac, had little time to recuperate from the recently concluded Virginia campaign. Word of the Confederate move into Maryland spread quickly, and in response, President Lincoln and General-in-Chief Henry Halleck restored George McClellan as head of the Army of the Potomac, commanding him to protect Washington from Lee's aggressive force. To this end, McClellan shuffled the Army of the Potomac into three 'Grand Divisions,' each consisting of two army corps. The Right Grand Division contained the I and IX Corps (commanded by Maj. Gens. Joseph Hooker and Jesse L. Reno, respectively), and was placed under the command of General Ambrose Burnside. The Highlanders remained in the First Division of the IX Corps, which was now led by General Orlando B. Willcox (in place of Isaac Ingalls Stevens), though they were moved from the Second to First Brigade. The First Brigade, commanded by Col. Benjamin C. Christ, consisted of the 79th New York, 28th Massachusetts, 50th Pennsylvania, and the 8th and 17th Michigan, while the Second Brigade under Col. Thomas Welsh contained the 46th New York and the 45th and 100th Pennsylvania.[19]

On September 7, General McClellan set the Army of the Potomac in pursuit of Lee's Confederates, who had reached Frederick, Maryland. At noon that day, the men of the 79th New York struck camp and began their northwesterly march. Though it had been only six days since their last fight, the Highlanders began the new campaign in relatively good spirits. In a minor stroke of good timing, the regiment welcomed some 70 new recruits from New York City the previous day, who, in addition to a number of returning stragglers, augmented their ranks to about 300 enlisted men.[20]

For the next four days, the First Division, IX Corps, made its way toward Frederick; Leesboro was reached on the night of September 7; Hyattstown on September 9; and New Market, some six miles from Frederick, on September 11.[21] The change of scenery offered by the Maryland countryside was welcomed by the men of the 79th New York, as Private Robert Davidson noted in his letter to the *Scottish-American Journal*: "I may mention that the 'smiling plenty' of the Maryland farms, and the hearty welcome accorded to us on our route by the inhabitants, afforded a decided and pleasant contrast to the many scenes of desolation and ruin through which we have recently passed."[22] Twenty-two-year-old Corporal William Todd, regimental historian of the 79th New York, recalled the switch to Maryland in equally positive terms: "We were in 'God's Country' now, and the change from Virginia was a pleasant one; the roads were good, the weather fine, and the men cheerful."[23]

By the time the 79th New York reached the outskirts of Frederick on September 11, the Confederates had moved on. Two days previous General Lee had issued Special Orders 191, in which he laid down the particulars for the next phase of the campaign. Lee boldly ordered his Army of Northern Virginia divided into two main segments: Maj. Gen. Thomas "Stonewall" Jackson, with three divisions, would proceed to Harpers Ferry, Virginia, and lay siege to its Federal garrison; Maj, Gen. James Longstreet, with two divisions, was to head northwest for Hagerstown, Maryland. The success of Lee's plan depended upon several factors, the primary being secrecy. Lee relied on both General J. E. B. Stuart's cavalry and South Mountain (a fifty mile ridge that could be crossed by an army at only a handful of passes and that now separated the Army of Northern Virginia from the Army of the Potomac) to screen his movements from the enemy. Any knowledge of his plan among his Union adversaries could spell disaster.[24]

This knowledge was delivered to General McClellan on September 13 when a copy of Lee's Special Orders 191, discovered by Union soldiers in a field on the outskirts of Frederick, was placed in his hands. McClellan now knew Lee's plan, the positions of his troops, and that only Stuart's cavalry and a division commanded by Confederate Maj. Gen. Daniel H. Hill protected Turner's Gap, the vital nearby pass in South Mountain. If McClellan could move his massive army with alacrity across South Mountain, he would come between Lee's divided force—Jackson and Longstreet were now some 25 miles apart—before they could reunite. If McClellan could move his army in time, the days of the Army of Northern Virginia and the Confederacy might be numbered.[25]

Those proved to be big "ifs" for George McClellan. The evening before McClellan's advantage was so fortuitously presented, the men of the 79th New York arrived at the heights east of Frederick, where they bivouacked for the night. Early the next morning, September 13, the Highlanders, along with a detachment of the 6th New York Cavalry and Capt. Asa M. Cook's 8th Massachusetts Battery, were ordered on a reconnaissance of the Hagerstown Road near Frederick "for the purpose of finding out the whereabouts of the enemy, and observing his movements." This they did, but encountering no enemy force by mid-afternoon, they returned to camp. Upon their arrival, however, the men of the 79th did not find the rest of their division, which earlier that day had advanced through Frederick and moved towards the base of South Mountain, settling a mile and a half east of the village of Middletown.[26]

Discovering the route taken by the First Division, the 79th New York immediately set out to rejoin their comrades. Tired from their day's work and out of rations, the Highlanders reached Frederick late in the day. Corporal Todd remembered the scene:

> We had marched a long distance out of our way in returning from picket duty, and when, at nightfall, we approached Frederick, the men were tired and hungry. On entering the city, however, the sight which greeted our eyes, drove all tired and hungry feelings from our minds. The balconies and door-steps of many of the houses were filled with ladies and children, dressed in white, with red and blue profusely displayed, waiting to receive us. . . .It was an inspiring sight, those loyal women, welcoming us with bright smiling faces, and words of kindly greeting—we were not tired![27]

Rejuvenated, the men of the 79th New York reached First Division headquarters early the next day.[28]

McClellan chose September 14 to probe the passes of South Mountain for a possible crossing. The nearby creases in the mountain range at Turner's and Fox's gaps were still held by D. H. Hill's Confederates and, though Hill was grossly outnumbered—only two of his five brigades were at hand that morning—the rough terrain of South Mountain favored the defenders. Through the ravines, woods, and undergrowth of Turner's Gap ran the National Road, from which two additional roads branched at the eastern base of South Mountain: the Old Sharpsburg Road broke to the south and ran west through South Mountain at Fox's Gap, nearly one mile from the pass at Turner's; the Old Hagerstown Road angled to the north a short distance and rejoined the National Road at the peak of South Mountain at Turner's. A number of lesser roads and paths snaked to and from the National and Old Sharpsburg Roads as they worked themselves toward the summit, making Hill's task of protecting both passes simultaneously much more difficult.

Though certainly not simple, General Hill's orders were clear: keep the Federals from crossing South Mountain in the vicinity of Turner's Gap until Jackson's operation against Harpers Ferry was concluded and the Army of Northern Virginia could again be consolidated. To this end, Hill spread his men to cover the various approaches, sending Brig. Gen. Samuel Garland's brigade of North Carolinians (consisting of the 5th, 12th, 13th, 20th and 23rd North Carolina) to Fox's Gap, and keeping Brig. Gen. Alfred H. Colquitt's brigade (13th Alabama, 6th, 23rd, 27th and 28th Georgia) to guard Turner's Gap.[29]

Due to its relative proximity to South Mountain (the bulk of the Army of the Potomac was still near Frederick), the IX Corps was charged with the task of leading the Union advance. With the support of General Alfred Pleasonton's cavalry, Brig. Gen. Jacob Cox's Kanawha Division, the IX Corps' lead element, was first up the slope. At mid-morning, Cox launched his division against Garland's Georgians at Fox's Gap, the sounds of which were heard several miles away by the Highlanders, who had not yet left their camp east of Middletown. The 79th New York and the rest of the Willcox's First Division departed for the front between 10:30 and 11:00 a.m., sent to support Cox's men at Fox's Gap.[30]

As the Highlanders began their advance toward the sound of the guns on South Mountain, they were provided a magnificent view. As Private Davidson recorded:

> The beauty of the scene breaks upon your vision in a moment, like a charm. You no sooner reach the crest of the North [Catoctin] Mountain than the long, deep valley, rich with the fruits of the earth, and studded with pretty cottages and farmhouses, opens to the view. Then the repose afforded to the eye by the dark, stern South Mountain on the other side of the valley forms a grand framework to the picture. I wished for a moment—begging Uncle Sam's pardon—that I had come on another mission, and that I could stay to breathe the free mountain air, in peace and quietness, for a while. But the turnpike was alive with armed men, the passes of South Mountain were crowded with Confederate forces, the boom of cannon quickly reached our ears, the word was given to 'fall in,' and away we went.[31]

Lt. Col. David Morrison, the forty-one year old native Scot and British Army veteran who commanded the 79th New York that day, had little time to take in the scenery, though he did note the temperament of the Highlanders. "Although my men were wearied and much fatigued from the effects of the preceding forty-eight hours' almost constant duty," he wrote, " when they found that the enemy was making a stand, their eagerness to face them was un-bounded, and they boldly pushed forward to the foot of the mountain."[32]

The First Division arrived at the foot of South Mountain sometime between 1:00 and 2:00 p.m. Initially, preparations were made to continue the division straight up the National Road for an attack upon the woods southeast of the Mountain House at Turner's Gap. Before Willcox's men could proceed, how-ever, General Burnside, commander of the Right Grand Division, arrived on the scene and ordered them up the Old Sharpsburg Road instead, so as to take a position near Cox's already engaged Kanawha Division at Fox's Gap.[33]

Cox's Ohioans had battled with Garland's North Carolinians at Fox's Gap for most of the morning, and with good results. The Confederates were pushed from the crest of South Mountain, and for a time late in the morning, Fox's Gap was in Union hands. Cox's men soon found themselves in a precarious position, however. Though they had driven back Garland's brigade, their promised rein-forcements—the remaining three divisions of IX Corps—had not yet arrived, and their ammunition was running dangerously low. Isolated at an exposed position at the top of the mountain, the Kanawha Division began receiving an intensified fire from nearby Confederate artillerists, who accurately lobbed shells amongst Cox's men. Cox had little choice but to withdraw his soldiers from Fox's Gap a short distance and regroup his forces. By noon, a lull had fallen over the battlefield, and a superb opportunity to exploit early gains at Fox's Gap was quickly slipping away.[34]

Upon receiving their new orders, the men of the First Division proceeded with all haste toward Cox's position at Fox's Gap. Given the rough terrain and steep slope of South Mountain, however, speed of movement was little more than wishful thinking. To reach the Old Sharpsburg Road from their position at the National Road, Willcox's men were required to turn left onto the Bolivar Road, which runs southward from the National Road and links up with the Old Sharpsburg about a mile distant from Fox's Gap, then turn right (west) upon Old Sharpsburg and climb the slope toward the contested pass. The First Division advanced in the direction of Fox's Gap with Christ's First Brigade in the lead, the regiments of which were deployed in column with the 79th New York in front.[35]

As the Highlanders struck off upon the Bolivar Road, they came into the range of the guns of Capt. John Lane's Georgia Battery, positioned across the National Road in the vicinity of Turner's Gap. "The enemy's guns were planted on the heights above," recalled Corporal Todd, "and their shot and shell were dropping about us as we marched along the road."[36] According to Private Davidson, the incoming rounds did little damage to the Highlanders' determina-tion: "As we advanced within range of the enemy's batteries, we were treated to shell, but the Seventy-Ninth marched steadily on without betraying the slightest emotion." Still, admitted Davidson, "The Confederate position was exceedingly strong, and we instinctively knew that desperate work was before us." The Old Sharpsburg Road soon was reached and, shortly after turning onto the rough mountain road, the men of 79th New York encountered a group of Union soldiers watching captured Confederates, the former being very pleased to see men from the First Division entering the fight. "As we passed by a guard over a crowd of prisoners we were congratulated on our arrival," noted Private David-son. "One enthusiastic volunteer [of the guard] cried out. . .'We charged on

[th]em and took 150 prisoners. But you'll find plenty of [th]em left,' he added, apologetically, as if he wouldn't rob us of our due for the world."[37]

It was 2:00 p.m. by the time the lead element of Willcox's First Division reached Cox's position. During the two-hour pause in the fight for Fox's Gap, Garland's beaten Confederates had received much-needed reinforcements in the form of two of D. H. Hill's remaining three brigades, all of which arrived in time for the renewed fight for South Mountain. Hill placed Brig. Gen. George Anderson's Brigade (2nd, 4th, 14th and 30th North Carolina) at Garland's former position, with Brig. Gen. Roswell Ripley's Brigade (4th and 44th Georgia, 1st and 3rd North Carolina) close behind. Hill's remaining brigade, commanded by Brig. Gen. Robert Rodes (3rd, 5th, 6th, 12th and 26th Alabama), was directed to reinforce Colquitt's Brigade at Turner's Gap. In addition, General Longstreet's two divisions were on their way from Hagerstown and expected to arrive sometime that afternoon.[38] Union victory at Fox's Gap was now not as certain as it had appeared to be several hours earlier.

The New Yorkers of the 79th were preceding up the Old Sharpsburg Road by Cook's 8th Massachusetts Battery, the unit that had accompanied them on their reconnaissance mission the previous day. The steep, rocky road made advancing tough enough for infantrymen, let alone a battery of artillery, and the Highlanders were thus obliged to assist the Massachusetts gunners and manhandle their pieces up the mountain and into position—a task that was accomplished in all possible haste and under the accurate fire of Confederate artillerists. Two guns of Cook's Battery were placed near the Martz farmhouse, located alongside Old Sharpsburg Road, some 400 yards from summit of South Mountain. Ordered to support Cook, Lt. Col. Morrison deployed the Highlanders roughly 100 yards to its rear.[39]

As the remaining soldiers of Willcox's division continued to labor up Old Sharpsburg Road, Cook's artillerists opened fire upon Lane's Battery, roughly a mile distant. One of Cook's guns was disabled in the resulting exchange and, as a replacement piece was ushered to the front, a previously unseen and much closer Confederate battery fired upon Cook's position. This unexpected fire of canister and shell came from Confederate Capt. J. W. Bondurant's guns, positioned less than 600 yards away in the woods near Daniel Wise's farmhouse, which sat at the mouth of Fox's Gap. "Then," noted Private Davidson, "the excitement commenced." Startled by Bondurant's deadly fire, Cook's panic-stricken gunners abandoned their pieces, some taking cover in nearby woods while others rushed their column of caissons and the disabled cannon back down the road from whence they had just come, a route still occupied by the

On September 13, 1862, Maj. Gen. George B. McClellan fortuitously came into possession of a copy of Robert E. Lee's Special Orders No. 191, which detailed the disposition of the Confederate Army of Northern Virginia. With this information, McClellan moved out against the divided Confederates the following day.

The wooded and difficult South Mountain range divided the opponents. McClellan's task was to seize the passes and force his way westward, which would place his army between Lee's divided divisions.

On September 14, Federal cavalry discovered D. H. Hill's division defending Fox's and Turner's Gaps. By midmorning, Jacob Cox's IX Corps division was advancing up wooded and rocky slopes, and by noon the rest of the IX Corps was moving forward to capture the crest of South Mountain.

The 79th New York "Highlanders," part of Benjamin Christ's brigade, Orlando Willcox's First Division, arrived on the scene and was immediately dispatched to protect Cook's 8th Massachusetts Battery. After securing the position, the regiment moved forward in a general assault that drove back the tenacious defenders and seized the crest of South Mountain. Uncharacteristically, the 79th endured light losses of only twelve wounded.

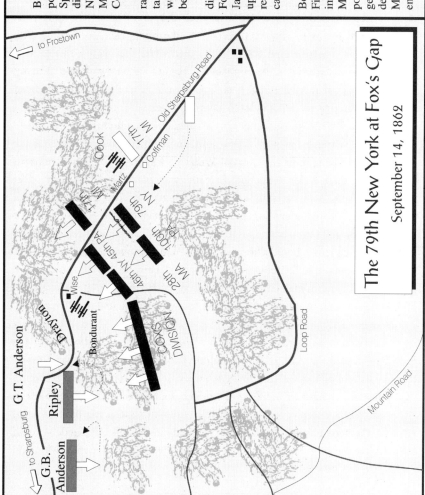

The 79th New York at Fox's Gap
September 14, 1862

approaching Union troops of the First Division. Confusion abounded, witnessed Private Davidson, for "[a]ll at once there appeared some danger of a stampede. . . .There was a rushing sound amongst the brush, and a cry arose that one of our batteries had been driven from its position, leaving two guns, and that the enemy were charging down upon us."[40]

Almost immediately, General Willcox, who had just arrived on the scene, ordered Lieutenant Colonel Morrison to hurry the 79th to the front of Cook's remaining pieces and to the left of the Old Sharpsburg Road. The 17th Michigan was similarly directed, although to the rear of Cook's battery and the right of Old Sharpsburg Road. Time was of the essence, as the enemy was now so close to Cook's remaining guns that a charge seemed realistic and not just the fantasy of panicked soldiers. Though executed under a heavy fire from Bondurant's pieces and Confederate infantry positioned along the crest, Morrison's orders were carried out and to good effect, recalled Corporal Todd. "The order was given at once for us to 'change direction by the right flank; forward; double quick!' and it was executed so speedily, that when the enemy saw it they halted." This move brought the Highlanders behind a stone wall, one of many found that day on the farm land near Fox's Gap, "where it would have been difficult for three times our number to have dislodged us," noted Todd.[41]

With the 79th New York and 17th Michigan so positioned, the immediate threat to Cook's guns was alleviated and, more importantly, a larger panic averted. The remaining infantrymen of Willcox's First Division were deployed. Colonel Thomas Welsh's Second Brigade was placed to the left of Old Sharpsburg Road, with the right of the 45th Pennsylvania adjacent to the road, and the left of the 46th New York extending to the men of Cox's division. As for the Second Brigade's remaining regiments, the 8th Michigan was sent off to the left to reinforce Cox's lines, while the 100th Pennsylvania was held in reserve. Of the regiments in Col. Benjamin Christ's First Brigade, the 79th New York and 17th Michigan remained in their positions near Cook's Battery, while the 50th Pennsylvania, like the 8th Michigan, was sent to Cox, and the 28th Massachusetts was held in reserve.[42]

Confederate artillerists maintained a "furious fire" upon the men of the First Division as they settled into position. Though the farm walls and rough terrain of the mountain offered Willcox's men some cover from the incoming projectiles, many hit their marks, and Union casualties began to increase steadily. Soon Willcox received orders to take Bondurant's menacing battery "at all hazards." Willcox found Morrison and informed him that his Highlanders would be used for the task. Morrison acted quickly. "Drawing his sword, Morrison ordered us to 'stand up and prepare to charge,'" recalled Corporal Todd. Continuing, he remembered that "[o]n seeing the line General Willcox asked: 'Is this your regiment?' 'Yes, General, but if you will give me more men we'll take the battery,' was Morrison's reply. 'No, I'll send another regiment, yours is too small.'" Willcox instead ordered the 45th Pennsylvania and 17th Michigan, both much stronger in number, to lead the charge of the Confederate guns, with the 79th New York following behind in support.[43]

By the time Willcox received orders to advance upon Bondurant's Battery, Longstreet's approaching divisions had arrived on the scene. A thankful Hill quickly steered the first pair of Longstreet's arriving brigades, those of Brig. Gen. Thomas F. Drayton and Col. George T. Anderson, to Fox's Gap. The regiments of Drayton's Brigade (50th and 51st Georgia, 15th South Carolina, and 3rd South Carolina Battalion) took positions near Bondurant's guns, and were sheltered by stone walls.[44]

Willcox issued the order to advance, the 46th New York, 45th Pennsylvania and 17th Michigan in front (left to right), with the 100th Pennsylvania and 79th New York, the latter positioned behind the 45th Pennsylvania, following in support. At least one of the Highlanders, Private Davidson, saw the advance as dictated by circumstances. Recalling the situation just prior to the order being given, Davidson wrote,

> The fire [from Confederate artillery] was indeed terrific, sweeping the road and the field in a way which seemed overpowering. Our batteries made but few replies, and there we lay, speculating on what was going to turn up. To retreat, we saw, would be utter destruction, to advance—well, there seemed nothing else for it. The enemy decided the question for us by advancing skirmishers, and opening upon us with musketry.[45]

As skirmishers from Drayton's Brigade began to advance toward their position, the men of Willcox's division left the relative protection of the walls and advanced up the slope of South Mountain. Willcox's men drove the Confederate skirmishers before them, but soon closed upon Drayton's main force. "Then commenced a terrible musketry fight," recorded Private Davidson. Elaborating, he wrote,

> If I had a <u>Tribune</u> philosopher at my elbow to supply the fitting adjective phrases I might attempt a description; but the sounds and sensations of a great musketry contest must after all be experienced to be appreciated. The file firing, before we got a full view of the ground, was splendid, and great in

volume. The enemy confident in the strength of their position, raised their well-known yelp, as our men advanced; but their cock-sure cries of joy were soon dissipated by the hurrahs of the Union troops, as they drove the Confederates pell-mell before them.[46]

Willcox's men succeeded in taking the crest of the mountain, though not in time to capture Bondurant's guns, which were quickly withdrawn in the face of the advancing Federals.[47] Nonetheless, Fox's Gap was now in Union hands.

Drayton's Confederates were overpowered by superior numbers and had broken in disorder from the crest, leaving many of their number—dead, wounded, and prisoners—behind. The Confederates quickly regrouped, however, and Drayton's men reformed in the woods and behind stone walls on the plateau and the opposite slope of the mountain. According to Private Davidson, "[w]e had gained the summit of the mountain, but the enemy still held the woods on the right of our front, and a stone wall skirting the road to the right. From this stone wall they poured in a murderous flanking fire."[48]

The Highlanders had come to a halt in a cornfield, still positioned behind the 45th Pennsylvania. To escape the renewed Confederate musketry fire, Lt. Col. Morrison ordered his men to lie down in the corn. "We lay down," recalled Corporal Todd, "some of us falling asleep while the bullets were cutting the tops of the corn-stalks above our heads."[49] Morrison then was approached by an aide to General Willcox, "crouching as near to the ground as possible in order to escape the deadly shower of bullets," with orders for an officer and 35 men to perform a reconnaissance mission of the enemy's new position. Morrison assigned the task to twenty-three-year-old Capt. William C. Clark of Company G. Clark, and his thin line struck off to the right and approached a Confederate battery, which opened fire on the small detachment of Highlanders as soon as they came into view. Clark's men were forced to ground, but were able to send back word of their position and the enemy in their front, who were close enough to be within earshot. Shortly after sunset, Clark and his brave band were relieved and personally thanked by their corps commander, Maj. Gen. Jesse Reno; they rejoined the regiment the next morning.[50]

Near dusk, the soldiers of the Brig. Gen. Samuel Sturgis' Second Division, IX Corps, arrived to relieve their comrades in Willcox's First Division, who withdrew from their hard-earned positions atop South Mountain. The 79th New York was not finished fighting for the day, however. Shortly after dark, the Highlanders and the 28th Massachusetts were ordered back to the front lines. Exactly where they were sent is uncertain, but it most likely was near their former position, now occupied by Sturgis' troops, at the crest of the mountain. Opposing them were the recently-arrived Confederates of Brig. Gen. John B. Hood's two brigades, commanded by Col. William T. Wofford and Evander M. Law. These two brigades had settled into a position along the Wood Road, which connected Fox's and Turner's Gaps by running between the Old Sharpsburg Road at Wise's Farm and the National Road east of the Mountain House.[51]

Between the fall of darkness and 10:00 p.m., a good many shots were exchanged between Union and Confederate troops stationed atop South Mountain. Though most of this renewed fire was nothing more than roughly-aimed musketry, one of the early volleys fired from Hood's Confederates surprised a segment of newly-arrived Union reinforcements from Sturgis' division. Alhough the exact location and regimental designations of these startled troops is unclear, they were somewhere to the rear of the 79th New York's forward position. Corporal Todd remembered the scene:

> At dark the regiment was moved forward beyond the other regiments of the brigade. . . .Just as this movement was completed the enemy fired a volley or two at our line, which frightened the troops in our rear more than it injured us, for two or three of the regiments became demoralized and fell back down the hill-side in some confusion. General Willcox, fearing that the whole line had fallen back, sent an aid to ascertain the extent of the panic, and when the officer found us quietly standing in line, it was from him we first learned of what had happened in our rear.[52]

General Willcox later credited the Highlanders for their composure under fire that night, as well as for their well executed and equally controlled stand in front of Cook's abandoned guns earlier in the fight. According to Private Davidson, "the steadiness which the Seventy-Ninth showed at a critical time. . .met with commendation from General Willcox, who expressed his acknowledgments to Lieutenant-Colonel Morrison. I believe the General gave the regiment credit for having prevented a disastrous stampede twice." Similarly, Morrison confirmed that "[o]n the field, I was complimented by General Willcox, who stated to me, that my regiment had, on two different occasions, saved the day by their unflinching and determined bravery."[53]

By 10:00 p.m., the firing atop South Mountain ceased and the fight for Fox's Gap came to an end. Lee ordered Hill's and Longstreet's exhausted soldiers to withdraw from South Mountain and proceed toward the town of Sharpsburg. There, Lee again would offer battle to the Army of the Potomac, but this time with the bulk of his entire Army of Northern Virginia present.[54]

Although the guns finally fell silent over the fields of Fox's Gap, it was not a time of rest for those Union troops, including the Highlanders, who were positioned on the front lines that night. "All about us lay the dead and dying," wrote Corporal Todd,

> while the groans and cries of the wounded sounded in our ears throughout the long hours of that weary night. Those in our immediate vicinity were relieved to the extent of our ability, but we were obliged to keep in line and under arms till daylight, and dared not wander far, even to give a drink of water to a tenth of those who moaned piteously for it. We expected. . .the enemy in our front would attempt to recover the lost ground during the night. The weather was cold and as we stood in line shivering and wishing for morning, we conversed in low tones with each other, congratulating ourselves on this our first victory in the new campaign.[55]

The fight for South Mountain was a Union victory, though not as complete as it could have been. To be sure, Union troops had gained control of the vital passes in South Mountain, but the slow-moving Army of the Potomac failed to exploit the enormous advantage in numbers it had held over the enemy on South Mountain. An opportunity to drive a wedge between Lee's divided Army of Northern Virginia was lost and the Confederates were allowed to withdraw and regroup to fight again.

As the sun rose on the morning of September 15, the carnage of the previous day's fighting became brutally apparent. "The morning broke upon a terrible spectacle," recorded Private Davidson. "The dead lay in heaps, the rebel killed far outnumbering ours. The road, the field, and the woods were strewn with corpses. The enemy's killed lay, as I have said, in heaps—absolutely piled up, just as they fell. In one group there were no fewer then nineteen dead bodies, one hanging upon a fence, the feet off the ground. . . .The spectacle was dreadful."[56] Corporal Todd confirmed the scene. "Morning of the 15th dawned at last, and on such a sight as none of us ever wished to look upon again," he wrote. "Behind and in front of us, but especially in the angles of the stone walls, the dead bodies of the enemy lay thick: near the gaps in the fences they were piled on top of each other like cord-wood dumped from a cart."[57]

Losses incurred by the IX Corps in the fight for Fox's Gap were 158 killed, 670 wounded, and 30 missing. Of this aggregate of 858, Cox's Kanawha Division and Willcox's First Division suffered the greatest numbers of casualties (356 and 355, respectively). Uncharacteristically, the 79th New York emerged relatively unscathed, as the regiment had but 12 wounded to show for their active participation in the fight, while their comrades in the 17th Michigan and

45th Pennsylvania lost over 130 men, mostly in the charge for Bondurant's guns.[58] Confederate casualties for Fox's Gap are harder to establish. A comparison between the overall Union and Confederate losses at Fox's and Turner's Gaps reveals that while the Federals lost some 1,800 men, the Confederates lost more, at least 2,300.[59]

The Highlanders received a much needed—albeit brief—respite on the morning of September 15. The rising sun revealed that the enemy, so close to their front the previous evening, had withdrawn. With the threat of renewed fighting gone, the weary New Yorkers went about getting breakfast. "We had had neither dinner nor supper the previous day," recalled Corporal Todd, "save perhaps a dry cracker or two, and were in a fit condition to enjoy a cup of coffee, even amidst such ghastly surroundings."[60] According to Lt. Col. Morrison, it was 9:00 a.m. when he received orders to move his regiment from the field. Morrison marched the 79th several hundred yards back down the slope, where the Highlanders stacked arms and enjoyed a well-deserved rest.[61] During their descent, the men of the 79th witnessed more grim scenes from the previous day's fighting. Corporal Todd remembered it well:

> We moved off the field, and on our way we saw many more evidences of the battle. At one angle of the stone walls fourteen bodies of the enemy were counted lying in a heap, just as they had fallen, apparently. . . .A curious sight presented itself in the body of a rebel straddling a stone wall: he must have been killed while in the act of climbing over, for with a leg on either side, the body was thrown slightly forward stiff in death. We were glad to leave these scenes behind us.[62]

The Highlanders' repose came to a quick end. The Army of the Potomac was ordered to pursue the Army of Northern Virginia, believed by McClellan to be in full retreat toward the Potomac River. Shortly after noon on the 15th, the IX Corps, now commanded by Brig. Gen. Jacob D. Cox (General Reno having been killed late in the day at Fox's Gap), began its westward advance along the Old Sharpsburg Road with orders to cross South Mountain at Fox's Gap. From there, it would continue toward the town of Sharpsburg, which lay just beyond Antietam Creek, some eight miles distant.[63]

Ninth Corps reached a position about a mile from Antietam Creek just before sundown. As it settled in for the night, the men of the First Division could plainly see their adversaries to the west; Lee's force was not retreating, despite what McClellan had initially believed. "The enemy appeared to be making a stand on the opposite bank of that stream," observed Corporal Todd, "and occasionally a shot or two from some of their guns yet remaining on this side would drop about us, but without doing any harm."[64]

Lee's Confederates indeed were making a stand to the west of Antietam Creek. Word of Stonewall Jackson's success at Harpers Ferry reached Lee earlier in the day, sealing his commitment to face the enemy at Sharpsburg. Like his previous order to divide the Army of Northern Virginia, Lee's decision on September 15 was fraught risk. With less than half of his army present, Lee was counting on McClellan's notorious lack of aggressiveness to prevent disaster. If the Army of the Potomac attacked in force before Jackson's men arrived from Harper's Ferry, Lee's Confederates at Sharpsburg—their backs to the Potomac River—would face annihilation.

Meanwhile, McClellan spent the day positioning his various corps along Antietam Creek's east bank. McClellan placed the IX Corps on the extreme left of his developing battle line, sending Hooker's I Corps, the other half of Burnside's Right Grand Division, off to the far right. McClellan's planned attack (at least initially) called for an advance on the far right (led by Hooker's I Corps), followed by an attack by the IX Corps on the left. With the Confederates so occupied, McClellan hoped a decisive blow could then be delivered by a thrust to the center of Lee's line.[65]

September 16 came and went without an attack by the Army of the Potomac. Instead, McClellan used the day to continue shifting troops in preparation for a fight. Not all of the Northern soldiers understood McClellan's actions—or lack thereof. "Tuesday the 16th was occupied in moving about, apparently to find some vantage ground," recorded Corporal Todd. "We moved down the stream and at night occupied a position. . .across the Rohrersville and Sharpsburg turnpike, near a stone bridge which spanned the stream, and in full view of the enemy, who were strongly posted on the opposite bank."[66] With the IX Corps in place opposite the Rohrbach Bridge (soon to be known as Burnside's Bridge), the Highlanders, held slightly back in a reserve position along with the rest of Willcox's First Division, spent an uncomfortable night in the rain. "Being without shelter," wrote Todd, "we received a good drenching."[67]

The Battle of Antietam commenced early on the morning of September 17 as the men of Hooker's I Corps advanced against the Confederate left, occupied by six of Stonewall Jackson's nine divisions, which had arrived the previous day from Harpers Ferry.[68] The fighting raged throughout the morning. To the south, however, the IX Corps saw little activity save for an occasional exchange of artillery fire with the Confederates to their front.[69]

Shortly before 10:00 a.m., Burnside received orders from McClellan to move his corps across Antietam Creek. Once a foothold was established on the west bank of the stream, the IX Corps would, according to McClellan's plan, be supported to the north from soldiers of the V Corps, who would cross the Antietam at the Middle Bridge. Burnside relayed the orders to Cox, who organized his divisions for the crossing.[70]

Though the Rohrbach Bridge's dimensions posed problems to the 12,500-man IX Corps—the bridge was no more than 12 feet wide with a 125 foot span—Cox's men also had to deal with well-protected Confederate infantryman occupying the wooded heights on the west bank. These Confederates—only 400-500 in number—belonged to the 2nd and 20th Georgia Infantry, Robert Toombs' Brigade, and were commanded by Col. Henry L. Benning. As at Fox's Gap, the terrain surrounding Rohrbach Bridge greatly favored the defensive. Benning's Georgians were positioned behind a stone wall, felled trees, and piled fence rails. Though heavily outnumbered, they posed a significant threat to any attempted crossing in their vicinity.[71]

From approximately 10:00 a.m. to 1:00 p.m., Federal soldiers from the Kanawha Division (now commanded by Col. Eliakim Scammon) and Sturgis' Second Division made successive and unsuccessful attempts to cross the bridge. A final and particularly determined attempt by two of Sturgis' regiments, the 51st Pennsylvania and 51st New York, coupled with a turning movement from Snavely's Ford, pried Benning's hardpressed Georgians to withdraw. The Federal success at the Rohrbach Bridge came at a high price: approximately 500 troops were killed or wounded during the several assaults, most of them on or in the vicinity of the bridge.[72]

During the fight for what would thereafter be known as Burnside's Bridge, the Highlanders and the rest of Willcox's First Division had remained in their reserve positions, some three-quarters of a mile to the east of Antietam Creek. With the bridge won, Willcox's men were brought quickly to the front. The First Division was ordered to cross the bridge and form on the extreme right of the IX Corps for a general advance toward Sharpsburg, a mile to the west. Cox's plan called for Brig. Gen. Isaac Rodman's Third Division to advance to the left of Willcox's men, the latter to follow the Rohrbach Bridge Road, with both divisions converging on the town of Sharpsburg. The First and Third Divisions would be supported by a brigade from the Kanawha Division, while Sturgis' Second Division would remain in a reserve position near the bridge.[73]

At 2:00 p.m., Willcox's men crossed the Antietam (which, according to Corporal Todd, was still "littered with the Union dead") and proceeded north-

ward along the Rohrbach Bridge Road to the point where the road turns westward on its path to Sharpsburg.[74] There, Willcox's two brigades were deployed
to either side of the road: Christ's First Brigade to the right, with the 79th New
York deployed along the line as skirmishers, followed by the 50th Pennsylvania,
17th Michigan, and 28th Massachusetts; Welsh's Second Brigade was deployed
to the left, the 100th Pennsylvania deployed as skirmishers, with the 45th Pennsylvania, 46th New York and 8th Michigan (transferred from the First to Second
Brigade the previous day) in support.[75]

The Highlanders, formed in a double skirmish line, led the advance of
Christ's brigade around 3:00 p.m. In their path were the fields, outbuildings, and
house of farmer Joseph Sherrick, whose property was inhabited by small band
of Confederates led by Col. F. W. McMaster and belonging to Brig. Gen. David
R. Jones' division of Longstreet's Command.. A much greater threat to the First
Division's advance, however, were the distant Confederate batteries and infantry
stationed on the heights to the east (present-day Cemetery Hill) and south (along
the Harpers Ferry Road), in perfect positions to rake the ground surrounding the
Rohrbach Bridge Road with shells and musketry fire.[76]

It was not long before the 79th New York received the full attention of the
Confederates to their front. As Lt. Col. Morrison recalled,

> No sooner had my regiment appeared in sight than the enemy opened a
> terrific fire of shell, grape, and canister, from a full battery, in position, on the
> heights directly in front [of what now is referred to as Cemetery Hill]. Stead-
> ily my line advanced, until within rifle range, when they commenced firing,
> still advancing, driving their skirmishers from the orchard near the gully, and
> the cornfield on the centre and right.[77]

Private Robert Davidson, for reasons unknown, was not with the 79th New York
that day. He was, however, in a position to view his comrades' advance through
the fields of the Sherrick farm: "The Seventy-Ninth crossed the [Rohrbach]
bridge, ascended the heights, and advanced upon the enemy in skirmishing order
. . . .The enemy's artillery poured in a terrific storm of grape and canister, and
our men had to do the best they could with their muskets. . . ." Recalling the
advance through the Sherrick farmland, Corporal Todd bluntly wrote, "It was a
terrible ordeal."[78]

The Highlanders successfully pushed McMaster's troops from their posi-
tions on the Sherrick farm back toward the base of Cemetery Hill, where the
Confederates were soon reinforced and reformed near a stone house beside the
Rohrbach Bridge Road, some 300 yards distant. In the meantime, the remaining

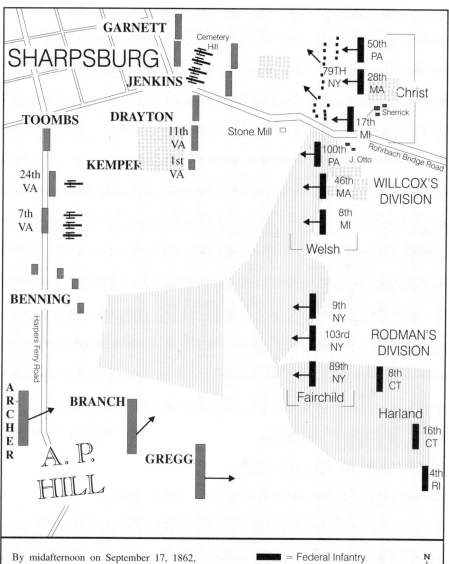

GARNETT

Cemetery Hill

SHARPSBURG

JENKINS

50th PA

79TH NY

28th MA

Christ

Sherrick

17th MI

Rohrbach Bridge Road

TOOMBS

DRAYTON

11th VA

Stone Mill

KEMPER

1st VA

100th PA

J. Otto

46th MA

WILLCOX'S DIVISION

24th VA

7th VA

8th MI

Welsh

BENNING

Harpers Ferry Road

9th NY

103rd NY

RODMAN'S DIVISION

89th NY

8th CT

Fairchild

ARCHER

BRANCH

Harland

16th CT

A. P. HILL

GREGG

4th RI

By midafternoon on September 17, 1862, Ambrose Burnside's IX Corps had finally crossed the Rohrbach Bridge. Two hours were consumed preparing for an attack against Lee's right flank, and the methodical advance began about 3:00 p.m. The 79th New York Highlanders covered Christ's front in a double rank of skirmishers. Although it looked as though the Federals were going to capture Sharpsburg and turn Lee's flank, A. P. Hill's Division arrived from Harpers Ferry and assaulted Burnside's left flank, driving it back and ending the battle.

■■■ = Federal Infantry
▬ = Confederate Infantry

N

The 79th New York at Antietam

September 17, 1862

(4:20 p.m. - 5:00 p.m.

regiments of Christ's brigade made their way toward the Highlanders' forward—and precarious—position at the Sherrick farm. This much larger Union force made a considerably better target for the Confederate gunners on the heights bordering Sharpsburg, giving the Highlanders a temporary respite from the heavy artillery fire, but at the expense of their trailing comrades.[79]

The difficulties facing Christ's men were not limited to the destructive fire of the Confederates in their front, though it was this fire that caused the First Brigade's advance to grind to a temporary halt by 3:30 p.m. The men of Christ's brigade had advanced well ahead of their supports from the left wing of the First Division, and Welsh's Second Brigade was a significant distance behind on their path to the left of the Old Rohrbach Road. This situation left Christ's men exposed and without support on the Sherrick farm. With Christ pinned-down by the Confederate fire (especially from the guns positioned along the Harpers Ferry Road), Welsh's soldiers quickly made up ground and moved into line with their comrades in the First Division. Their actions absorbed the deadly attention of the menacing Confederate artillerists on the Sharpsburg heights.[80]

With Welsh's brigade up, the advance of the First Division resumed en mass. The Highlanders moved forward, supported on their left by Welsh's men and on their right by the regulars of the 2nd United States Infantry. Back in August 1861, the 2nd U.S. Infantry had been among those regular troops ordered by McClellan to surround and quell the mutinous soldiers of the 79th New York; on this afternoon, the 2nd U.S. Infantry, part of V Corps, was one of several regular infantry regiments probing the Confederate center—significantly less reinforcement than McClellan had promised to send in support of IX Corps during its advance. Still, the 2nd U.S. joined the right wing of the Highlanders' skirmish line and, with the aid of Welsh's flanking force, helped Christ's men force the Confederates from their position near the stone house and back towards Sharpsburg.[81]

With the Confederates driven from their forward position, all that stood between Willcox's First Division and Sharpsburg were Confederate cannons and the Virginia infantrymen of Brig. Gen. Richard B. Garnett's Brigade atop Cemetery Hill. The Highlanders, with the assistance of the 2nd U.S., succeeded in gaining a fence rail bordering the cornfield at the base of the hill. From this position, the men of the 79th directed their fire at the Confederate gunners. "I advanced. . .up to the fence at the cornfield," reported Lt. Col. Morrison, "when, by the galling fire of my men, the enemy were obliged to change the position of their guns."[82] The Confederate position was rapidly becoming untenable. Seeking to exploit the situation, Christ sent forward the 17th Michigan, supported by the 50th Pennsylvania and 28th Massachusetts, to capture the guns. The move was just moments too late, and the pieces were withdrawn from the heights before they could be taken.[83]

By this time, a relatively clear path to the town of Sharpsburg was open, as was a golden opportunity to turn Lee's right and cut his army off from its sole route of retreat over the Potomac River. A fortuitous set of circumstances, however, interceded to prevent a decisive defeat of Lee's army. The First Division's participation in the battle essentially ended with the Confederate evacuation of (present-day) Cemetery Hill. As its soldiers held on to their hard-fought territorial gains, Rodman's Third Division, which anchored both the left of the IX Corps and McClellan's entire line of battle, were flanked by A. P. Hill's arriving Light Division, which reached the field about 3:30 p.m. after a grueling 17-mile forced march from Harpers Ferry. Hill quickly threw his brigades into the action, and Rodman's men began to retreat in the face of this new Confederate pressure. The Federal withdrawal, however, exposed the left flank of Willcox's First Division. With their ammunition all but gone and now under threat of being cut off from the rest of the withdrawing IX Corps, Welsh's and Christ's brigades were ordered to relinquish their positions on the outskirts of Sharpsburg around 4:30 p.m. The Federals fell back and took up a new position along the western bank of Antietam Creek, the same ground upon which they had formed for their advance along the Rohrbach Bridge Road some two hours earlier.[84]

With darkness quickly approaching, Willcox established his lines for the night. Welsh's and Christ's brigades still straddled the Old Rohrbach Bridge Road (to the left and right, respectively), while Sturgis' Second Division and the Kanawha Division formed to the south. The Highlanders, who received fresh supplies of ammunition upon reaching Antietam Creek, remained on the skirmish line, where they spent the entire night getting what sleep they could, fully expecting a renewal of the fighting early the next morning.[85] However, nothing of importance occurred on the Highlanders' watch that evening, as the Battle of Antietam had concluded with the falling sun. The Army of Northern Virginia, though badly battered and organizationally eviscerated, had not been destroyed. Despite the advice of some of his generals, Lee consolidated his position and remained in place throughout September 18, daring McClellan to attack him. True to form, McClellan did not renew the fight, much to the chagrin of many of his soldiers, including Highlander William Todd. Writing after the war as the historian of his regiment, Corporal Todd remembered how the men felt the day after the battle:

The next morning we expected to renew the battle, but all remained quiet along the line, except for the exchange of shot between picket lines. The enemy could be distinctly seen occupyingthe position they held late the previous afternoon, and we wondered why McClellan did not at once press forward and secure the fruits of the victory won the day before. We all believed that a decisive victory was within our grasp, and chafed at the apparently uncalled-for delay. All day long we remained in a state of inactivity, believing that the enemy was employing the time in so strengthening his position that it would only be by a great sacrifice of life his lines could be forced. We did not dream that Lee would be allowed to escape.[86]

Escape Lee did, withdrawing his men back across the Potomac River during the night of September 18, thus ending the Maryland Campaign.

Losses at Antietam were enormous. Twelve hours of fighting around the small town of Sharpsburg had produced near 23,000 casualties. While the Army of the Potomac lost some 12,400 men killed, wounded and missing (25% of those engaged), the Army of Northern Virginia lost near 10,300 (roughly 30% of those engaged).[87] In Willcox's First Division of IX Corps, Christ's brigade suffered 244 total casualties, while Welsh's brigade lost an aggregate 93 men. The remaining three divisions of IX Corps suffered 2,011 killed, wounded and missing between them.[88] The Confederate units facing IX Corps on September 17 inflicted many more casualties than they themselves incurred: together, the commands of D. R. Jones and A. P. Hill lost approximately 1,000 men.[89]

The 79th New York suffered 32 casualties on September 17, including its first fatalities of the campaign. Five Highlanders had lost their lives in the advance toward Sharpsburg, while 27 others were wounded, bringing the total number of casualties incurred by the 79th New York during the Antietam Campaign to 44, approximately 15% of the regiment's strength.[90]

The 79th New York's soldiers remained in the vicinity of Sharpsburg for several weeks after the battle, their time spent on picket duty, drill, recuperation and "the hum-drum duties of camp life." On September 30, the arrival of new recruits and the return of veterans from sick-leave brought the Highlanders' ranks back up to approximately 300 officers and enlisted men, most of whom would see a good deal more fighting before returning to civilian life.[91] Not until October 26 did the 79th's stay in Maryland come to an end, when the IX Corps, along with the rest of the Army of the Potomac, was sent back to Virginia.[92]

The 79th New York went on to carve out a distinguished career in the Western Theater, assigned to the IX Corps for the balance of the war. Held in reserve at the December 13 Battle of Fredericksburg, the Highlanders were shipped to Louisville, Kentucky in March 1863 and assisted in the protection of area rail lines from Confederate guerrillas of Gen. John Hunt Morgan's command. In June 1863, the Highlanders accompanied the IX Corps to Mississippi, where they were attached to Maj. Gen. William T. Sherman's force and saw minor fighting near Vicksburg. The hot summer fighting was followed by a return to Kentucky in August 1863, where the New Yorkers prepared for their part in Burnside's invasion of East Tennessee. The move into the rough Tennessee country resulted in their participation at the Battles of Blue Springs (October 10) and Fort Sanders (November 29). In the latter action, the 79th New York played an instrumental part in the repulse of Longstreet's Corps, a significant victory that thwarted Confederate plans to retake Knoxville.

The 79th New York returned to Virginia in the spring of 1864. After minor action in the Wilderness, the Highlanders saw their last serious fighting of the war at Spotsylvania on May 9. Nine days later, their three-year terms expired. The men of the 79th New York returned home, where they were each issued glengarry caps—courtesy of the local Caledonian Club—for their march through the city. About 100 Highlanders whose terms of service had not yet expired were reformed into a two-company battalion and sent back to Virginia where they served as the provost guard for the XVIII and IX Corps before participating in the Petersburg Campaign.[93]

After the war, the 79th New York was reinstated to the First Division, New York State Militia, and again donned their pre-war Scottish garb. The post-war 79th N.Y.S.M did not last, however, as waning interest by veterans, lack of new recruits and a cost-conscious governor led to the regiment's disbandment in 1876.[94]

The 1862 Maryland Campaign was not the bloodiest nor the most trying experience for the 79th New York Highlanders. In fact, their 15% casualty rate at the battles of South Mountain and Antietam was well under the average figure for Union forces engaged, and lower than the regiment's previous casualty rates at the battles of First Bull Run and Secessionville. However, if one examines the regiment's participation in the Maryland Campaign in a broader context, including their previous service in Pope's Virginia Campaign, the Highlanders' efforts and sacrifice become much more impressive. In less than a month of almost constant campaigning and fighting, the Highlanders lost 149 men, or roughly 27% of the regiment's aggregate casualties for the entire war.[95] It was with

first-hand knowledge of this broader context that Lt. Col. David Morrison
drafted the following congratulatory order, read aloud to the Highlanders shortly
after the Battle of Antietam:

> It is with much pleasure that the Lieutenant-Colonel commanding observes
> the present splendid discipline of the regiment. Soldiers of the Seventy-Ninth,
> within the last few weeks, you have passed through the most trying times you
> have ever experienced. You have not only fought many battles, but endured
> untold hardships. You have accomplished many marches, by day and by
> night—many of you without shoes, and all poorly clothed. You have endured
> both hunger and thirst with scarcely a murmur of complaint. On the field of
> Chantilly you were the first to meet the enemy. You fought like heroes, and,
> although many of our brave comrades fell—among the rest our gallant and
> beloved General [Stevens]—the object of the fight was accomplished. On the
> battle-field of South Mountain you saved the day by your steady conduct; and
> in the last great battle you elicited, by your intrepid action, the admiration of
> the Brigadier General commanding. But, fellow-soldiers, it is not by your
> good fighting alone that you have shown your good discipline. I have not had
> occasion to punish a single man for disobedience or misconduct; and in
> expressing the deep satisfaction I feel over this happy circumstance I can only
> express the hope that you will one and all persevere in that course of good
> behaviour and correct deportment which is at all times and under all circum-
> stances the highest praise and honor of the brave soldier.[96]

Notes

1. *Scottish-American Journal* (New York), August 1, 1861, October 2, 1862.

2. John P. Severin and Frederick P. Todd, "79th Regiment, New York State Militia,
1860-1861." *Military Collector and Historian*, 8 (1956), p. 20.

3. Severin and Todd, "79th Regiment," p. 20; *Scottish-American Journal*, December 25, 1858, January 15, 1859.

4. Michael J. McAfee, "79th Regiment, New York State Militia." *Military Images
Magazine*, 11 (September-October 1989), p. 28.

5. *New York Military Gazette*, November 13, 1858.

6. McAfee, "79th Regiment, New York State Militia," p. 29.

7. *Scottish-American Journal*, April 25, 1861.

8. *Scottish-American Journal*, May 16, 1861.

9. See Ella Lonn, *Foreigners in the Union Army and Navy* (Baton Rouge, 1951), p.
130, for a brief analysis of the regiment's ethnic make-up.

10. William Todd, *The Seventy-Ninth Highlanders: New York Volunteers, 1861-1865* (Albany, 1886), pp. 24-41; William F. Fox, *Regimental Losses in the American Civil War, 1861-1865* (Dayton, 1974), p. 426.

11. Jeffry D. Wert, "Mutiny in the Army." *Civil War Times Illustrated*, 24 (April 1985), pp. 13-15; Todd, *Highlanders*, pp. 52-55; William C. Lusk, ed., *War Letters of William Thompson Lusk* (New York, 1911), pp. 67-74; *New York Herald*, August 17, 1861.

12. Ibid.

13. *War of the Rebellion: Official Records of the Union and Confederate Armies*, 128 vols. (Washington, 1880-1901), series I, vol. 14, pp. 51, 62-63, 90. Hereinafter cited as *OR*. All references are to series I unless otherwise noted. For more information on the fascinating Secessionville campaign, see Patrick Brennan, Secessionville: Assault on Charleston (Savas, 1996). Brennan's study is one of the best campaign histories ever published.

14. See Todd, *Highlanders*, pp. 192-210.

15. Frederick Phisterer, *New York in the War of the Rebellion: 1861 to 1865*, 6 vols. (Albany, 1912), vol. 4, p. 2842; *Scottish-American Journal*, November 6, 1862. See Todd, *Highlanders*, pp. 211-225, for a detailed account of the 79th New York at the Battle of Chantilly; George Ryerson to brother, September 10, 1862, Ryerson papers, in private possession.

16. Lusk, *War Letters*, p. 190; Alexander Campbell to wife, September 9, 1862, Campbell Family Papers, 1860 to 1886, South Carolina Department of Archives and History, Columbia, South Carolina.

17. Stephen W. Sears, *Landscape Turned Red: The Battle of Antietam* (New York, 1983), pp. 64-66.

18. Sears, *Landscape Turned Red*, pp. 69, 72; Todd, *Highlanders*, p. 225; *Scottish-American Journal*, September 11, 1861.

19. Sears, *Landscape Turned Red*, p. 364; Frederick H. Dyer, *A Compendium of the War of the Rebellion*, 2 vols. (Des Moines, 1908), vol. 1, pp. 313-314.

20. Todd, *Highlanders*, pp. 226-228.

21. John W. Shildt, *The Ninth Corps at Antietam* (Gaithersburg, 1994), pp. 55-61; Todd, *Highlanders*, pp. 228-229.

22. *Scottish-American Journal*, October 2, 1862.

23. *Annual Report of the Adjutant-General of the State of New York for the Year 1901* (Albany, 1902), p. 1054 (hereinafter cited as *Annual Report*); Todd, *Highlanders*, pp. 227-228.

24. Sears, *Landscape Turned Red*, pp. 82, 90-91.

25. Ibid., pp. 112, 116.

26. *Scottish-American Journal*, October 9, 1862; *OR* 19, 432.

27. Todd, *Highlanders*, pp. 229-230.

28. *Scottish-American Journal*, October 9, 1862.

29. Sears, *Landscape Turned Red*, pp. 126, 128-129, 371.

30. Sears, *Landscape Turned Red*, p. 133; Todd, *Highlanders*, p. 230.

31. *Scottish-American Journal*, October 2, 1862.

32. *Scottish-American Journal*, October 9, 1862.

33. Ezra A. Carman, "History of the Antietam Campaign," Ezra Carman Papers, Manuscript Division, Library of Congress, p. 449 (hereinafter cited as "Antietam Campaign").

34. For a detailed account of the early fight for Fox's Gap, see D. Scott Hartwig, "'My God! Be Careful!': Morning Battle at Fox's Gap, September 14, 1862." *Civil War Regiments: A Journal of the American Civil War*, Vol. 5, no. 3 (Fall 1997), pp. 27-55.

35. *Scottish-American Journal*, October 2, 1862.

36. Todd, *Highlanders*, p. 230.

37. *Scottish-American Journal*, October 2, 1862.

38. Sears, *Landscape Turned Red*, pp. 134, 371.

39. *Scottish-American Journal*, October 9, 1862; Carman, "Antietam Campaign," p. 449; *OR* 19, p. 433.

40. Carman, "Antietam Campaign," p. 450; *Scottish-American Journal*, October 2, 1862; *OR* 19, pp. 433-434, 437.

41. *OR* 19, p. 428; *Scottish-American Journal*, October 9, 1862; Todd, *Highlanders*, pp. 231-232.

42. In actuality, only about 100 men from the 8th Michigan were sent to reinforce Cox; the remainder of the regiment had broken and fled to the rear during the panicked withdraw of Cook's caissons. Carman, "Antietam Campaign," pp. 450-451; *OR* 19, pp. 428, 437, 461.

43. Todd, *Highlanders*, p. 232; *OR* 19, p. 428. In his account of the action at Fox's Gap, Todd consistently misspelled his division commander's surname. I have silently corrected this particular misspelling in all passages used from Todd's, Davidson's and Morrison's writings.

44. Sears, *Landscape Turned Red*, pp. 134, 368; Carman, "Antietam Campaign," p. 451.

45. *Scottish-American Journal*, October 2, 1862.

46. Ibid.

47. Carman, "Antietam Campaign," pp. 454-455.

48. Ibid., p. 454; *Scottish-American Journal*, October 2, 1862.

49. *Scottish-American Journal*, October 9, 1862; Todd, *Highlanders*, p. 233.

50. Todd, *Highlanders*, pp. 233-234; *Annual Report*, p. 836; *Scottish-American Journal*, October 9, 1862.

51. *OR* 19, pp. 438, 440, 460; Todd, *Highlanders*, p. 234; Hartwig, "Fox's Gap," pp. 32-33.

52. Todd, *Highlanders*, pp. 234-235. Not surprisingly, darkness and the quickness of the panic among Sturgis' men caused those in the 79th New York to have varying recollections of the event. Lt. Col. Morrison recalled that "the enemy advanced in force, driving before them two regiments which were on my front." Private Davidson did not

note any panicked Union troops (either to the rear or front of their position), but rather insisted that "the enemy made three distinct attempts in the darkness to dislodge our troops, but were each time repulsed with great slaughter." Given the evidence, Todd's account of the night's events appears to hold the most truth. *Scottish-American Journal*, October 2 & 9, 1862.

53. *Scottish-American Journal*, October 2 & 9, 1862.

54. Sears, *Landscape Turned Red*, pp. 150-151.

55. Todd, *Highlanders*, p. 235.

56. *Scottish-American Journal*, October 2, 1862.

57. Todd, *Highlanders*, p. 236.

58. *OR* 19, pp. 186-187.

59. Sears, *Landscape Turned Red*, p. 143; Shildt, *Ninth Corps*, p. 84.

60. Todd, *Highlanders*, p. 236.

61. *Scottish-American Journal*, October 9, 1862.

62. Todd, *Highlanders*, p. 236.

63. *OR* 19, pp. 28-29, 418.

64. Todd, *Highlanders*, p. 237; *OR* 19, p. 418.

65. Sears, *Landscape Turned Red*, pp. 169-173.

66. Todd, *Highlanders*, p. 237.

67. *OR* 19, pp. 423-424; Todd, *Highlanders*, p. 237.

68. Sears, *Landscape Turned Red*, pp. 164-165, 180-181.

69. Ibid., pp. 180-254.

70. *OR* 19, p. 424; Sears, *Landscape Turned Red*, p. 261. Controversy has surrounded the exact timing of McClellan's orders to Burnside to advance, and the resulting delay in IX Corps' Rohrbach Bridge crossing. See Sears, *Landscape Turned Red*, pages 353-357 for a concise analysis of the debate; also see elsewhere in this issue of *Civil War Regiments*, pp. 88-118, B. Keith Toney, "The Attack and Defense of Burnside's Bridge," for a good discussion of the timing controversy and a solid examination of the Confederate perspective of Burnside's attack.

71. Sears, *Landscape Turned Red*, p. 260.

72. Ibid., pp. 262-267.

73. *OR* 19, pp. 425-426; Sears, *Landscape Turned Red*, pp. 276-277.

74. Todd, *Highlanders*, p. 242.

75. *OR* 19, pp. 177, 430.

76. Todd, *Highlanders*, p. 243; Sears, *Landscape Turned Red*, p. 279.

77. *Scottish-American Journal*, October 9, 1862.

78. *Scottish-American Journal*, October 2, 1862; Todd, *Highlanders*, p. 243.

79. *OR* 19, pp. 430, 438; Sears, *Landscape Turned Red*, pp. 279-280.

80. *OR* 19, pp. 430, 438.

81. Sears, *Landscape Turned Red*, pp. 279-281; Timothy J. Reese, *Sykes' Regular Infantry Division, 1861-1864: A History of Regular United States Infantry Operations in*

the Civil War's Easter Theater (Jefferson, N.C., 1990), p. 143; *Scottish-American Journal*, October 9, 1862; *OR* 19, pp. 362-363.

82. *Scottish-American Journal*, October 9,1862.

83. *OR* 19, pp. 438-439.

84. Sears, *Landscape Turned Red*, pp. 281-289; *OR* 19, pp. 431, 439; Todd, *Highlanders*, p. 243.

85. *OR* 19, p. 426; *Scottish-American Journal*, October 9, 1862; Todd, *Highlanders*, p. 243.

86. Todd, *Highlanders*, pp. 243-244.

87. Sears, *Landscape Turned Red*, pp. 294, 296.

88. Ibid., pp. 196-198.

89. Sears, *Landscape Turned Red*, p. 292.

90. *OR* 19, pp. 186, 196.

91. Todd, *Highlanders*, p. 246.

92. *Scottish-American Journal*, November 20, 1862.

93. For a discussion of the rest of 79th's war service see Todd, *Highlanders*, pp. 257-486.

94. Todd, *Highlanders*, p. 487; *New York Times*, Dec 21, 1875.

95. Phisterer, *New York in the War of the Rebellion*, vol. 4, p. 2842.

96. *Scottish-American Journal*, November 6, 1862.

"Always the bridge! If the bridge is lost, all is lost!"

"Dying As Brave Men Should Die"
The Attack and Defense of Burnside's Bridge

B. Keith Toney

By 10:00 a.m. on the morning of September 17, 1862, the sounds of battle had been rolling over the hills and valleys of the farmland surrounding the tiny Maryland village of Sharpsburg for nearly five hours. Major General George McClellan had started the day's action by throwing Brig. Gen. Joseph Hooker's I Corps against the Confederate left flank at 5:30. Four hours later, the Federals were having a go at the Confederate center, positioned along a sunken farm lane. As the morning moved inexorably along, the only place that remained quiet was the Confederate right flank. That, however, was about to change, and along with it would change the name of a stone arch spanning Antietam Creek, the new name to be etched forever into the nation's history.

Robert E. Lee entrusted his right to Maj. Gen. David R. "Neighbor" Jones, a 37-year old South Carolinian. Jones had graduated from West Point 41st of 59 cadets in the famed Class of 1846, and had served faithfully in the Old Army until his native state left the Union. "Neighbor"—he received his nickname at West Point for his friendly, out-going nature—soon followed suit, resigning his commission and joining General P. G. T. Beauregard at Charleston Harbor, where he served as Beauregard's chief of staff. Jones was on hand when Fort Sumter fell. By the time of First Manassas, he had been promoted to brigadier general, and a subsequent promotion to major general came in March 1862. Even though signs of the heart disease that eventually would kill him had already appeared, Jones led his division ably, if not spectacularly, during the Seven Days' Battles, and had raised his stock immeasurably during the Second

Manassas Campaign when he held Thoroughfare Gap open for James Longstreet's approach.[1]

General Jones would need every bit of military skill he could muster outside Sharpsburg, as well as a liberal dose of luck, to accomplish the daunting task Lee had given him. Even though on paper Jones had six brigades under his command, a summer of hard campaigning had whittled their cumulative strength down to less than 2,500 men. More than 12,000 Federal troops were aligned against him.[2]

While the numerical odds were against Jones, they were decidedly in his favor when it came to the terrain. From the heights south and east of the

Maj. Gen. David R. Jones

Generals in Gray

village of Sharpsburg, where Jones formed his main line of defense, the ground sloped downwards through a series of peaks and valleys to Antietam Creek, some 3/4 of a mile away.[3] Along the creekbank, the key point was a triple-arched stone bridge 125 feet long and 12 feet wide, known locally as the lower (or Rohrbach) bridge. Before long, the bridge would bear the name by which it is known today: Burnside's Bridge.[4]

A number of factors made the area around the bridge favorable for Jones' first line of defense. While several fords were available within a mile on either side of the stone structure, the bridge itself was obviously the best and most logical crossing point for any Federal troops that might attack Jones' front. Situated in a narrow valley, with the west bank rising sharply from the water's edge to a bluff some 100 feet high, the bridge was the crossing point for a dirt road leading from the south known alternately as the Rohrbach or Rohrersville Road. The road entered the valley some 300 yards downstream from the bridge, with a post and rail fence bordering the eastern side of the road for most of its length. East of the road an open field ran fairly level for about 100 yards before rising abruptly to a height of 100 feet, so that the crest of the bluffs on either side of the creek were about level. Thus, Union soldiers advancing to cross the

Brig. Gen. Robert Toombs

Generals in Gray

bridge would be exposed in an open field of fire for anywhere from 100 to over 300 yards.[5]

Jones gave the task of defending the bridge to his most controversial subordinate, Brig. Gen. Robert Toombs. Given his past record and volatile nature, Toombs was a most unusual choice to undertake so important a task. Fifty-two years old at the time of the battle, Toombs had served almost half his life in the public eye. He entered politics in 1837 when he was elected to the first of six terms in the Georgia state legislature before being sent by his constituents to represent them in Congress in 1844.[6] He served as representative until he was elected United States Senator in 1853,

a capacity in which he served until 1861, when he returned to Georgia to serve as a delegate to the secession convention in Montgomery, Alabama.[7] There, Toombs would be disappointed. He expected to be chosen as the first president of the new Confederate States of America, and instead ended up with the position of Secretary of State. The fiery politician served in that post for only five months before resigning to accept a commission as brigadier general in command of a brigade of Georgians, a decision no doubt made easier by two factors: the desire to gain the political mileage that military service could provide, and a desire to leave the cabinet of Jefferson Davis, who Toombs had come to hate.[8]

As accomplished a leader as Toombs was in the political arena, he would prove to be nearly as spectacular in his ineptness as a battlefield commander. Fellow Georgian Thomas Cobb said of Toombs, "I have sergeants in my legion in whose military capacity I have more confidence." G. Moxley Sorrel, who had extensive dealings with Toombs in his role as aide-de-camp to James Longstreet, echoed Cobb's sentiments, writing, "He was once and for all a politician, and in the wrong shop with a sword and uniform on."[9]

Toombs' contempt for professional soldiers, especially West Pointers, was near legendary. One of his oft-quoted sayings later in life was that the epitaph of the Confederacy should be "Died of West Point."[10] On another occasion, in a letter detailing the retreat from Yorktown written to his life-long friend and fellow Georgian Vice-President Alexander Stephens, Toombs launched into another attack against West Pointers. "Science will do anything but fight." he wrote. "It will burn, retreat, curse, swear, get drunk, strip soldiers, anything but fight."[11]

By the opening of the Maryland campaign, Toombs' military career could best be measured by the number of controversies and contentious incidents it spawned, rather than any tangible achievements. General Joseph Johnston had placed Toombs under arrest in 1861 for disobeying orders while the army was encamped near Manassas.[12] During the Seven Days' Battles on the morning of June 28, Toombs launched an attack without orders and went so far as to order Brig. Gen. George T. "Tige" Anderson's brigade to support him. When his commander, Maj. Gen. John Magruder, found out what Toombs had done, he ordered the attack canceled, but not before a number of men had been killed or wounded in a senseless action. Somehow Toombs escaped official reprimand for his incompetence, though the incident played a role in General Lee's later efforts to have Magruder transferred from his command.[13] Three days later on July 1, the Battle of Malvern Hill brought forth another chapter in Toombs' checkered military career. After he lost control of his brigade, Maj. Gen. D. H. Hill, whose troops Toombs was supposed to be supporting, rallied the Georgians himself and sent them forward. Hill publicly censured Toombs on the battlefield, accusing him of pretending to want to fight but not doing so when confronted by the enemy. Toombs was so enraged by this accusation of cowardice he challenged Hill to a duel, which the hot-tempered North Carolinian declined for religious, to say nothing of realistic, reasons.[14]

At Second Manassas, Toombs found himself once again running afoul of a superior officer, although this time it was his corps commander, James Longstreet. Toombs took it upon himself to move two of his regiments, which Longstreet had personally positioned to guard a ford. The move left the crossing undefended and open for use by the Federals—an invitation which was accepted. When Longstreet found out what Toombs had done, he placed him under arrest. It was only after Toombs had admitted his mistake and apologized to Longstreet that he was released to join his brigade on the battlefield, where he arrived too late to lead them into the fight.[15] For all his contentiousness, though, Toombs had his supporters, both within and outside the army. Oddly enough, one of them was General Longstreet, who said, "If Toombs had been educated at

West Point, where he could have learned self-control, he would have been as distinguished as a soldier as he was as a civilian."[16]

Toombs later claimed that as the army entered Maryland, Major General Jones had appointed him to command a division consisting of his own, Thomas F. Drayton's, and George T. Anderson's brigades. Given his dismal military record—and the telling fact that neither Longstreet nor Jones made mention of Toombs having a division, referring instead in their reports to "Jones and his six brigades"—such a claim seems baseless.[17] Regardless of what size force Toombs may have thought he commanded in his own mind, the fact remained that as 10:00 a.m. approached on Wednesday, September 17, 1862, he had no more than 500 to 550 men to defend one of the most critical points on the battlefield.[18]

Through a combination of fate and his own failings, Robert Toombs had managed to miss most of the major battles that had occurred since he entered the army. He had written to his wife that his enemies were trying to drive him out of the service, but he wouldn't resign until he had distinguished himself in a great battle. "The day after such an event" he said, "I will retire if I live through it."[19] The great battle was upon him; the rest was now up to Toombs.

Across the way, on the east side of the Antietam, Toombs' opponent that day was wrestling with his own personal demons. Major General Ambrose E. Burnside, commander of the Federal IX Corps, graduated from West Point in 1847, the year after David R. Jones left the institution. The two had been friends at the academy, and Burnside enjoyed much the same reputation as an affable and out-going fellow. On the morning of September 17, however, it wasn't Neighbor Jones troubling Burnside's mind as much as it was another of Jones' old classmates, Burnside's commander and closest friend, George Brinton McClellan.

The trouble had begun on September 15, when Burnside was, in McClellan's opinion, inordinately slow in moving IX Corps in pursuit of the Confederates after the Battle of South Mountain the previous day. McClellan had called Burnside to task for the tardiness in a manner quite unlike anything to which "Burn" was accustomed in his dealings with "Little Mac." The situation was further exacerbated when, on the 16th, Joe Hooker's I Corps was removed from Burnside's control as wing commander without explanation by McClellan. Hooker was posted on the Union right and told to expect his orders directly from the army commander. Burnside was furious over this very public slight, and blamed Hooker for scheming to achieve a more independent command.[20]

To make matters worse, matters on the Union side of Antietam Creek were further clouded that morning with a situation not unlike that perceived by Robert Toombs. Where Toombs may have believed he commanded an organization larger than he actually did, Burnside persisted in claiming control over a now non-existent command. As his IX Corps arrived in the vicinity of Sharpsburg on September 15, Brig. Gen. Jacob Cox, whose Kanawha Division had been loosely attached to IX Corps prior to South Mountain, assumed that the temporary command he had exercised over the corps during the battle of September 14 had ended. Cox was surprised when Burnside informed him the next day that since the order removing I Corps from Burnside's command said nothing about removing Burnside as wing commander, Cox should continue to command IX Corps while he, Burnside, continued to command the phantom right wing of the army.[21] Rather than discuss the absurdity of such an arrangement, Cox tried tactfully to point out instead that it would be better for Burnside to command the corps since, if for no other reason, Cox's divisional staff was not large enough to perform the duties necessary. Not to worry, replied Burnside, he would place his own staff at Cox's disposal.[22] From the tone of his report of the incident, Cox may have left the meeting thinking, "why not?" Burnside certainly would not need a very large staff to service an imaginary wing command.

Of all the issues and controversies swirling around the Rohrbach Bridge portion of the battle, one of the most important was this question: what was the objective of IX Corps on the morning of September 17, 1862? Evidently, no one, including Burnside and Cox, was quite sure. McClellan had not held a meeting with his corps commanders prior to the battle to outline his plan, nor had he bothered to let them know individually what was going on, other than issuing fairly vague orders regarding their specific duties.[23] The matter becomes even more confusing since McClellan filed two reports on the battle, one dated October 15, 1862, which McClellan termed his "preliminary report," and his "official" report of August 4, 1863, written after he had been relieved of command. Except for the re-occurrence of names and places, one could easily believe the two reports were written about two different battles rather than the same action.

Since the report of October 15 was written when events were fresh in McClellan's mind and also before he had a number of personal axes to grind, this earlier account is generally accepted as the more accurate of the pair. McClellan states in this report that his plan was to attack the enemy's left and to create a diversion on the right, ". . .with the hope of something more," he added rather vaguely, "by assailing the enemy's right." McClellan stated further that should one or both of the flank attacks succeed, he would then attack the center ". . .with any reserve I might then have on hand."[24]

Of course, this plan as outlined was not even remotely similar to what actually happened during the battle, but the idea that IX Corps' objective was to create a diversion is supported by Brigadier General Cox. In his report dated September 23, Cox stated that IX Corps' attack ". . .had the effect of a most powerful diversion in favor of the center and right of the army. . . ."[25] Cox later reinforced the diversionary role assigned to IX Corps in his account of the battle written after the war.[26]

The mechanics of the movement got underway about 7:00 a.m. With the fighting on the Federal right flank already in full swing, Burnside received word from McClellan to prepare to advance, but to await further orders before moving to the attack. Burnside read the order and passed it on to Cox, who issued the necessary orders to move IX Corps into position.[27]

If uncertainty as to McClellan's expectations was the order of the day for the Federals, Brigadier General Toombs faced no such difficulties. His objective, which had been explained to him in detail, was precise and easy to understand: delay any enemy attempt to cross the Antietam and move against the Confederate right. Although he commanded defensible ground, General Jones appreciated the fact that the Federals had the capacity to throw overwhelming numbers against his thinly-spread defense. He therefore planned a classic defense-in-depth, and gave explicit orders as to how it should be conducted. In his report, Toombs says he was ordered by Jones:

> . . .to occupy the most eligible position I could find on the Antietam. . .in order to prevent the enemy from crossing the river. From this position I was ordered to fall back when it should become necessary, by my right flank, and to hold a hill about 400 yards below the bridge. . .as long as it might be practicable, and then to fall back and take position on your right in line of battle. . .about 600 or 800 yards in rear of the bridge.[28]

Toombs, in turn, entrusted the defense of the bridge to his most capable commander, Col. Henry Benning. The 48-year old Benning had been a justice on the Georgia Supreme Court before the war, and was an avowed secessionist. Judge Benning was given serious consideration as a candidate for a cabinet post in the newly-formed Confederate government, but chose instead to offer his services to the military. After raising a regiment in his hometown of Columbus, he was appointed colonel of the 17th Georgia Regiment. Known as "Old Rock" to his men, the six-foot tall Benning spoke with a deep, gutteral voice which inspired confidence.[29]

Living up to the high benchmark implied by his sobriquet looked to be almost impossible on the morning of September 17. Benning had only a few men with whom to work, and he set out to make the best of a difficult situation. There were two obvious crossing points that had to be defended: the bridge itself, and Snavely's Ford, about one and a half miles downstream.[30] When dawn broke over Sharpsburg that morning, Benning wasn't overly concerned with Snavely's Ford since Brig. Gen. John G. Walker's Division was positioned to defend against any incursion from that direction. As the tactical situation worsened on the northern end of the field, however, Lee sent word to Walker around 9:00 a.m. to move rapidly to the left in support of Stonewall Jackson's hard-pressed troops.[31] With the departure of Walker, Henry Benning suddenly found himself defending Snavely's Ford as well as the bridge and its approaches.

Benning deployed Col. John B. Cummings' 20th Georgia Infantry, about 220 men, immediately opposite the head of the bridge, with the wings of the regiment extending a short distance on either side of it. The left flank of the 20th rested about 40 yards north of the bridge, with a thin skirmish line extending another 200 yards north along the creek. Some of the Georgians took advantage of the trees lining the creek bank to secure a better vantage point for shooting at any enemy who dared approach the bridge. Almost directly opposite the head of the bridge and some two-thirds of the way up the slope was an old stone quarry. Colonel Cummings placed one company, 25 to 30 men, in the quarry itself, where the rock to construct the bridge had been extracted.[32]

To the right of the 20th was Lt. Col. William R. Holmes' 2nd Georgia Infantry, with a strength of only 120 men. The 2nd extended the line south below the quarry for 300 yards to where the Antietam bends back to the west. Posted near the crest of the ridge behind a hastily constructed breastwork of fence rails and tree limbs, as well as behind the trees along the slope of the creek bank, the 2nd Georgia was well-positioned to challenge any troops who tried to approach along the Rohrersville Road.[33]

The other two regiments of Toombs' Brigade, the 15th and 17th Georgia, had been detailed to guard the wagon trains. In order to augment Benning's meager force, Toombs was assigned the 50th Georgia Infantry from Drayton's Brigade, about 100 men under Lt. Col. Frank Kearse, as well as one company of South Carolinians from Jenkins' Brigade. Benning placed half of the South

Colonel George Crook
(after his promotion to major general later in
the war)

USAMHI

Carolina company to the right of the 2nd Georgia, with the 50th Georgia next in line. To the right of Kearse's regiment Benning positioned the other half-company of South Carolinians.[34] With the departure of Walker's Division, this small force, no more than 130-140 men, had the responsibility of guarding nearly a mile of ground along the banks of the Antietam, as well as Snavely's Ford. The 2nd and 20th Georgia, by comparison, were posted along a front totalling about 900 yards, which worked out to an average of one man every eight feet.[35] The disparity in these assignments was a calculated risk, but a logical one since the bridge posed the greater threat to Lee's right flank and would thus likely be the focal point of any attempted crossing.

As Benning deployed his men, Burnside and Cox spent three hours as spectators at the Henry Rohrbach farm, observing from afar the drama playing out across the creek around the Dunker Church and Sunken Road. The pair of generals watched as division after division of their comrades moved forward and engaged the enemy. When, they wondered anxiously, would their turn come? The answer arrived at 10:00 a.m., when an aide from McClellan's headquarters reached them. In an order dated 9:10 a.m,. Burnside was directed to begin his attack. He was also informed that reinforcements would be sent once he had gained control of the bridge.

Part of the blame aimed at Burnside through the years has centered around McClellan's later claims that he sent the order to advance at 8:00 a.m., and that Burnside's delay in carrying out the order was instrumental in the Army of the Potomac's failure to achieve a decisive victory. McClellan's assertion is incorrect. McClellan confirmed that in his initial report on the battle, Burnside received the document at 10:00 a.m., and the time written on the order was an hour and ten minutes later than when McClellan claimed to have sent it.[36]

Burnside examined the directive and passed it along to Cox, telling him to give the honor of assaulting the bridge to Col. George Crook's brigade from the Kanawha Division. Burnside thereafter ordered his close personal friend, Col. Henry W. Kingsbury, Jr., to move his 11th Connecticut Infantry forward as skirmishers and provide a covering fire for Crook's assault on the bridge. Kingsbury's 440-man regiment had been detached from Brig. Gen. Isaac Rodman's division for this duty.[37] The long hours of waiting were over; Burnside was ready to take his bridge.

In his autobiography, George Crook claimed a Captain Christ from Cox's staff delivered the order to him that, "The general wishes you to take the bridge," to which Crook queried, "What bridge?" When the captain said he didn't know, Crook asked him the location of the stream, and received the same reply. According to Crook, he then ". . .had to get a good many men killed in acquiring the information which should have been supplied me from division headquarters."[38]

It is hard to reconcile this claim—as well as others made by Crook—with the fact that when the entire corps was moved forward and put on stand-by at 7:00 a.m., Crook sent companies F and I of the 11th Ohio Infantry forward as skirmishers. These two companies drove in the skirmish line that Benning had placed on the east side of the creek along the Rohrersville Road.[39] If in fact Crook had no idea where his objective was despite having sent out skirmishers, it just adds to the uncharacteristic ineptness he displayed that day.

The plan of attack was for the 11th Connecticut to gain a position from which it could provide a covering fire while Crook's Ohio brigade rushed down the slope of the hill directly opposite the bridge and stormed across. The situation swiftly moved from bad to worse almost immediately. Henry Kingsbury led the 11th Connecticut forward over a high knoll immediately southeast of the bridge. As soon as it came in view and started down the open slope of the knoll toward the bridge road, Kingsbury's men came under the withering fire of the 2nd Georgia. While it was obvious to all that any direct attempt to storm the bridge would not be easy, it quickly became apparent that the difficulty of the task greatly increased when Confederate batteries well behind the defenders opened fire, their guns zeroed in on the approaches to the bridge.[40]

The men of the 11th rushed down the slope toward the road as comrades began to fall around them. The left and center companies forced their way over the rail fence bordering the bridge road, formed a line along the eastern creek bank, and returned fire at the Georgians. The soldiers on the right of the regiment, however, found themselves pinned down in the open by the storm of bullets and shells raining in on top of them. As casualties began to mount, they slowly inched their way toward the foot of the bridge.[41]

The commander of Company A, Capt. John Griswold, moved forward from the creek bank with his company in an attempt to ford the stream. It did not take long for him to discover that this plan was not going to work, for the swiftly-running water was nearly four feet deep, and the increased fire from the Confederates threatened to slaughter his men in the stream. Any doubt Griswold may have had evaporated when those soldiers who entered the water were cut down. Captain Griswold was one of the casualties. After he was shot, he managed to struggle to the far bank before falling dead from his wounds.[42]

The right flank of the regiment fared no better. Some accounts have Colonel Kingsbury making it as far as the foot of the bridge, but if true, it was a position he did not hold long. The terrific fire from Benning's Georgians forced the 11th Connecticut to withdraw just ten minutes after its advance began, leaving 139 of its 440 men (31.59%) on the field—including Kingsbury, who was mortally wounded. Ironically, the fallen Kingsbury's brother-in-law was none other than Confederate general David R. Jones. It was later said that Jones was devastated when he received the news of Kingsbury's death, and the shock of the loss of his sister's husband played a role in his own death from a stroke a few months later.[43]

As the 11th Connecticut was being chopped to pieces by Benning, George Crook moved his brigade to the attack. An already difficult task was made impossible by the way Crook deployed his troops, which best can be described as piecemeal and confused. His first mistake was the decision to hold the largest of his three regiments, the 800 men of the 36th Ohio, in reserve at the Henry Rohrbach farm. The initial attack was made by four companies from Lt. Col. Gottfried Becker's 28th Ohio, whose soldiers advanced over the crest of the hill opposite the bridge and started down the slope, only to quickly fall back when they came under fire from the men of the 20th Georgia stationed in the old quarry. With this initial attempt repulsed, Colonel Crook placed two 20-lb. Parrott rifles from Capt. Seth Simmonds' Kentucky battery on the crest of the hill where the 28th Ohio lay, and ordered five companies of the regiment to support the battery.[44]

Crook then ordered his smallest regiment, the 11th Ohio, to try its luck at taking the bridge. Lt. Col. A. H. Coleman led his men forward, but his fortunes quickly soured. For some reason, probably a simple misunderstanding of orders, the right wing of the regiment veered off to the right, toward the two skirmish companies (F and I) which had been sent out previously and were still in position under the cover of some trees on the crest of the hill overlooking the bridge. The left wing moved straight down the slope and into the open, where it was met with the same heavy fire that had demolished the 11th Connecticut. These men had gotten no closer than 100 yards of the bridge when Lieutenant Colonel Coleman fell mortally wounded. Coleman's loss and the heavy wall of fire threw the soldiers into mass confusion. Major Lyman Jackson, realizing that he was in what he described as a "useless position," was able to re-gain control and moved the left wing back up the slope under a covering fire provided by what was left of the 11th Connecticut. Jackson managed to extract his men and move them to the right, where they reformed with the rest of the regiment.[45]

As if the task given the 11th Ohio was not difficult enough, the support Colonel Crook had promised Coleman never materialized. Crook had told Coleman that the five companies of the 28th Ohio that were not busy guarding Simmonds' guns would support and cooperate with him during his attack. The problem was that Colonel Crook, who personally led the five Ohio companies, was unable to bring them out overlooking the bridge as he planned. Instead, he became confused and emerged 300 or 400 yards north of where he was supposed to be. Crook placed the five companies behind a low ridge and fence about 50 yards from the creek, where they would spend the next two hours or so trading shots with skirmishers from the 20th Georgia sheltered in the trees on the opposite bank. Crook's companies finally crossed the creek unopposed when the Confederates withdrew at 1:00 p.m.[46]

George Crook had a long and illustrious career with the army ahead of him, but his performance on September 17 left much to be desired. After the five companies from the 28th Ohio had gone to ground north of the bridge, Crook reported back to Burnside and Cox that he was pinned down and could do nothing further—despite the fact he had lost less than 42 of the 1,200 men he had taken forward, and the 800 men from the 36th Ohio were still marking time in reserve.[47] One can only imagine the reaction of the survivors from other brigades and regiments who assaulted the bridge that day—many of whom lost in excess of 30% casualties—when they learned that Crook's brigade suffered but 67 casualties out of 2,005 men, or 3.3%.[48]

When it became obvious that Crook's attack was a failure, Burnside turned to Brig. Gen. Samuel Sturgis to force the issue. Sturgis had moved his division, which consisted of the brigades of Brig. Gen. James Nagle and Col. Edward Ferrero, into a position where they could support and exploit whatever success

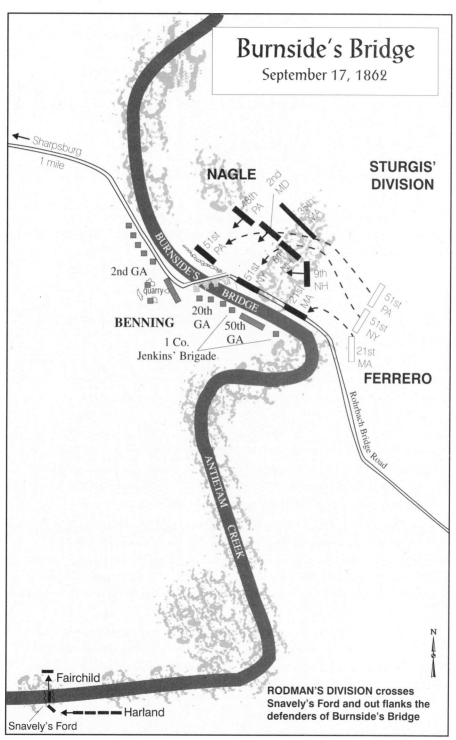

Burnside's Bridge
September 17, 1862

Sharpsburg
1 mile

NAGLE

2nd
MD

STURGIS'
DIVISION

48th
PA

35th
MA

51st
PA

BURNSIDE'S

2nd GA

6th
NH

51st
NY

9th
NH

quarry

BRIDGE

21st
MA

51st
PA

BENNING

20th
GA

50th
GA

51st
NY

1 Co.
Jenkins' Brigade

21st
MA

FERRERO

ANTIETAM

Rohrbach Bridge Road

CREEK

N

Fairchild

RODMAN'S DIVISION crosses
Snavely's Ford and out flanks the
defenders of Burnside's Bridge

Harland

Snavely's Ford

Theodore P. Savas

Crook's attack might gain. Since Nagle's brigade was formed in a cornfield on the Rohrbach farm and was closest to the bridge, it was given the dubious honor of leading the attack.[49]

Before Nagle went in, Burnside ordered every gun that could be brought to bear to fire on the Georgians. For several minutes, guns from Simmonds', Cook's, Benjamin's, and McMullen's batteries rained iron down upon Benning's men. Eshelman's and Richardson's Confederate batteries of the Washington Artillery, posted northwest of the bridge in support of Benning, did what they could to return the fire. Armed with smooth-bore Napoleons and howitzers, however, they were unable to reach the longer-range rifled guns the Federals were employing. As a result, the Southern gunners could offer little more than loud moral support to their comrades huddled along the creekbank.[50]

By the time the Federal artillery slackened, Sturgis had no doubt about the importance of his mission. Not only had Cox given him the order to take the bridge, but Burnside had as well. As Sturgis said in his report, "The importance of carrying it without delay was impressed upon me by General Burnside, and I went in person to the vicinity of the bridge and ordered the 2nd Maryland, Colonel Duryea, and Colonel Griffin, 6th New Hampshire, to move over at a double-quick and with bayonets fixed."[51]

Nagle's brigade formed for the attack in Rohrbach's cornfield southeast of the bridge. The 2nd Maryland, about 150 men under Col. Jacob Duryea, was deployed in an old lane running through the cornfield to a point nearly intersecting the bridge road with the rest of the brigade in line behind and to its left. In an effort to lessen the distance it would have to advance along the bridge road exposing themselves to the enfilading fire of the Georgians, the 2nd Maryland, followed by Col. S. G. Griffin's 6th New Hampshire (also about 150 men), moved back through the cornfield and behind a plowed hill closer to the bridge. There, the soldiers fixed bayonets and prepared themselves for the charge.[52]

While these two regiments were getting ready for the advance, the remaining pair of regiments of the brigade, the 9th New Hampshire and 48th Pennsylvania, were moving to a position which would allow them to provide covering fire for the assault on the bridge. Apparently there was some confusion on the part of the 48th Pennsylvania in its efforts to get into position. A surgeon with the 2nd Maryland, Theodore Dimon, recalled overhearing shouts and looking around to see General Sturgis berating the 48th's Col. Joshua K. Sigfried. "God damn you to hell, sir, don't you understand the English language? I ordered you to advance in line and support the 2nd Maryland, and what in hell are you doing flanking around in this corn?"[53] Colonel Sigfried understood Sturgis well enough this time around, and his 48th Pennsylvania moved to a position on the hill overlooking the bridge near the five companies of the 28th Ohio who were supporting the two guns of Simmonds' battery.[54]

Colonel Enoch Fellows led his 9th New Hampshire Regiment to a position along the bridge road near the big bend in the creek. Seeking what little shelter they could behind the post and rail fence bordering the road, the men from the 9th began trading volleys with the Georgians and South Carolinians across the creek. As soon as the 9th's soldiers marched into sight, Confederate artillery opened fire. Ignoring protocol, the lieutenant colonel of the regiment, H. B. Titus, set aside his sword, picked up the rifle from a dead soldier, and joined his troops on the firing line until he was severely wounded.[55]

By this time the 2nd Maryland and 6th New Hampshire were moving to the attack. Formed in column of fours, with the 2nd Maryland in the van, the two regiments hurried down toward the bridge road from the hill where they had formed. A group of officers ran ahead of the column and served as pioneers, opening a section in the stout chestnut post and rail fence through which the column could file.[56] Once again, as soon as blue uniforms presented themselves as targets, Benning's men opened fire. Soldiers were falling rapidly by the time the column reached the opening in the fence. Those waiting to pass through the broken rails fence into the road watched the slaughter ahead and began shying away, threatening to break ranks and dash back for the safety of the hill they had just left. Colonel Duryea rushed toward the head of the column, shoving men back into line and shouting, "What the hell you doing there? Straighten that line, there. Forward!" In this fashion, Colonel Duryea got his regiment moving.[57]

By the time the head of the column had reached a point about halfway between where it had entered the road and the foot of the bridge, the opposite creek bank was a solid sheet of smoke and flame from the muzzles of the stalwart Georgians, who were firing as fast as they could load. Since the distance was only about 100 yards, the effect of the Confederate fire was utterly devastating. Fully one-third of the Marylanders fell dead or wounded. The head of the column made it to within 250 feet of the bridge before the men broke and began scrambling for whatever cover they could find. Eventually the regiment reformed on the plowed hill near the spot where it had begun its charge. It remained there, trading long range shots with the Confederates, until its men ran out of ammunition.[58]

Pressing close behind the 2nd Maryland, the 6th New Hampshire fared no better. One of the officers of the regiment claimed that of the first 100 men through the fence and into the road, 90% of them fell killed or wounded. This figure probably takes into account the casualties of the 2nd Maryland as well,

since the 6th New Hampshire, advancing behind the Marylanders, suffered considerably
less than 90 casualties in total. Still, the fire
of the Georgians was severe enough that the
6th New Hampshire quickly fell back and
took a position to the right of the 2nd Maryland on the plowed hill.[59]

Colonel Edward Ferero
(after his promotion to major general
later in the war)

USAMHI

By now it was between 11:30 and noon.
In less than two hours, Henry Benning had
staved off two attacks, both of which outnumbered him three to one. The question
now was what would come next, and how
much longer could "Old Rock" hold on?
Ambrose Burnside probably was asking
himself the same question. Several accounts
mention that on three or four occasions, messengers from McClellan appeared at
Burnside's headquarters with communiques ordering him to take the bridge at
all costs. It was becoming apparent that the mission of IX Corps had changed in
McClellan's mind from that of a diversion to one having the utmost importance
on the outcome of the battle.

Accordingly, Burnside stepped in again, bypassing the chain of command
that he had established by sending a message directly to General Sturgis: the
bridge was to be taken at all hazards. Sturgis, in turn, assigned the task to the
commander of his other brigade, Col. Edward Ferrero.[60]

In a war filled with colorful characters, Ferrero still managed to stand out.
Born in Spain to Italian parents, his family emigrated to the United States when
Ferrero was a baby. He grew up in New York City, following his father's
footsteps to become a dance instructor, which included a position as dance and
fencing instructor at West Point. A popular figure with the New York society
crowd, Ferrero parlayed his reputation and his membership in a local militia unit
into the colonelcy of the 51st New York Regiment when it was formed. By the
time of Second Manassas, he commanded the brigade which he led onto the
battlefield at Antietam.[61]

Sturgis directed Ferrero to give the task of taking the bridge to Col. John
Hartranft's 51st Pennsylvania Infantry, and Col. Robert Potter's 51st New York
Infantry. Both regimental commanders had good reputations, and both would
later rise to prominence during the war. Ferrero called his brigade to attention
and announced, probably for dramatic effect, that General Burnside himself had

requested the two 51sts take the bridge. Corporal Lewis Patterson, of Company I, 51st Pennsylvania, broke the quiet by shouting, "Will you give us our whiskey, colonel, if we take it?" Ferrero had recently cut off the regiment's whiskey ration as a disciplinary measure. Without hesitating he called back, "Yes, by God! You shall have as much as you want, if you take the bridge. . .if I have to send to New York to get it and pay for it out of my own purse. Will you take it?"[62] With a resounding roar, the men replied in the affirmative. If the principle of God and country were not enough to get the job done, Ferrero was willing to give John Barleycorn a crack at it.

After seeing how futile the attack along the bridge road had been, it was decided the next attempt should be a frontal rush down the hill opposite the bridge, not unlike what Crook was supposed to have attempted. The men of the two 51sts dropped their knapsacks and moved from where they had been resting in the Rohrbach cornfield to a position behind where the 48th Pennsylvania still was trading shots with the enemy. There they formed in preparation for the attack, the New Yorkers on the left and the Pennsylvanians on the right. Each regiment carried 335 men into the fight.[63]

As before, the artillery paved the way for the assault. George Crook had managed to get two howitzers from Simmonds' Battery down the slope behind where his five companies of the 28th Ohio still lay nearly 400 yards above the bridge. Captain George Durell's Battery D, Pennsylvania Light Artillery and Capt. Joseph Clark, Jr.'s Battery E, 4th U.S., had also moved into position to add their support to the attack.[64]

The other two regiments of the brigade, Col. William Clark's 21st Massachusetts (150 men) and Lt. Col. Sumner Carruth's 35th Massachusetts (800 men) moved into position to support the attack. The 21st Massachusetts moved down to the foot of the plowed hill and took a position along the post and rail fence bordering the road, a good position which allowed them to pour a covering fire into Benning's men. The 35th Massachusetts moved in behind the two 51sts, ready to follow close behind them as they closed on the bridge.[65]

The Pennsylvanians and New Yorkers moved forward side by side down the slope of the hill. Picking up speed as they descended, the two regiments charged over the open field toward the bridge 300 yards away. Every other regiment in Nagle's and Ferrero's brigades able to do so fired as rapidly as possible in an attempt to smother their opposition.[66]

As they neared the bridge, the men of the 51st Pennsylvania discovered they had a problem. Not only was the fire from the opposite bank still as hot as it had ever been, but the fence which ran along the bridge road turned on an angle and connected with the northern, or upper, bridge abutment, barring their access to the span. Without orders, the Pennsylvanians began moving to the right, dashing for the cover of the stone wall that ran for some distance northward along the creek bank. Colonel Hartranft could do little more than move down to the wall with his men and survey the situation. As he pondered his next move, Hartranft got some men to pull down the fence rails by the bridge abutment to create an opening.[67]

On the left, the 51st New York faced a similar problem, and the sudden departure of the Pennsylvanians exposed his right flank. Colonel Potter shifted his men to the left, where some of them tore down a few rails to forge an opening into the bridge road. As handfuls of his New Yorkers forced their way through the opening, others climbed over the fence, and in this manner Potter positioned his men along the fence on the creek side of the road, extending south from the bridge. Unfortunately, the post and rail fence offered little protection from the whizzing minie balls—and almost nothing in comparison to the stone wall their Pennsylvania comrades had gained—but it was better than nothing. Colonel Potter knew his men would not be able to hold on long, exposed as they were to the devastating fire. It was at this moment, as if an unspoken prayer was being answered, that Potter noticed an amazing thing: the Confederate fire was beginning to slacken. Staring through the thick clouds of powder smoke, Potter could make out Confederates stealing away from their rifle pits by twos and threes. The enemy was falling back.[68]

While he will never be known as Horatius, Colonel Benning demonstrated that his nickname "Old Rock" was an apt description. Benning had held out as long as he could, probably longer than Toombs or anyone had ever expected he would. With his ammunition running desperately low, however, and with a report that he was about to be out-flanked from the direction of Snavely's Ford, Benning knew it was time to retreat.[69]

Whether it was Potter who saw the opportunity and told Hartranft he was leading his men across (as Potter later claimed), or whether it was Hartranft who started his regiment with the New Yorkers then moving in unison (as Hartranft later asserted), is immaterial and impossible to establish. Regardless of how it happened, the two columns filed through the fence openings and with their colors leading the way, dashed onto the bridge. A few shots greeted the mass of men as they started across the span. By the time they were half way across, the firing had all but ceased. Colonel Hartranft, his voice hoarse from shouting orders over the din of battle, leaned against the bridge abutment and croaked at his men as they crowded into the opening, "Come on, boys, for I can't halloo any more!" as he fanned his hat at them as if to help them over.

It was about 1:00 p.m. Three hours after receiving the order to attack, General Burnside had his bridge. Despite the fact the Georgians were beginning to retreat before the final rush was made, the stone span had been gained at a dear price: of the 670 men from the two 51sts who made the charge, 207 of them were dead or wounded.[70]

Not all of Benning's men were able to make good their escape. As the 2nd Georgia began falling back, someone noticed that Company D, the right flank element, was not with them. Apparently the company missed the order to retreat in all the noise and confusion. Lieutenant H. H. Perry was sent back to retrieve the lost soldiers, but before he could do so a number of them were captured or wounded.[71] The commander of the 2nd Georgia, Lt. Col. William R. Holmes, shouted for some of his men to follow him and rashly ran down to the creek bank. At the water's edge he shook his sword and yelled at the Federals until he fell, riddled with bullets.[72] On Holmes' left, Lieutenant McCrimmon and 16 men from Company H of the 20th Georgia were captured. Soldiers from the five companies of the 28th Ohio had forded the creek upstream and rushed in behind the Confederates while their attention was focused on the men rushing across the bridge. Troops from the 51st Pennsylvania surrounded the prisoners and threatened to shoot them on the spot, saying they had "fought too long against such odds." Lieutenant Colonel Thomas Bell rode amongst them and calmed the men down before sending the prisoners to the rear. As the captives were crossing the bridge they had defended for so long, they saw yet one more Federal fall. Lieutenant Colonel Bell, who had walked his horse down to the creek for a drink, was struck in the temple by a fragment from an exploding shell and mortally wounded.[73]

Colonel Edward Ferrero had accomplished what two other brigade commanders had failed to do. Many young officers were probably surprised and found it ironic that the man who had taught them the intricacies of the waltz at West Point was the one who managed to capture the bridge. For Ferrero, even though he would rise to the rank of brevet major general before war's end, the capture of Burnside's Bridge was the high point of his military career. Unfortunately for Ferrero, he is better remembered for being drunk in a bunker when his division lost nearly 3,800 casualties in the disastrous assault on the "Crater" at Petersburg on July 30, 1864. Still, fate seemed kind to Edward Ferrero, as he returned to New York after the war and took up his old trade, enjoying a long and lucrative career leasing and managing a number of popular ballrooms.[74] Ironic indeed that the conqueror of Burnside's Bridge became the 19th-century's version of Arthur Murray.

While Ferrero played a significant role in opening Burnside's avenue to Sharpsburg, it is important to keep in mind that it was more than the charge of his two 51st regiments that broke the Confederate defense at the bridge. The report of Federals threatening their right flank played a key role in Benning's and Toombs' decision to retire to a new position. That threat was supplied by the division of Brig. Gen. Isaac Rodman, a key element in Ambrose Burnside's plan to cross Antietam Creek.

It was no secret to anyone that the bridge was the logical place to cross the waterway, and the Federal high command naturally assumed it would be heavily defended. Burnside therefore planned to cross a large force over a ford local farmers informed him was south of the bridge. Such a move would turn the left flank of the enemy and make an assault on the bridge easier and perhaps even unnecessary. Burnside positioned the division of Brig. Gen. Isaac Rodman, along with Col. Eliakim Scammon's brigade (commanded at Antietam by Col. Hugh Ewing) overlooking the ford on the night of the 16th, so they would be ready to move quickly when the order came on the 17th.[75]

Or so Burnside thought. The problem was that neither Ambrose Burnside nor his subordinates had made a personal reconaissance to determine the actual location of Snavely's Ford. Instead, the mission was left to some young engineers from General McClellan's staff sent by "Little Mac" for this purpose on the 16th. The staff engineers led Rodman through the dusk on the 16th to a spot two-thirds of a mile below the bridge where, they confidently informed the general, he could cross the Antietam.[76]

The next morning, Rodman's men awoke to a Confederate artillery bombardment against their position. Rodman pulled his division back from the bluff on which they were situated to the cover of the hill and awaited orders. A few hours later, about 10:30 a.m., orders arrived for him to attack. Rodman moved his two brigades, Col. Harrison Fairchild's and Col. Edward Harland's, plus Ewing's attached brigade, 800 yards up to the point the engineers had designated as the ford. A dismayed Rodman found the ford situated at the foot of a steep bluff over 160 feet high and well-defended by the skirmish line of the 50th Georgia. While it might suffice for getting a wagon load of hay across the creek, as a crossing point for 3,200 men it was useless. The general positioned five naval howitzers under the command of Capt. J. R. Whiting to drive back the enemy skirmish line and also deliver an enfilading fire into the ranks of the 2nd Georgia Regiment.[77]

Unable to cross the creek, Rodman ordered Colonel Harland to send out a scouting party to find the ford local farmers had described. Harland detached Capt. C. L. Upham and two companies of the 8th Connecticut for the mission. Upham returned soon thereafter and reported he had found the ford easily enough. The problem was getting to it. Upham's two companies had easily worked their way along the dense undergrowth lining the creek bank, but the division would have to take a much longer route over open, plowed fields, a march of over two miles from where they had started the morning. Out of viable options, Rodman wasted no time in getting the march underway.[78]

While Isaac Rodman was trying to find a place to cross the Antietam, Burnside and Cox were wondering what had become of the flanking division. Rodman's column was an integral part of Burnside's plan. General Cox later explained that it was so important, the assault on the bridge would have been delayed until Rodman sent word he was across and in position, had it not been for McClellan's repeated orders to take the bridge.[79]

After the unexpected two mile march, Rodman's division finally reached Snavely's Ford sometime between noon and 12:30 p.m. Captain Whiting's howitzers were once again placed where they could provide a covering fire for the crossing, with the 8th Connecticut from Harland's brigade was detailed to support the guns. As the troops scaled the hill overlooking the ford, they could see smoke rising over the trees from the fight raging at the bridge. Colonel Fairchild gave the orders for Lt. Col. Edgar Kimball to lead his 9th New York across the ford. The 373 New Yorkers entered the hip-deep stream and made it halfway across before the South Carolinians and Georgians opened on them. Without pausing to return fire, the men of the 9th New York slogged across the creek and filed to the right as soon as they reached the west bank, where they took cover under the brow of a 185-foot high bluff rising above the ford. Union troops were across the Antietam on the southern end of the battlefield.[80]

The right flank of the Confederate line had been resting on the bluff under which the New Yorkers were seeking shelter, but as soon as they saw the Union troops appear on the opposite bank and start down to the ford, the half-company of South Carolinians and some of the 50th Georgia men dashed for a stone wall about 165 yards across a plowed field from the ford. It was from this relatively strong position that the Confederates had opened fire when the crossing began. General Rodman, who had personally accompanied the 9th New York on its crossing, hastily organized the regiment into two wings and started each segment scaling the cliff. Fairchild's other two regiments, Maj. Edward Jardine's 89th New York (368 men) and Maj. Benjamin Ringold's 103rd New York (202 men), followed behind the 9th, their crossing also contested by the Confederates posted behind the stone wall. As soon as they reached the western bank, General Rodman sent these two regiments scurrying up the cliff also.[81]

Colonel Harland's brigade followed close on the heels of Fairchild. Colonel William Steere led his 4th Rhode Island across the ford first, followed by Col. Francis Beach's 16th Connecticut. Both regiments turned to the left as they emerged from the stream and fanned out in a battle line, the 4th Rhode Island on the right and the 16th Connecticut passing behind them to take a position on Colonel Steere's left. Steere also sent out Company H to the front and Company K to the left to drive the Confederate skirmish line from their position behind the stone wall. On the left, Colonel Beach sent two companies from the 16th Connecticut out past the Snavely farm buildings to picket a farm lane which led from the Snavely farm towards Myers' Ford, located some 700 yards below Snavely's. The two companies had not been gone long, however, before they came tumbling back to rejoin the 16th Connecticut, driven in by the fire from Eshelman's Battery, which earlier had been shifted to the right to add some muscle to the defense of Snavely's Ford.[82]

Eshelman's fire drove the soldiers of the 16th Connecticut out of their position and forced them to shift to the right and pass behind the 4th Rhode Island. This exposed the left flank of the Rhode Islanders to the artillery fire, which in turn caused them to shift right as well. Fortunately for both of these regiments and the 8th Connecticut, which by then had left its position in support of Whiting's howitzers and were in the process of crossing the ford, an unidentified Union battery of rifles opened on Eshelman and drove the Confederate gunners to seek cover.[83]

While Harland was getting his brigade across, Fairchild was extending his line toward the bridge, feeling for the flank of the rest of IX Corps. It was not long before contact was made with skirmishers from the 48th Pennsylvania. As Fairchild and Harland moved right, Col. Hugh Ewing brought Scammon's brigade of the Kanawha Division across Snavely's Ford and further extended the line to the left. By 2:00 p.m., Burnside had an unbroken line extending for nearly one and a half miles, stretching from just north of the lower bridge road leading from Sharpsburg to the bridge to Snavely's Ford.[84]

While Rodman was busy crossing at Snavely's Ford, the rest of IX Corps' soldiers were crossing the bridge and firmly establishing their presence on the west side of the Antietam. Substantial criticism has been heaped upon Ambrose Burnside on a variety of issues. By far the most difficult of Burnside's decisions to explain or defend is the one to use the bridge exclusively for getting the rest of the corps across the creek. Although he captured the bridge at 1:00 p.m., the bottleneck at the stone span delayed his advance toward Sharpsburg for two critical hours. It would have been a simple matter to march his men across the creek—which was from knee to chest deep—at virtually any location. Yet Burnside chose to send everything across the bridge: men, supply wagons, and artillery. It was a minor logistical miracle that in two hours he managed to cross, over a 12-foot wide bridge, more than 3,200 men in columns of four, as well as the wagons and artillery. But this does not excuse the fact that there was no reason for the bridge to be the sole access to the other side of the Antietam. While it is true the Federals were harrassed by artillery fire during the crossing, there is certainly no reason to think this fire would have had any greater effect if troops were fording the stream rather than crossing the bridge. Burnside's only plausible excuse centers on the uncertainty of what IX Corps' mission was that day. General McClellan, however, had already made it clear through the course of the late morning and early afternoon that his vision of what Burnside was expected to accomplish had changed.

Between 1:00 and 3:00 p.m. Brig. Gen. Orlando Willcox's division crossed the bridge and took a position on the right of the corps, with Col. Benjamin Christ's brigade deployed on the right of the bridge road leading from town, and Col. Thomas Welch's brigade aligned on the left. Rodman's division pressed north from Snavely's Ford and formed the left flank of Burnside's line. Sturgis, whose troops had taken the bridge and had expended most of their ammunition in the effort, was re-supplied and placed in reserve.[85] Finally, at 3:00 p.m. or shortly thereafter, IX Corps began moving forward.

For the Confederates, the two hour delay in Burnside's advance was a godsend. As it stood, however, General David R. Jones had few resources with which to hold the right flank of Lee's army. Worse still, he could not expect any reinforcements from the left. Jones aligned his thin division with the brigades of Brig. Gen. Richard Garnett and Micah Jenkins (commanded by Col. Joseph Walker) on the left of his line. Garnett and Walker offered a spirited defense and did a good job slowing down Welch and Christ as the two Union brigades slowly made their advance across the Sherrick and Otto farms.

On Jones' right flank, however, matters were not proceeding nearly as well. There, the brigades of Thomas Drayton and James Kemper tried to stem the advance of Burnside's Federals, but the steady movement of Rodman's division across the fields and through the valleys and ravines southwest of Sharpsburg was too powerful to resist. The Confedeates put up a stout defense, and in places the fighting devolved into hand-to-hand combat with clubbed muskets and bayonets. But sheer numbers carried the day, and the Confederates finally broke and ran for the rear. Ambrose Burnside was just a few minutes away from capturing Sharpsburg, gaining Lee's rear, and cutting off the Army of Northern Virginia's path of retreat to Virginia.[86]

One organization, however, stood in Burnside's way: the small brigade—or what was left of it—of Robert Toombs. When Colonel Benning retired from the bridge, he initially had led his men back to the position designated by Toombs behind a stone wall about half a mile in front of Jones' main battle line. By the time Benning reached this point, Toombs' other two regiments, the 15th Georgia under Col. W. T. Millican, and the Benning's own 17th Georgia (temporarily commanded by Capt. J. A. McGregor) accompanied by five companies of the 11th Georgia Regiment from Col. George T. Anderson's brigade, had reached the battlefield. The 20th Georgia and the 2nd Georgia, their cartridge boxes empty after their stand at the bridge, retired to refill them. By the time Kemper and Drayton's lines had broken, Toombs had pulled back to a position on the far right of Jones' line.[87]

Desperate to stem the tide sweeping towards Sharpsburg, Jones ordered Toombs to attack and throw them back. Henry Benning had been magnificent in his defense of the bridge; now, however, the spotlight fell squarely on Robert Toombs. The opportunity he had so fervently wished for, to distinguish himself in military glory, had finally arrived. Despite the arrival of his other two regiments, Toombs still had less than 500 men. To his credit, the fiery politician-turned-soldier did not hesitate in his duty. If Harvey Hill had wondered how much sand the little Georgian possessed at Malvern Hill, there was no questioning Toombs now. He guided his men to within 100 yards of the 8th Connecticut (which was leading Harland's brigade) and opened fire. The Federals tried to continue pressing forward, and did so for another 20 yards or so. The two lines were almost toe-to-toe, loading and firing as rapidly as they could. Toombs rode his horse up and down his line like a man possessed, urging his boys to stand firm and pour it on them. He had sent a message back to Jones requesting artillery support, and just as the fighting reached a crescendo, shells began whistling into the Federal ranks.[88]

And then, up came Hill. The march of Maj. Gen. A. P. Hill's Light Division, which covered the 17 miles from Harpers Ferry in eight hours and arrived on the Union flank in precisely the nick of time, has been recounted many times. The grueling march, with the sound of battle reverberating in the distance, is the stuff of which legends are made. Certainly the importance of Hill's timely arrival to the survival of Robert E. Lee's army cannot be overstated. An important aspect of this story, however, has been lost in the dramatics of the moment. But for Robert Toombs, Henry Benning, and their soldiers, we would not have in our minds the dramatic image of a red-shirted Hill driving his column speedily along with the flat of his sword, rescuing the army at the last possible moment. Exactly what would have happened had Toombs' men not fought so long and hard is impossible to know. Perhaps large segments of George McClellan's army would have been waiting at Boteler's Ford when Hill crossed, ready to exact a heavy toll.

Even if Hill had not reached the battlefield in time, the attack and defense of Burnside Bridge would still be regarded as one of the most stubbornly contested actions of the entire war. Perhaps the epitaph of every man, both North and South, who fell in the deadly combat over that stone arch on September 17, 1862, was best written by David R. Jones. In his official report, Jones expressed his regret at the deaths of the 2nd Georgia's Lt. Col. William R. Holmes and the 15th Georgia's Col. W. T. Millican by writing that they fell ". . .dying as brave men should die."[89]

Post-war photograph of Burnside's Bridge

Antietam National Battlefield

By applying the principles of war to the fight for Burnside's Bridge, it is easy to discern why the Confederates did well there. The application of these principles also reveals, however, that Ambrose Burnside is not quite the affable incompetent history that has thus far portrayed him to be. The principles of war are as follows: (1) Objective (directing the operation toward a clearly defined objective); (2) Offensive (seize and exploit the initiative); (3) Mass (concentrate power); (4) Economy of force; (5) Maneuver; (6) Unity of command (insure unity of effort under a responsible commander); (7) Security; (8) Surprise; (9) Simplicity (prepare clear and concise orders and plans).

If we assess Burnside's performance through an objective lens, it is easy to reach the conclusion that Burnside embarked on a fairly sound plan for achieving his primary objective, i.e., that of creating a diversion on the Confederate right and getting his troops across the Antietam. The plan of attack called for a concentrated effort of artillery and infantry to force the crossing at the bridge, while a turning movement was being undertaken by Rodman at Snavely's Ford (principles 1, 2, 3, 5, 8). Both the first and third efforts to take the bridge (Crook's and Ferrero's) were meant to be a concentrated effort taking advantage of superior firepower and numbers (and the latter effort in fact succeeded). The failure to employ principles 6, 7, and 9 (unity of command, security, and simplicity) have already been discussed, and it is apparent that the awkward command structure brought on by Burnside's insistence that Cox act as corps commander, the lack of reconnaisance, and the lack of a clear plan, certainly had an effect on the day's events. And, of course, once the bridge had been taken, practically every one of the principles was abandoned.

The Confederates, on the other hand, applied these principles well. Toombs and Benning knew exactly what was expected of them at all times, and they accomplished their task by a good understanding of how to use the terrain to their advantage to offset their serious lack of numbers (principles 1, 3, 4, 5, 6, 7, and 9).

When viewed separate from the struggle for the heights and village of Sharpsburg, the attack and defense of Burnside's Bridge emerges as one of the best fought and most hotly contested actions of the Battle of Antietam. The casualties alone—approximately 500 Union and 120 Confederate—hardly do justice to the ferocity of the combat that took place. The tribute Henry Benning paid to his men could be expressed equally by the Union commanders. Speaking of the valiant stand his troops made, Benning said, "During the long and terrible fire not a man, except a wounded one, fell out and went to the rear—not a man."[90]

It is perhaps proper that the fight for the bridge should be viewed separately, since the role of IX Corps changed so dramatically in the mind of George McClellan through the course of the day. While indeed IX Corps' assault on the town was but a continuation of the fight for the bridge, the two were every bit as diverse as, say, the fight for McPherson's Ridge and the fight for the Lutheran Seminary on the first day at Gettysburg.

When A. P. Hill's counter-attack drove the soldiers of IX Corps back to the bridge they had struggled so hard to gain, Burnside requested the reinforcements General McClellan had been promising him since before the first attack was made at 10:00 a.m. If he was not reinforced, warned Burnside, he would be forced to relinquish all the ground he had gained that bloody day. McClellan replied that he had no reinforcements to send. In a melodramatic postscript, McClellan shouted to the courier as he rode away, "Tell him if he cannot hold his ground, then the bridge, to the last man! Always the bridge! If the bridge is lost, all is lost!"[91]

Certainly, more than 600 dead and wounded American fighting men and millions of visitors to Antietam agree.

Notes

The author wishes to thank Ranger-Historian Paul Chiles and Park Historian Ted Alexander from Antietam National Battlefield for their invaluable assistance in writing of this article.

1. Ezra J. Warner, *Generals In Gray*, (Baton Rouge, 1959), pp. 163-164.

2. U.S. War Department, *The War of the Rebellion: The Official Records of the Union and Confederate Armies*, 128 vols., (Washington, D.C. 1890-1901), series I, Vol. 19, pt. 1, p. 886 (hereinafter cited as *OR*; all references are to series I unless otherwise noted); John Michael Priest, *Antietam: The Soldiers' Battle*, (Shippensburg, 1989), pp. 339-341.

3. Map of the Battlefield of Antietam, surveyed by Lt. Col. E. B. Cope, position of troops by General E. A. Carman, (Washington, D.C., 1904), Map # 9. Hereinafter cited as Cope.

4. Stephen W. Sears, *Landscape Turned Red: The Battle of Antietam*, (New Haven, 1983), p. 260.

5. Cope, map # 9; Sears, *Landscape Turned Red*, pp. 260; *OR* 19, pt. 1, p. 890.

6. Peter S. Carmichael, "Robert Augustus Toombs", in William C. Davis and Julie Hoffman, eds., *The Confederate General*, 6 vols., (Harrisburg, 1991), vol. 6, p. 50.

7. Charles C. Jones, Jr., "Brig. Gen. Robert Toombs—An Address Delivered Before the Confederate Survivors Association in Augusta, Ga, at its 8th Annual Meeting, on Memorial Day", April 26,1886, *Southern Historical Society Papers*, vol. 14, pp. 298-299.

8. Carmichael, "Robert Augustus Toombs,", p. 50.

9. Ibid.

10. Ibid.

11. Douglas S. Freeman, *Lee's Lieutenants: A Study in Command*, 3 vols. (New York, 1942), vol. 1, p. 625.

12. Ibid.

13. Ibid, pp. 544-546

14. Ibid, pp. 626-628

15. Freeman, *Lee's Lieutenants*, vol. 2, pp. 61-62.

16. Carmichael, "Robert Augustus Toombs," p. 51.

17. Freeman, *Lee's Lieutenants*, vol. 2, pp. 218-219.

18. OR 19, pt 1, pp 889; Priest, *Antietam: The Soldiers' Battle*, p. 218.

19. Freeman, *Lee's Lieutenants*, vol. 2, p. 218.

20. Sears, *Landscape Turned Red*, pp. 170-171.

21. Jacob D. Cox, "The Battle of Antietam," in Robert U. Johnson and Clarence C. Buel, eds., *Battles and Leaders of the Civil War*, 4 vols., (New York, 1884-1889), vol. 2, pp. 630-632.

22. Ibid.

23. Sears, *Landscape Turned Red*, p. 169.

24. *OR* 19, pt. 1, p. 30.

25. *OR* 19, pt. 1, p. 426.

26. Cox, "The Battle of Antietam," pp. 633-634.

27. General Ezra Carman Manuscript, Antietam National Battlefield Library, Sharpsburg, Md, Chapter 21, p. 4. Hereinafter cited as Carman. All references to chapter 21 unless otherwise noted; *OR* 19, pt. 1, p. 424.

28. *OR* 19, pt. 1, p. 888.

29. Lawrence L. Hewitt, "Henry Lewis Benning", *The Confederate General*, vol 1, pp. 100-101; Freeman, *Lee's Lieutenants*, vol. 2, p. 219.

30. Cope, map # 9.

31. *OR* 19, pt. 1, p. 914.

32. *OR* 19, pt. 1, pp. 888-889; Carman, pp. 8-9.

33. Ibid.

34. Ibid.

35. Priest, *Antietam: The Soldiers' Battle*, p. 218.

36. *OR* 51, pt 1, pp 844; *OR* 19, pt 1, pp. 31, 63, 419; Cox, "The Battle of Antietam," pp. 647-648.

37. *OR* 19, pt 1, p. 419; Carman, p. 5.

38. *General George Crook: His Autobiography*, edited by Martin F. Schmitt (Norman, 1946), p. 97.

39. *OR* 19, pt. 1, p. 890; Priest, *Antietam: The Soldiers' Battle*, p. 217; Carman. p 5.

40. *OR* 19, pt. 1, pp. 424-425; Carman, pp. 11-12. The hill from which the Southern batteries fired is now the National Cemetery.

41. Ibid; William Frassanito, *Antietam: The Photographic Legacy of America's Bloodiest Day* (New York, 1978), p. 230.

42. Ibid

43. Ibid; Sears, *Landscape Turned Red*, pp. 262-263; James Longstreet, *From Manassas to Appomattox*, (Philadelphia, 1895), pp. 262-263.

44) Carman, pp. 12-14.

45. Ibid; *OR* 19, pt. 1, p. 473.

46. Carman, pp. 12-14; Cox, "The Battle of Antietam," p. 651.

47. *OR* 19, pt. 1, pp. 419, 425; Vertical Files, 11th, 28th, and 36th Ohio Regiments, Antietam National Battlefield Library.

48. Vertical Files, 11th, 28th, and 36th Ohio Regiments, Antietam National Battlefield Library

49. *OR* 19, pt 1, pp. 419, 444; Carman, p. 14.

50. *OR* 19, pt 1, pp. 444, 850-851; Carman, p. 15; Cope, map # 9.

51. *OR* 19, pt. 1, p. 444.

52. Carman, p. 16.

53. Theodore Dimon, "A Federal Surgeon at Sharpsburg," *Civil War History*, vol. 6, no. 2, (June 1960), pp. 141-142.

54. Carman, p. 16.

55. Edward O. Lord, *History of the Ninth Regiment New Hampshire Volunteers in the War of the Rebellion*, (Concord, 1895), pp. 110, 125.

56. Carman, p. 16.

57. Ibid; Dimon, "A Federal Surgeon at Sharpsburg," pp. 140-142.

58. Carman, pp. 16-17; *OR* 19, pt 1, pp 446-447; Cope, map # 10.

59. Ibid; Lyman Jackman, *History of the 6th New Hampshire Regiment in the War For the Union*, (Concord, 1891), pp. 103-104.

60. *OR* 19, p. 1, pp. 419, 444.

61. Ezra J. Warner, *Generals in Blue*, (Baton Rouge, 1964), pp. 150-151.

62. OR 19, pt. 1, p. 444; Thomas H. Parker, *History of the 51st Regiment of P.V. and V.V.*, (Philadelphia, 1869), pp. 230-231.

63. Carman, pp. 17-18.

64. Ibid; Cope, map # 11.

65. Ibid; Priest, *Antietam: The Soldiers' Battle*, p. 340.

66. Carman, pp. 18-19.

67. Ibid; James V. Murfin, *The Gleam of Bayonets*, (New York, 1965), p. 275.

68. Ibid.

69. Carman, p. 19; *OR* 19, pt. 1, p. 890; "The Burke Sharpshooters," *Confederate Veteran*, vol. 32, p. 464; Henry L. Benning, "Notes by General H.L. Benning on Battle of Sharpsburg," *Southern Historical Society Papers*, vol. 16, p. 393.

70. Carman, p. 19-20; Murfin, *Gleam of Bayonets*, pp. 275-276; Dimon, "A Federal Surgeon at Sharpsburg," p. 144; Priest, *Antietam: The Soldiers' Battle*, p. 340.

71. "The Burke Sharpshooters," pp. 464-465.

72. Carman, pp. 22-23.

73. Benning, "Notes on Battle of Sharpsburg," p. 393.

74. Warner, *Generals in Blue*, pp. 150-151.

75. Cox, "The Battle of Antietam," p. 650.

76. Carman, p. 25; Sears, *Landscape Turned Red*, p. 259.

77. Carman, pp. 25-27; *OR* 19, pt. 1, pp. 450-451.

78. Ibid; Sears, *Landscape Turned Red*, p. 262.

79. Cox, "The Battle of Antietam," p. 651.

80. Carman, pp. 27-28; *OR* 19, pt. 1, pp 452-453; Priest, *Antietam: The Soldiers' Battle*, p. 340; Cope, map # 11.

81. Ibid.

82. Carman, pp. 28-29; *OR* 19, pt. 1, pp. 451, 453, 850-851; Cope, map # 11.

83. Ibid.

84. Ibid.

85. *OR* 19, pt. 1, p. 425; Sears, *Landscape Turned Red*, pp. 267-269 .

86. Sears, *Landscape Turned Red*, pp. 277-284; Alexander Hunter, "A High Private's Sketch of Sharpsburg, Paper no. 2," *Southern Historical Society Papers*, vol. 11, pp 16-17; John Dooley, *John Dooley, Confederate Soldier: His War Journal*, edited by Joseph T. Durkin, S.J., (Georgetown, 1945), pp. 45-47.

87. Sears, *Landscape Turned Red*, pp. 277-284; *OR* 19, pt. 1, pp. 886, 890-891; Benning, "Notes on Battle of Sharpsburg," pp. 393-394.

88) *OR* 19, pt. 1, pp. 453-454, 851, 886-887, 891-892; Dooley, John Dooley, Confederate Soldier, pp. 46-47; Benning, "Notes on Battle of Sharpsburg," pp. 393-395.

89. *OR* 19, pt. 1, p. 887.

90. Carman, pp. 21-22.

91. Sears, *Landscape Turned Red*, pp. 291-292.

"I felt that I would give all the world to be able to shoot the advancing foe."

BAPTISM OF FIRE

The 118th ("Corn Exchange") Pennsylvania Infantry at the Battle of Shepherdstown

Mark A. Snell

B y the summer of 1862, few Northern recruits were enlisting to replace the tens of thousands of soldiers killed or maimed during the bloody spring and early summer campaigns. Major General George McClellan's Peninsula Campaign had teetered on the brink of success at the gates of Richmond before finally tumbling down like a house of cards. In the Western Theater, the April slaughter suffered by U. S. Grant at Shiloh, although an important Union victory, also thinned the army's ranks.

Just before these campaigns, however, in March 1862, many in the North believed that the prospects for a relatively easy victory were visible on the horizon. As a result, Secretary of War Edwin Stanton ordered U. S. Army recruiting offices closed. The horrendous casualties suffered by McClellan and Grant revealed the lack of wisdom in this decision and convinced nearly everyone that the war would not be over by the end of summer. Concerned that a call for recruits by the Federal government would be interpreted as a sign of panic, President Lincoln worked out a deal allowing the Northern governors to formally "request" that the President call upon the states for 300,000 new three-year volunteers. In July, Lincoln assigned each state a quota based on population. If the quotas were not met, the governors would draft their enrolled militia for nine-months' service.[1]

It was under these circumstances that the 118th Pennsylvania Infantry Regiment was raised. Young men were not so eager to don a uniform as they had been a year earlier, and thus it became necessary to devise means to entice them to enlist. Patriotism was one way to get a young man's blood stirring. Money was another. Believing the latter would prove more fruitful than the former, the Philadelphia banking firm known as the Corn Exchange agreed to subsidize a bounty to entice the young men to sign up. At a meeting of the Corn Exchange Association on July 24, 1862, a resolution was passed to "collect, by voluntary subscription, the amount of means necessary to organize said regiment, and to consult with and aid in all proper ways the officers that may be selected to put the regiment in fighting trim."[2]

A special committee was set up within the Corn Exchange Association to ensure that the resolution was carried out. The Association offered a modest bounty in addition to the bonus being given by the United States Government. The total bounty of $160, along with one month's pay in advance, induced 960 men to enlist in the regiment in the incredibly short period of just thirty days.[3] This achievement is even more amazing when one realizes that Northern state governments had to resort to conscription because men were not joining the army as quickly as they had earlier in the war.

In addition to providing a bounty, the Corn Exchange Association gave each recruit a rubber blanket, toiletries, and "other articles of comfort and convenience." The colonel of the new regiment was Charles Mallet Prevost, who had been a member of the Corn Exchange Association before the war and a veteran of McClellan's Peninsula Campaign. The forty-four year old Prevost was at home in Philadelphia convalescing from an illness he contracted in Virginia when he was appointed to command the 118th Pennsylvania.[4]

. In early August, the governor of Pennsylvania authorized the regiment to begin recruiting. Ten recruiting offices, one for each company in the regiment, were scattered around the city of Philadelphia. Once enlisted, the new recruits were sent to the "camp of rendezvous and instruction" on the outskirts of Philadelphia near the falls of the Schuykill River. One of the young sergeants who was detailed to be the clerk of the camp commandant also was a veteran. Sergeant J. Rudhall White, who had been a clerk in civilian life, had seen action at the Battle of Bull Run—allegedly as a Confederates soldier. According to the 118th's regimental historian,

> White was a handsome soldierly man of scarce twenty summers. A native of Warrenton, Virginia, at the breaking out of the war he was a young lieutenant in the Black Horse Cavalry [1st Virginia] . . . subsequently famous in all the campaigns of Virginia. Differing in sentiments from his friends and his family, sacrificing the ties of home and friendship, he determined to defend his convictions with his sword. Firm in his belief that the unrighteous attempt to

Colonel Charles Mallet Prevost, Commander, 118th Pennsylvania Infantry

History of the 118th P.V.

disrupt the gov't. should be suppressed, imbued with the highest patriotism, he sought service in the Union Army.[5]

Sergeant (later Lieutenant) J. Rudhall White

History of the 118th P.V.

As the men arrived at "Camp Union," uniforms were issued and the process of learning close-order drill began. The regiment's historian later wrote that "[t]he drill in the 'facings' disclosed the fact that many, otherwise intelligent, were not certain as to which was their right hand or their left. Consequently, when the order 'Right Face!' was given, face met face in inquiring astonishment, and frantic attempts to obey the order made still greater confusion." With practice, the men became proficient, and soon company and battalion drills were learned. On one clear August day, the men moved out smartly in battalion drill. With their band blaring and the colors of the regiment unfurled, the men looked quite martial—until one of the soldiers stepped on a nest of yellow jackets. The regiment's historian remembered that "another nest was disturbed, and still others; the music increased. The yellow jackets made a spirited attack. The regiment hesitated, faltered, wavered, fled!—fled in confusion covered with stings instead of glory. The Corn Exchange Regiment had suffered its first defeat."[6]

Weapons training and marksmanship in the 118th Pennsylvania apparently received much less attention than learning to maneuver, primarily because the unit's arms (British Enfields) were issued sporadically and late in the training cycle. For example, companies C, E, I, and K were issued their rifles on August 15, but five more days days passed before companies A, B, and H received theirs. Companies D and G, however, did not receive their Enfields until the end of the month.[7]

Only a few weeks after training began—and the day after the final two companies were issued rifles—the regiment was mustered into Federal service on August 31. The Pennsylvanians departed Camp Union on September 1 for

Washington, D.C. The haste to muster in and transfer the regiment to the District of Columbia is explained in part because Maj. Gen. John Pope's Army of Virginia had been thrashed at the Battle of Second Bull Run, and the nation's capital was in peril. By September 3, the Corn Exchange Regiment was encamped near Fort Albany, on Arlington Heights, overlooking the Potomac River.[8] The arrival of other reinforcements and Washington's defenses, among other reasons, precluded a Confederate move in that direction. As a result, the regiment's members remained in the Washington area where they practiced the art of soldiering.

Their sojourn there did not last long. On September 6, the 118th's soldiers were issued forty rounds of ammunition—apparently their first issue of live rounds.[9] Six days later on September 12, the 118th Pennsylvania was assigned to the 1st Brigade, 1st Division, V Corps, Army of the Potomac. Their brigade, a large and eclectic mixture of troops commanded by Col. James Barnes, consisted of the 18th and 22nd Massachusetts, the 13th and 25th New York, the 1st Michigan, the 2nd Maine, and the 2nd Company, Massachusetts Sharpshooters. The 118th's sister units had fought in the battles on the Virginia Peninsula during the spring and summer of 1862, and had recently participated in the Second Bull Run debacle.[10]

Unbeknownst to the Pennsylvanians, they were heading into western Maryland to oppose Lee's Army of Northern Virginia, which was raiding north of the Potomac River in search of a victory on Northern soil. By this time Lincoln had wisely rid himself of the thoroughly disgraced John Pope in favor of George McClellan, whose organizational skills had quickly returned the army to its former fighting trim. The march of the brigade from Washington to western Maryland took its toll on the new soldiers. The other veterans in Barnes' brigade were accustomed to long marches and had learned to carry only necessary items in the blanket rolls slung over their shoulders. The men of the 118th, however, carried extraneous items and other impedimenta in cumbersome knapsacks. The rookies quickly learned from their veteran brethren, and before too many hours had passed the roadside was littered with knapsacks and other items of questionable value to a soldier engaged in active campaigning. Still, the toilsome march and extreme heat took its toll, and the Pennsylvania regiment lost virtually all semblance of organization. Men fell out of the march by the score from heat prostration or sheer exhaustion. One tired Corn Exchange straggler came upon his division commander, Maj. Gen. George Morrell, and asked him: "General, can you tell me where the 118th Pennsylvania is?" The general replied, "Certainly, my man. Everywhere between here and Washington."[11]

By the morning of September 13, most of the stragglers had caught up (or had been corralled) by the 118th's officers. The following evening, the Corn Exchange Regiment camped on the outskirts of Frederick on the banks of the Monocacy River. Much of the day and a sizable portion of the army had been utilized to force the passes of South Mountain, which were stubbornly held by elements of Lee's army. The efforts reached fruition at dark when the Confederates abandoned their delaying action and fell back west of the South Mountain range. As most of McClellan's army continued its pursuit of the enemy the next day, the 118th remained in camp. On September 16, it marched with the rest of the brigade through Turner's Gap and camped at Keedysville that evening.[12]

In a bold and hazardous decision, Lee decided to offer McClellan battle at Sharpsburg. The fighting raged from daybreak through dusk on September 17, and when the battle finally and mercifully ended, more Americans had been killed or wounded than any day in the country's history. Fortunately for the green Pennsylvanians and most of the rest of their V Corps comrades, McClellan had not seen fit to utilize their services, and they spent the day in reserve.

The next day, Barnes' brigade was moved towards the Federal left, near Burnside Bridge, where the soldiers witnessed the aftermath of the battle. The carnage made an indelible impression on the men who, only a few weeks before, plied their civilian trades back in the City of Brotherly Love. One soldier remembered the scene well:

> On the morning of the 18th the command was moved off some miles toward the left, in the direction where Burnside had made the desperate fight for the stone bridge. . . .Some of the route was over a portion of the field where the battle had waged fiercely. . . .Down the slope of the road, approaching the bridge, the numbers of the slain increased; abandoned muskets and cartridge-boxes lay everywhere, and the ground, furrowed and upturned by shot and shell, showed the heavy work of the enemy's guns. Just at the entrance of the bridge a man lay stretched upon his back, unconscious, but moaning, a minnie-ball imbedded in his forehead.[13]

While traversing the southern edge of the battlefield, the Pennsylvanians passed a house that reportedly still contained Confederate sharpshooters. Not entirely convinced that Southerners remained in the house, Cpl. Richard E. Sandford of Company E climbed a fence for a better look. A shot rang out, and Corporal Sandford fell with a bullet wound that necessitated the amputation of one of his legs at mid-thigh. Sandford was discharged for disability at Philadelphia on March 16, 1863. He was the 118th's first battle-related casualty.[14]

Lee had defiantly remained in position throughout the 18th, daring McClellan to renew his assaults. Other than sporadic skirmishing, no serious fighting took place. That night, Lee was allowed to withdraw his shattered army unmolested across the Potomac River at Boteler's Ford (also known as Blackford's, Pack Horse, or Shepherdstown Ford), about a mile and a half downstream from Shepherdstown, (West) Virginia. Jeb Stuart and his Confederate cavalry division crossed about a mile upstream from Shepherdstown.[15]

With the exception of an artillery battery and some wagons of wounded men from Brig. Gen. John G. Walker's Division of James Longstreet's command, by the morning of the 19th the Army of Northern Virginia was safely on the south bank of the Potomac. As Lee sat on his mount Traveler in the middle of the river, Walker rode up to inform him that his unit was the last of the army to cross. Lee's reply evinced his concern and appreciation of the disaster that had threatened to engulf his army north of the river when he sighed, "Thank God." Although it appeared as though the Maryland Campaign was over, a bloody postscript was about to be played out.[16]

Sitting on the bluffs on the Virginia side of the river was a rear guard of Col. Thomas Munford's cavalry brigade, two depleted infantry brigades, and a powerful collection of artillery. The whole was commanded by the chief of the Army of Northern Virginia's artillery, Brig. Gen. William Nelson Pendleton. The nucleus of the artillery force guarding the ford was composed of Maj. William Nelson's Battalion of the army's reserve artillery, which had not been employed at Antietam. Batteries from other commands were commandeered as they reached the far bank of the river until a minimum of 44 guns had been deployed to guard the ford. Short range cannons were stacked in the middle of the line, while the longer range rifled pieces were positioned to strengthen its flanks.[17]

Pendleton, whose attributes did not include the ability to make sound military judgments, had been instructed to guard the ford until nightfall. Lee did not believe McClellan would pursue the Army of Northern Virginia. According to the commanding general, "a few guns and a small cavalry force [would be] sufficient to hold the fords."[18] If this was true, Pendleton obviously possessed enough of an armed force to stop any Union probe in his direction. Besides, the terrain alone was a formidable enough obstacle to make any attack difficult and probably impossible. Running parallel to the river was the road to Shepherdstown, and directly above this road were steep and treacherous cliffs, rising as high as 80 to 100 feet. Most of the vegetation was cleared along the bluffs, making for excellent fields of fire for the Confederate artillery positioned along the crest. A belt of woods ran parallel to the bluffs about 3/4 of a mile behind the river. Approximately a quarter of a mile upstream from the ford was an old mill dam, which had once provided power to the now-abandoned Boteler's Cement Mill. Several empty mill buildings were clustered along the Shepherdstown Road in the vicinity of the dam, along with mill-related structures such as kilns (used for lime burning, an essential ingredient in cement). At the ford's exit, a road running perpendicular to the Shepherdstown Road ascended the bluffs. With the exception of a few ravines, this road (known then as the Charlestown Road and today as Trough Road) was the only practical means for a sizable body of soldiers to reach the top of the bluffs. Pendleton's column, it seemed, was holding an impregnable position.

Lee's estimate of the situation, however, was wrong. In spite of this imposing terrain and the presence of the Confederate rear guard, McClellan ordered a pursuit by his cavalry and elements of V Corps. By evening of the 19th, Union artillery on the Maryland side of the Potomac River was pummeling Pendleton's guns. To make matters worse, the Confederate artillery was running out of ammunition. Pendleton ordered his pieces to begin withdrawing. As they prepared to move rearward, a party of 500 hand picked men from the 2nd Brigade of Morrell's division—including several soldiers from the 118th Pennsylvania—splashed across the river under the covering fire of 4th Michigan Infantry and the 1st United States' Sharpshooters, who had taken position in the empty Chesapeake and Ohio Canal that paralleled the river on the Maryland side.[19]

Although General Pendleton tried to rally the infantry and cavalry, the deteriorating situation appeared, to him at least, hopeless. As his men contested the assault, the artillery general rode rearward seeking help. At about 1:00 a.m. on the morning of September 20, the frustrated officer finally rode up to Robert E. Lee's headquarters. In his exhausted despair, Pendleton erroneously informed Lee that a Union force had stormed his rear guard and captured all of the artillery. "All?" asked Lee increduously. "Yes, General, I fear all."[20] Pendleton's credibility with the army took a sharp turn downward when his panicked assessment of the situation turned out to be almost completely incorrect. In fact, only four or five guns had been abandoned to the enemy. The 500-man Federal attack force had merely staged a cross-river raid, and darkness prevented the Union commanders from capitalizing on their success.[21]

The minor success, however, prompted further action the following day, and on September 20, Maj. Gen. Fitz John Porter pushed a large part of his V Corps across the Potomac. Marching in the wake of screening Union cavalry, three brigades from V Corps' 2nd Division, commanded by Brig. Gen. George

Sykes, together with Col. James Barnes' brigade of the 1st Division, were assembled for the proposed crossing.[22] At 8:00 a.m., by the time the Unionists were beginning to cross, Confederate reinforcements were arriving in the vicinity of Boteler's Ford. During his late-night ride, Pendleton had stopped at Maj. Gen. Thomas J. "Stonewall" Jackson's headquarters before galloping on to find Lee. Pendleton's news of the loss of his guns disgusted Jackson, who decided to take action to protect the army's rear. Without waiting for daylight, Stonewall dispatched three divisions toward the ford.[23]

The Northern cavalry crossed the river first, followed by Sykes' Division. Once across, Sykes' infantrymen pushed up the Charlestown Road and began fanning out at the top of the bluffs, where they soon encountered Jackson's men. Outnumbered, the Federals began to fall back toward the Potomac. Barnes' brigade, meanwhile, also had crossed over the river, with the 118th Pennsylvania bringing up the rear. Once his regiments were organized on the southern bank, Barnes led them out to reconnoiter toward Shepherdstown. As the men moved past the old cement mill towards Shepherdstown, Sykes gave the order for his own division to withdraw. Shortly thereafter, one of Sykes' staff officers came riding down the road and announced to Barnes that the Confederates were advancing in force. The colonel immediately ordered his brigade to take a position on the bluffs next to the road. The 18th Massachusetts, the first regiment in line, reached the top first, followed by the 25th and 13th New York regiments, which ascended the heights behind it. The New Yorkers deployed on the right of the 18th, "a few rods distant," Barnes later reported.[24]

As these three regiments were aligning themselves, Barnes turned to Colonel Prevost, the 118th Pennsylvania's commander, and asked, "Can you get your regiment on the top of the cliff?" "I will try sir," Prevost answered.[25] Barnes told him to follow the route of the two New York outfits and to take position on their left flank. The brigade's remaining regiments scaled the heights where the 18th Massachusetts made its climb. When these last regiments reached the top, the 1st Michigan and 22nd Massachusetts took up a position between the 18th Massachusetts and the 118th Pennsylvania, while the 2nd Maine planted itself on the far left of the line beyond the 18th Massachusetts.[26] The nature of the rugged terrain, however, did not allow the flanks of the various units to connect with each other.

The Corn Exchange soldiers had just formed their line of battle when one of the 118th's lieutenants ran up to Prevost and informed him that one of Barnes' staff officers had given the order to retreat. "From whom did you say you heard this?" Prevost barked. The acting assistant adjutant of the brigade,

Maj. Gen. A. P. Hill

The pugnacious Hill's Light Division blunted the Federal thrust over the Potomac River and threw it back with heavy losses.

Generals in Gray

Brig. Gen. James Archer

Archer took command of three of Hill's brigades at Shepherdstown. Archer later reported that the advance of his command "was made under the heaviest artillery fire I have ever witnessed."

Generals in Gray

came the lieutenant's response. "I do not receive orders in that way," retorted Prevost. "If Colonel Barnes has any orders to give me, let his aide come to me."[27]

The brigade was in a difficult situation, and this was most certainly not the time for Prevost to insist on military protocol. Sykes' Division was already beginning to retreat across the Potomac, and the other regiments in Barnes' brigade were preparing to do likewise. From his location on the right center of the line, however, Prevost probably could not see the other retiring units. Yet, if Prevost ordered a retreat based upon a junior officer's verbal order, and if that order turned out to be exaggerated or false, his actions could spell disaster for the brigade. As the colonel was pondering his unappealing options, circumstances beyond his control engulfed the situation.

Directly in front of the Corn Exchange Regiment, Ambrose P. Hill's Light Division was stepping out of the woods and pushing across the fields towards the Philadelphians. Union artillery on the Maryland shore zeroed-in on the advancing Confederate line, but the Southerners continued their advance. Brigadier General James J. Archer, who took command of the three brigades on the left of Hill's line, later reported that "[t]he advance of my command was made under the heaviest artillery fire I have ever witnessed."[28] Undeterred and screaming the Rebel yell, Archer's men rushed forward and delivered a devastating volley into the center of the Pennsylvanians' line.[29]

The Federals, who had not yet fired their rifles in anger—and few if any had enjoyed the benefits of small arms training—were suddenly on the receiving end of a full-scale assault by one of the best divisions in Lee's army. To their chagrin, some of the men discovered for the first time that their Enfields were defective. On some of the weapons, weak mainsprings failed to provide enough force to the hammer, which was needed to explode the percussion cap and thus ignite the gunpowder. On others, the cone (or nipple) was defective, and shattered under the force of the striking hammer. The men panicked. Some picked up the weapons of their fallen comrades. Others rushed to their officers to find out what could be done. The center of the line began to waiver as the Confederates closed the distance between them.[30]

Colonel Prevost attempted to rally his men and hold them in line. He snatched the regimental flag and exhorted them to hold firm, but a musket ball ripped into his shoulder. Unable to remain in command, Prevost was carried down the ravine, where he was met by a concerned Colonel Barnes. "Where is your regiment?" Barnes inquired. "Fighting desperately at the top of the hill, sir, where you placed it," replied the wounded officer. "Why, I gave you orders to retire in good order." Prevost responded: "I never received them, sir." Prevost then told Barnes that his men were being terribly cut up and should be relieved. "I will do so myself," promised the brigade commander.[31]

By now, however, it was too late for an orderly withdrawal. The 118th's Lt. Col. James Gwyn took over for the wounded Prevost and ordered his men to fix bayonets. In the confusion of the moment, few heard or heeded him. Spontaneously, perhaps, some 200 members of the regiment left their position and charged out to meet the enemy, but the Unionists were heavily outnumbered and quickly flanked on both sides. Bullets began knocking many of them to the ground, and others fell back in confusion. The Corn Exchange Regiment's cohesion and order evaporated.

Contemporary depiction of soldiers from Berdan's Sharpshooters and the 5th New York Infantry firing from the bed of the C & O Canal

Harper's Weekly

Major Charles P. Herring

History of the 118th P.V.

The Philadelphians made a mad rush for the ravine. Some headed in the wrong direction, only to fall from the high cliffs to their death.[32] Hill's men were hot on their heels, shooting into the backs of the retreating Federals. As the soldiers of the 118th stumbled and tumbled down the ravine toward the Potomac, Confederate infantrymen lined the tops of the bluffs and poured a plunging fire into them.[33] Captain Courtney M. O'Callaghan, the 23-year old commander of Company I, was seriously hurt when he fell down side of the cliff. His injuries were so severe he was never able to return to active duty.[34]

While their comrades were being slaughtered along the cliff sides, other members from the regiment ran down the road towards the mill. Still others attemped to hide in the kilns along the river's edge. Private Joe Meehan of Company A described his own personal ordeal:

There was considerable confusion among our men and much noise, from the suddenness with which we found ourselves called into a brisk fight. A cry reached me about this time to fix bayonets. Who gave it I do not know. I shouted the order loudly to those about me. Captain O'Neil, who was near me, asked me what I said. I replied: 'They are calling to fix bayonets.' He raised his voice and called out: 'Fix bayonets;' but there were few besides myself who did it. The rebels were now approaching quite close. I had broken the nipple of my gun and had picked up another gun lying near me, but, as with the first one, I had great trouble in getting it to go off. It made me very angry; I felt that I would give all the world to be able to shoot the advancing foe. I had fired but about a half-dozen shots, when as many again could have been got off had the guns been good for anything.

I had taken a pin out and cleaned the nipple, and had raised my rifle for a shot when I felt what seemed like a blow with a heavy fist on my left shoulder from behind. I did not realize at first that I was shot, feeling no particular pain, but my almost useless arm soon told me what it was. I called to our orderly-sergeant that I was shot. He made no reply, probably not understanding me.

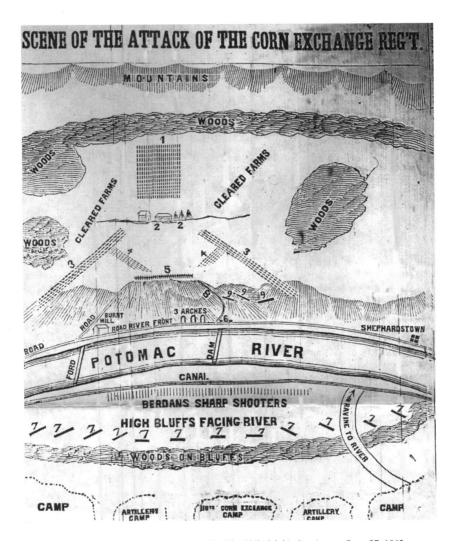

Crude map (not to scale) that appeared in *The Philadelphia Inquirer* on Sept. 27, 1862.

The numbers were keyed to a legend that accompanied the map, as follows: "1. Solid column of Rebels advancing from wood on double quick. 2. Farm house and barn with hay stacks half mile back. 3. Columns of Rebels advancing in triangle. 4. Rebels advance with white flag. 5. 118th, Corn Exchange, in battle line. 6. Col. Barnes' position. 7. Batteries in position in ploughed [sic] fields commanding opposite heights covering retreat. 8. Path which the 118th, Corn Exchange, ascended. 9. The New York 13th and 25th, and 18th Michigan in battle line." In addition to the fact that there are no mountains in the vicinity of Shepherdstown as appears on this map, there is no evidence that the Confederates ever showed a white flag during the battle, as the caption keyed to no. 4 indicates.

I then took my first look back of me, and found myself very nearly alone. Two wounded men, McElroy and Tibben, of Company A, were right behind me on the ground. I passed them both, and began to descend the hill with numerous others. There was great disorder. About half-way down, among the brush, an officer was trying to stem the tide of descent. I slid down the slope, with my one free arm to aid me, and reaching the road at the bottom of the bluff ran a short distance till I came to three archways in the hill. Into the first of these I got for protection. Two other wounded men were there and three others, one of whom was John Bray, one of my tent-mates. Our artillery at this time was shelling the heights to cover our retreat. The shells fell short, and one of them exploded in the archway next to me, tearing almost off the leg of Corporal James Wilson, who was therein for shelter.[35]

During the complete confusion that ruled that morning, some Pennsylvanians attempted escape by running across the slippery and dilapidated mill dam. Their effort was supported by the green-clad marksmen in Hiram Berdan's Sharpshooters, who used the dry bed of the C & O Canal as protection to lay down an effective covering fire. Other Corn Exchange boys tried to swim to safety. John Rudhall White, the ex-Confederate who recently had been promoted to 2nd lieutenant, swam the entire way across and stepped out of the water unscathed. As he ascended the bank of the C & O Canal he was heard to say, "Thank God! I am over at last." White had just uttered those words when a bullet ripped into his back and tore into his bowels. He died shortly thereafter.[36]

On the Virginia side of the Potomac, one of the 118th's color bearers stood like a stunned deer at the water's edge, unable to will himself to make the attempt. Major Charles P. Herring ripped the flag from his grasp and passed it to Pvt. William Hummel of Company D. Herring pushed Hummel into the river and together, the two men swam across, attracting a storm of bullets until they reached safety. The 118th's other flag was spotted floating in the Potomac above the dam. Captain Frank A. Donaldson, commander of Company H, had to yell several times at passing soldiers to pick up the banner before someone finally stopped and retrieved it.[37]

The Battle of Shepherdstown was a disaster for Union arms. Bodies in blue uniforms floated down the river and lay thickly along the breast of the dam. The next day, Union burial parties under a flag of truce were sent over to gather the slain. Years later, a veteran of the 12th New York Infantry, who had served on the burial detail that day, recalled the scene:

I do not know how many was buried by our party, but I know that it was more than we expected to find. Many of the bodies were recovered from almost inaccessible places, where they lodged among the bushy undergrowth on the side of the bluff, some having apparently been killed by the fall. Some, I believe, were killed by the bayonet. Numbers were found, with their knapsacks still slung, lying in several feet of water, where they had been shot down while trying to cross the river. Scores of muskets and knapsacks were found at one place, where the owners had left them before trying to swim across the deeper water of the dam. In spite of repeated and emphatic warnings, I could not resist the temptation, when none of the guards were looking, to try and exchange my warn and battered cap for a shiny new one I found lying among the rocks. I snatched it up, only to find that it had been pierced from front to rear by a bullet and the inside still reeking with blood and brains. It is needless to say I left it where it was found.[38]

Lieutenant Colonel James Gwyn

History of the 118th P.V.

And so the Corn Exchange Regiment underwent its baptism of fire. The engagement extracted a frightful cost. Of the 737 men in the 118th Pennsylvania, 63 were killed, 101 were wounded, and 105 were listed as either captured or missing, for a total of 269 casualties (approximately 36%). Many of the wounded, such as 19-year old Pvt. Chancellor Benjamin, died as a result of their injuries.[39] Total Union losses at the Battle of Shepherdstown were 363 (71 killed, 161 wounded, 131 captured or missing).[40] A. P. Hill's Division suffered 261 casualties (30 killed, 231 wounded), surprisingly high given the nature and course of the engagement.[41] The total loss for both sides (624) made the Battle of Shepherdstown the bloodiest fight ever waged in what would become the state of West Virginia.[42]

The debacle shocked the citizenry in Philadelphia. The *Philadelphia Inquirer* demanded to know,. "Whose fault was it?" The *Inquirer's* special correspondent insisted "in the name of humanity, justice and honor, that this dreadful culpability shall be fixed upon the guilty and incompetent party." Comparing the slaughter of the 118th to a similar tragedy suffered by the Philadelphia-recruited 71st Pennsylvania Infantry at Ball's Bluff, Virginia, the previous October, the reporter commented, "This is the second time the flower of Philadelphia, who have gallantly rushed to their country's defense, have been uselessly slaughtered on the banks of the Potomac. Ball's Bluff and Blackford's Ford have been too deeply ensanguined with Philadelphia blood for our people to permit this terrible responsibility to be shifted or shirked."[43] Private Charles C. Brown of the 13th New York also compared it to the October 1861 battle when he wrote that "it was almost another Balls Bluff affair." Brown, too, was not sure who was to blame for the debacle. "Whose blunder brought on the catastrophe I cannot say," Brown told a lady friend, but "[o]ne thing I know [it] was a blunder."[44]

The truth probably would not have satisfied the passionate Philadelphians, for it was neither Barnes' nor Prevost's fault. The pursuit was generally well designed, but an odd set of circumstances conspired to the detriment of the Pennsylvanians. The terrain was difficult, the order to fall back was misunderstood or never received, and the green regiment with defective weapons was suddenly confronted by a large veteran division of Confederates sweeping into their line. Unfortunately, many young men died as a result. On one matter everyone could agree: the 118th Pennsylvania, Private Brown informed his friend, fought ". . .bravely, and their first fight, too."[45]

In the weeks after the battle, Lieutenant Colonel Gwyn, who remained in command of the 118th while the wounded Prevost recuperated, attempted to get his regiment's defective muskets exchanged. He was adamant that they be replaced with Springfields. When Lt. George Batchelder, the division ordnance officer, issued new Enfields to the regiment on September 28, Gwynn sent him a terse message: "I have the honor to report that the muskets sent to this regiment this a.m. are the same as those that we have had in use, and have found them entirely useless. I herewith return the same with 75 others of the same kind, and request that you will furnish us with good arms immediately, or as soon as convenient."[46] The ordnance officer was sympathetic to Gwyn's situation, especially in light of the catastrophe the regiment had recently suffered partly as a result of the defective Enfields. "I have but 500 Sprinfields wherewith to supply XVI regiments, " Batchelder replied to Gwyn:

> When those already having Spfds. are supplied their deficiencies, the 118th shall have the balance. Meanwhile I have applied for Springfield Rifles to equip your whole regiment, and hope soon to be able to do so. The rifles sent you are Enfield but not of the same poor quality you now have.[47]

For the next several weeks, the men of the Corn Exchange Regiment bivouacked on the Maryland shore across the river from the scene of their horrific
fight. While in camp, the regiment received visitors from their hometown, including a delegation from the Corn Exchange Association bearing "about a ton
of medical and other stores for the 'boys' of their regiment." Relatives of those
killed in the affair also came to retrieve the bodies of their loved ones. The father
of Capt. Courtland Saunders, commander of Company C, took his son's remains
back to Philadelphia on September 26. John Ricketts had to arrange for the
removal of his son's remains under a flag of truce. Once the body of Capt.
Joseph Ricketts, Company K's commander, had been found, it was brought to
Sharpsburg and temporarily interred in a church cemetery until arrangements
were made to transport the captain's remains back to Philadelphia.[48]

Under Colonel Gwyn's stewardship, the 118th would go on to fight—with
Springfield rifles—in virtually all of the Army of the Potomac's major battles.
Its performance at Shepherdstown, however, haunted the regiment until the end
of the war. By the time the Corn Exchange boys mustered out of service, 1,493
men had served in her ranks. Of these, 125 were killed or died of wounds, and
232 others were wounded.[49] Over half of the men killed or mortally wounded
fell at Shepherdstown.

Colonel Prevost suffered an unusually cruel fate. He never fully recovered
from his Shepherdstown wound, and he never returned to command the regiment. The injury necessitated his resignation from the army on September 30,
1863, although he was breveted to brigadier general on July 16, 1867, with an
effective date of March 13, 1863. The bullet that had smashed his shoulder
could not be fully extracted, for it had lodged near his spine. As the years
passed, his pain and suffering continued to intensify. By 1877 the lead missile
was causing nerve damage, and Prevost lost most of his vision and the partial
use of his arms and legs. The projectile continued to irritate the area around the
spine and caused further disability. By 1878, Prevost was completely blind and
his legs totally paralyzed. The long-suffering officer lingered for another nine
years before finally succumbing on November 5, 1887. His death was directly
attributable to the wound he had suffered more than a quarter century earlier.[50]

Although the 118th Pennsylvania suffered only a few casualties at the
Battle of Gettysburg, its veterans chose that field to erect a monument to honor
their fallen comrades. (In fact, they placed not one but three such monuments at
Gettysburg.)[51] The Battle of Shepherdstown, however, would long be remembered by the Corn Exchange veterans as their most devastating fight. In 1897,

on the 35th anniversary of the battle, the regiment's surviving veterans assembled on the battlefield at Shepherdstown. There, Company A's Joseph Meehan recited a poem entitled "35 Years Ago." As the graying warriors stood on the banks of the Potomac River, Meehan read his touching verses, two of which memorialized the regiment's actions in September 1862:

> Antietam Field and Shepherdstown!
> Our losses date from you,
> We know 'tis vain, yet still we call
> give back the brave we knew.
> Our memory's map we trace again
> the bloody field they trod,
> Alas! We see again the slain
> We placed beneath the sod.
>
> Yes, five and thirty years have flown
> since you, together came,
> Upon this field, where well you won
> your legacy of fame.
> You're met to talk the battle o'er,
> to talk of actions won,
> Beneath the flag which on this ground
> Flashed in the light of sun.[52]

If the Corn Exchange regiment's soldiers could view the Shepherdstown Battlefield today, they would find it barely recognizable. Although the area has not undergone much development since the war, trees and other vegetation have changed the landscape from its 1862 appearance. The ruins of the cement mill are constantly being vandalized—both by humans and by nature. Visitors to the battlefield (which is in private ownership) will find only three iron War Department tablets (at the intersection of the Charlestown and Shepherdstown' roads near the ford) out of the five that originally marked the site. Sadly, one of the pair of missing tablets describes the actions of the 118th Pennsylvania.

If they even consider the fighting at Shepherdstown, most students of the Civil War think of it as an insignificant postscript to the Battle of Antietam. Yet, for the soldiers of the Corn Exchange regiment, the battle at the cement mill was both their baptism of fire and costliest engagement. Shepherdstown was as hal-

Post-war photograph of Private Joseph Meehan, Company A, 118th P. V.

History of the 118th P.V.

lowed to the 118th's veterans as Gettysburg was to the 20th Maine, or Second Manassas to the 5th New York. Thus it is somewhat ironic that the site of the 118th's sacrifice has fallen to such neglect. The battlefield's current condition and its lack of proper historical interpretation directly contradicts the last two lines in the final verse of Private Meehan's moving poem:

> O heroes of the Corn Exchange!
> O veterans of the line!
> Accept this day so long so dear to you,
> this little wreath of mine.
> Though you may never hear again
> The stirring battle drum,
> Your noble deeds the Land will crown
> A thousand years to come.[53]

Notes

The author would like to thank Mark Bell of Gettysburg National Military Park and Michael Musick of the National Archives for their assistance. Both men went "above and beyond the call of duty."

1. James McPherson, *Battle Cry of Freedom: The Civil War Era* (New York, 1988), pp. 401-402. On July 2, Lincoln made his call for 300,000 volunteers for three-years' service. When the states' quotas were not met, the Militia Act of 1862, passed by Congress on July 17, allowed the Federal government to impose on the states for 300,000 militiamen, drafted for nine months' active service. These 300,000 were in addition to the 300,000 three-year volunteers, and shortfalls in the latter category would have to be compensated by drafting additional men for a period of nine months.

2. J. L. Smith, *History of the Corn Exchange Regiment, 118th Pennsylvania Volunteers* (Philadelphia, 1888), p. 4.

3. A recruiting advertisement for Company A, which appeared in the August 7, 1862, edition of the *Philadelphia Inquirer,* announced: "Bounty $160—$100 paid each recruit as follows, $2 when the recruit is mustered in, $10 when sent to camp, $25 when the regiment is formed, $13 one month's pay in advance, and $25, one fourth of government bounty of $100."

4. Smith, *History of the Corn Exchange Regiment*, p. 4.

5. Ibid., p. 70. White's name, however, does not appear in the muster rolls of the 1st Virginia Cavalry, also known as the "Black Horse Cavalry."

6. Ibid., p. 13.

7. "Histories of commands from their organization to March 31, 1863," Record Group 94, Entry 120, National Archives and Records Administration, Washington, D.C. No record was found concerning the date that Company F was issued its weapons.

8. Smith, *History of the Corn Exchange Regiment*, p. 20; *Supplement to the Official Records of the Union and Confederate Armies*, (Wilmington, NC, 1998), vol. 62, pt. 2, p. 57.

9. General Order No. 2, Hqrs. 118th P.V., Ft. Albany, Sept. 6, 1862, in "Regimental Order Book, 118th P.V." RG 94, National Archives.

10. Smith, *History of the Corn Exchange Regiment*, p. 25; "Special Orders No. 3, Headquarters [Army of the Potomac], Washington, September 6, 1862," U. S. War Department, *War of the Rebellion: Official Records of the Union and Confederate Armies*, 128 vols. (Washington, D. C., 1890-1901), series I, vol. 19, pt. 2, pp. 197-98. Hereinafter cited as *OR*. All references are to series I unless otherwise noted.

11. Smith, *History of the Corn Exchange Regiment*, p. 30.

12. Ibid., p. 32.

13. Ibid., pp. 46-47.

14. Ibid., p. 50.

15. Dennis P. Kelly, "'Destructive Chastisement': The Battle of Shepherdstown," *Civil War Times Illustrated* (November, 1981), p. 9.

16. Ibid.

17. "Report of Brig. Gen. William N. Pendleton, C. S. Army, Chief of Artillery, of operations August 20-September 24," *OR* 19, pt. 1, pp. 830-31.

18. R. H. Chilton, Assistant Adjutant General, to Brig. Gen. Pendleton, September 19, 1862. *OR* 19, pt. 2, p. 612.

19. William H. Powell, *The Fifth Army Corps (Army of the Potomac): A Record of the Operations during the Civil War in the United States of America* (Dayton, 1984), pp. 293-94; "Report of Maj. Gen. Fitz-John Porter, U. S. Army, commanding Fifth Army Corps, of the battle of Antietam, skirmish at Blackford's or Boteler's Ford, and actions near Shepherdstown," *OR* 19, pt. 1, pp. 339-340.

20. Kelly, "Shepherdstown," p. 14.

21. "Report of Maj. Gen. Fitz-John Porter, U. S. Army, commanding Fifth Army Corps, of the battle of Antietam, skirmish at Blackford's or Boteler's Ford, and actions near Shepherdstown," *OR* 19, pt. 1, p. 340. According to Porter, only five Confederate cannons were captured.

22. Ibid.

23. Kelly, "Shepherdstown," p. 14.

24. "Report of Col. James Barnes, Eighteenth Massachusetts Infantry, commanding First Brigade, First Division, of action near Shepherdstown," *OR* 19, pt. 1, pp. 345-46.

25. Smith, *History of the Corn Exchange Regiment*, p. 59.

26. Barnes' Report, *OR* 19, pt. 1, p. 346

27. Smith, *History of the Corn Exchange Regiment*, pp. 60-61.

28. "Report of Brig. Gen. James J. Archer, C. S. Army, commanding brigade, of operations September 14-20," *OR* 19, pt. 1, pp. 1001-1002.

29. Ibid.; "Report of Brig. Gen. James H. Lane, C. S. Army, commanding Branch's brigade, of operations September 2-20," *OR* 19, pt. 1, p. 986.

30. Smith, *History of the Corn Exchange Regiment*, p. 61. Apparently, the chain-of-command was aware that many of the Enfields might not work in a combat situation. In his official report, General Porter wrote that "[t]hese defective arms had been reported to the General-in-Chief, but all efforts to replace them had failed." *OR* 19, pt. 1, p. 340 (footnote).

31. Ibid., p. 64.

32. "Report of Lieut. Col. James Gwyn, One hundred and eighteenth Pennsylvania Infantry, of action near Shepherdstown," *OR* 19, pt. 1, pp. 348-49; Smith, *History of the Corn Exchange Regiment*, p. 65.

33. Gwyn's Report, *OR* 19, pt. 1, pp. 348-49; "Our Shepherdstown Letter," *Philadelphia Inquirer*, September 26, 1862.

34. Compiled Service Record of Captain Courtney M. O' Callagahan, 118th Pennsylvania Infantry, National Archives.

35. Quoted in Smith, *History of the Corn Exchange Regiment*, pp. 82-84.

36. Smith, *History of the Corn Exchange Regiment*, pp. 69-70.

37. Richard A. Sauers, *Advance the Colors: Pennsylvania's Civil War Battle Flags*, vol. 2. (Harrisburg, 1991), p. 388.

38. C. W. Greene, "Fighting Them Over: What Our Veterans Have to Say About Their Old Campaigns. The 118th PA. The Bloody Fight at Shepherdstown Ford." *National Tribune*, January 14, 1886.

39. Compiled Service Record of Private Chancellor Benjamin, 118th Pennsylvania Infantry, National Archives. Benjamin passed away from "chronic diarrhea" on November 22, 1862, while recuperating from his Shepherdstown injury. "Return of Casualties in the Union forces in the skirmishes at Sharpsburg, Shepherdstown Ford, and near Williamsport, Md., September 19, action near Shepherdstown, Va., September 20, 1862, and general summary for the campaign," *OR* 19, pt. 1, p. 204.

40. "Return of Casualties in the Union forces. . . ," *OR* 19, pt. 1, p. 204. A 1905 edition of the 118th's regimental history claimed that the 118th's casualty figures were inflated in this report, with the "actual" number being only 209 casualties. This figure is suspect, however, as the author was trying to demonstrate that the 118th did not get as shot up as they had been portrayed. See *History of the 118th P.V* (Philadelphia, 1905), p. 94.)

41. "Report of Maj. Gen. Ambrose P. Hill, C. S. Army, commanding Light Division, of operations September 2-November 3," *OR* 19, pt. 1, p. 982. Confederate losses do not include casualties sustained on September 19. Although Southern losses appear

remarkably high, the majority probably occurred as a result of artillery fire from across the river.

42. The Battle of Droop Mountain on November 6, 1863, normally is cited as the "bloodiest" battle fought in West Virginia, but the total losses for both sides was less than 400 casualties (including captured and missing). At the "siege" of Harpers Ferry from September 14-15, 1862, Union and Confederate forces suffered less than 300 casualties combined (not counting the 12,737 Union soldiers who were surrendered), and the majority of those casualties occurred on Maryland Heights, not in West Virginia. The number of killed and wounded at Shepherdstown (624) makes this battle the bloodiest battle on what now is West Virginia soil.

43. *Philadelphia Inquirer*, September 26, 1862.

44. Charles Brown to "Caroline," September 22, 1862, in Katherine Macpherson, compiler, *Excerpts from the Civil War Letters of Charles Curtis Brown of Rochester, 13th Regiment N.Y. Infantry, 22nd Regiment N.Y. Cavalry* (Albany, OR, 1997), pp. 74-75.

45. Ibid.

46. Gwyn to Batchelder, September 28, 1862, in Regimental Order Book, 118th P.V., RG 94, National Archives.

47. Batchelder to Gwyn, September 28, 1862 (emphasis in original). Ibid.

48. *Philadelphia Inquirer*, September 26, 1862.

49. These numbers were based on tabulations from the company rosters found in Smith, *History of the Corn Exchange Regiment*, pp. 681-743. They differ substantially from the totals found in William F. Fox, *Regimental Losses in the American Civil War, 1861-1865* (Dayton, 1974), p. 203. Fox's numbers are less accurate than the tabulations taken from company rosters.

50. Compiled Service Record and Pension File of Charles M. Prevost, 118th Pennsylvania Infantry, National Archives.

51. 118th Pennsylvania Infantry file, vertical file collection, Gettysburg National Military Park Library.

52. "Thirty-fifth Annual Reunion of the 118th Regiment Pennsylvania Volunteers (Corn Exchange) held on the Battlefield of Shepherdstown, West Virginia, September 20, 1897" (n.p., 1897). Civil War Library and Museum, Philadelphia, PA.

53. Ibid. Both the 20th Maine and 5th New York played minor roles in the Shepherdstown battle.

". . .not a sight becoming a country that calls itself Christian."

DESTRUCTION, DISEASE, AND DEATH

The Battle of Antietam and the Sharpsburg Civilians

Ted Alexander

O n the morning of September 18, 1862, the people of the small farming community of Sharpsburg, Maryland, awoke to some of the worst carnage ever witnessed on the North American continent. The horrendous Battle of Antietam, fought the day before, is well known as the bloodiest single day's battle in American history. What is largely overlooked is that Sharpsburg was the first established community in the history of the Republic to sustain such intensive and multi-level abuse resulting from a large, highly-concentrated land battle of this size.[1]

Private Daniel Faust of Company H, 96th Pennsylvania, was a new recruit who, together along with his regiment, missed the battle. When he marched through Sharpsburg nearly three weeks later the damage was still very much apparent: "[A]t Sharpsburg the houses are rittled [sic] with balls and shells nearly all the gimleys [sic]. . .of the brick houses are all racket [sic] and the streets are laying full [of] shels [sic] and balls I never seen such a sight."[2] One could not escape the aftermath of the awful conflict that had taken place. The dead and wounded were everywhere. Private William H. Groninger, Company I, 126th Pennsylvania, had arrived on the field with his regiment on September 18. While he had been fortunate enough to have missed the battle, he arrived just in time to experience its morbid residue, and it left an indelible imprint on his memory that he vividly recalled some sixty-five years later:

We suffered much from thirst, and I took a number of canteens of my comrades, and went into town. A gate standing open showed me a draw well. At the windless was a dead man, his blood covering everything. I left the well in a hurry. A door was open; in the house lay two more dead men, a cannon ball having passed thru the corner of the house killing them."[3]

Sharpsburg, founded in 1763, is located in what is often called the Antietam, or Hagerstown Valley. This valley is the southern extension of the Cumberland Valley, which runs north to the Susquehanna River. South of Sharpsburg, across the Potomac River, the region becomes the Shenandoah Valley. It is about forty miles wide, bounded by the South Mountain range to the east and North Mountain range to the west. The entire geographical feature is part of what is known as The Great Valley, which divides the Eastern Seaboard from New York to Alabama. Sharpsburg is approximately 25 miles south of the Mason-Dixon Line.

Settlers arrived in the area as early as the 1740s, when the region around Sharpsburg was still part of Frederick County. Later, Sharpsburg became part of Washington County after it was organized in 1776. Hagerstown (the county seat about twelve miles to the northwest) and Sharpsburg are the oldest towns in Washington County. Both were formally laid out in 1763, although settlements existed there before that time.[4]

Sharpsburg was founded by Joseph Chapline, a member of a prominent Maryland colonial family, and named for Chapline's old friend, Maryland Governor Horatio Sharpe. The town was laid out around a water supply known as "The Great Spring," which still can be viewed today. In the 1930s, a memorial wall was built around the spring, and tradition has it that both Union and Confederate soldiers used it during and after the battle. Because of the water power generated by nearby Antietam Creek, grist mills were a major industry in the Sharpsburg area from colonial days until the early 20th century. Agriculture was the main industry for this part of Washington County, but the close proximity of the Chesapeake & Ohio Canal brought other forms of commerce to the town. By the 1850s Sharpsburg had a cooper's shop, a tannery and four shoe shops. Commerce was further facilitated by the completion of the Sharpsburg-Hagerstown Toll Pike in 1860. The streets were dirt and no attempt at standardized sidewalks seems to have been made until 18 years after the battle. At the time of the war, the population of the town exceeded 1,300 citizens.[5]

When John Trowbridge visited the town in 1865 he wrote that Sharpsburg was a "tossed and broken sort of place, that looks as if the solid ground swell of the earth had moved on and jostled it since the foundations were laid. As you go

up and down the hilly streets, the pavements, composed of fragments of lime-
stone slabs, thrust up such abrupt fangs and angles at you that it is necessary to
tread with exceeding caution."[6]

The Sharpsburg area had been settled a little more than 100 years before the
Battle of Antietam. Germans comprised the major European ethnic group to
settle there. It is estimated that during the 1700s, about 70 percent of all Ger-
man-speaking immigrants settled in Pennsylvania. From there many migrated to
western Maryland and Virginia's Shenandoah Valley. Thus, the German settlers
of these regions are frequently referred to as "Pennsylvania Germans."[7] "Pennsylvania German" is a broad term that includes immigrants from the Palatinate
(sometimes called Palatines), Alsace/Lorraine on the French-German border,
and Switzerland. The German immigrants called themselves the "Deutsche,"
which was bastardized in English to "Dutch."[8]

One of these "Dutch" was a chemist by the name of Dr. Christopher Cruss.
He had a farm as early as the 1760s on what became the north end of Antietam
Battlefield. After going through several owners, the property was purchased at
public sale in 1844 by David R. Miller at $53 per acre. Miller transferred the
deed to his father, John Miller, who owned the farm until his death in 1882. His
son David lived there and came to think of it as his own. At the time of the
battle, the farm sprawled across 260 acres. The most prominent landmark on the
site was a field of approximately 20 acres, which would gain immortality in the
battle as "The Cornfield." David Miller's grandparents had emigrated from
Germany in the 1760s. Their son John served as an officer in the War of 1812
and was a prosperous Sharpsburg businessman who owned several farms, a
hotel and grist mill. The Millers were Democrats and evidence suggests they
were strongly anti-Lincoln.[9]

A misnomer concerning the Germans is that they were all "Plain People" or
"Sect People" (members of the Dunker, Mennonite or Amish sect). While it is
true that the first sizable influx of Germans were Mennonite families to Pennsylvania in 1716, these so-called "Plain People" were a noticeable minority, both in
Pennsylvania and western Maryland.[10] The large majority, as many as 90 percent of German immigrants, were known as the "Church People" (members of
the Lutheran and Reformed churches). So it was with the citizens of Sharpsburg
and the surrounding countryside. Thus, while some noted area families were
Dunkers, most of the other farm families were not.[11]

The Germans contributed much to the culture of the region, the least of
which was their vernacular style of architecture developed by the early settlers
around Lancaster County, Pennsylvania. It spread with them in their migration

through Maryland and into the Shenandoah Valley, and was characterized by large stone farm houses and barns. Typical of this is the "Pennsylvania German bank barn," which normally is a two-level building. The first level was used for livestock, while the upper level was reserved for hay and grain. Confederate soldiers from the deep South and frontier states (such as Texas) were in awe of such structures. After Antietam, most of these barns served as field hospitals, and several were destroyed by fire during the battle.[12]

Today, visitors to the battlefield can see a number of these stout buildings both inside and outside the National Park boundary. One of the most prominent is the Piper barn, built in the late 18th century. Participants in the battle, however, would have seen a much smaller structure than what exists today. In 1898, a 60 by 44 foot wood-frame addition was built onto the north end, thus making it much larger than it was during the war.[13]

Another ethnic group that came over at the same time as the Germans were the French Huguenots. Some of the well known families of Sharpsburg, the Prys, Roulettes and Mummas, for example, traced their roots to this heritage. While the origin of the term "Huguenot" is unknown, it was first applied to French Protestants during the religious struggles of the 16th century. Religious persecution in France led to the dispersion of these people across Europe and around the world. Many Huguenots came directly to America. Others settled in parts of Germany and Switzerland and were amalgamated into those Germanic populations by the time they arrived in this country.[14]

The Roulettes were typical of French Huguenot settlement in this part of America. They descended from Jean Louis Roulette, a noted French engraver under the Italian masters in the early 1600s. The Roulettes settled in Maryland in the mid-18th century. The Roulette Farm is located in the center of Antietam Battlefield just north of the "Sunken Road." It was a homestead as early as 1748, and the first owner was noted Maryland frontiersman Thomas Cresap. From 1748 to 1804 the property went through some five different owners. John Miller purchased the farm on September 27, 1804. His daughter, Margaret A. Miller, married William Roulette in 1847. Accounts suggest that Roulette acquired the farm in 1853 either by purchase or via a wedding dowry. At the time of the battle, William Roulette was 37 years old and his wife was 32. They had six children and belonged to the Reformed Church. William, a staunch Republican, was a county commissioner.

Such large families were the norm for farm families of the mid 19th century. Like all people of their era, death was ever present. Infant mortality was high and not unexpected. When President Lincoln visited Antietam battlefield about two weeks after the fight, he was still in mourning over the death of his own young son Willie. So it was with the Roulettes. One son, Otho Williams, was not yet three when he died in 1856. Daughter Carrie May died on October 26, 1862. Thus, the family not only had to deal with the aftermath of battle and its destruction to their farm, but also with the death of their youngest daughter just five weeks later.[15]

The Mummas were another family with Huguenot roots who gained prominence in the Sharpsburg area. Like many Huguenots, they had commingled with German Protestants prior to coming to America. The Mummas, who settled near Sharpsburg, were Dunkers. Jacob Mumma was born in Cumberland County, Pennsylvania, in 1766. He moved to Washington County, Maryland, and purchased the Christian Orndorff farm and mill in 1796, which was located along

Mr. & Mrs. Samuel Mumma, circa 1850

Antietam National Battlefield

Antietam Creek at the site of the Middle Bridge. Later, Mumma purchased two adjoining properties. In 1831, he turned the farm over to his youngest son, Samuel, before dying nine years later in 1840.

Samuel was the owner of the Mumma Farm on Antietam Battlefield. Like his father, Samuel was married twice. His first wife, Barbara Hertzler, bore him five children between 1824 and 1833. All were males except the last born, Catherine, who died in infancy. In 1834, Mumma married Elizabeth Miller. This union brought forth 11 children—six boys and five girls—between 1835 and 1859. The Mumma house, barn, and spring house were probably built in the 1790s next to high ground sometimes referred to as "Smith's Hill." On the hill west of the house and barn is the Mumma family cemetery, established by the Smith and Orndorff families sometime in the 1700s (prior to the arrival of the Mummas). Later, Mr. Mumma allowed fellow members of the nearby Dunker Church to be laid to rest in the cemetery. (There are approximately 336 interments in the cemetery.) The stone wall around the grave yard, built in the 1870s, did not exist at the time of the battle. Mumma's most lasting contribution, in terms of the Antietam story, was his donation of the land for the Dunker Church.[16]

Other ethnic groups to settle in the Antietam Valley included the English and Irish Catholics. Some of the more prominent families in the community were English and members of the Episcopal Church, which was one of the first denominations established in Washington County. St. James School, seven miles north of Sharpsburg, was founded as an Episcopal Boys School before the war. Many of its students joined the Confederate army when the war broke out. These same boys came back to worship in September 1862 wearing Confederate uniforms.[17]

Construction of the National Road and the Chesapeake and Ohio Canal brought Irish Catholic laborers to Washington County in the early decades of the 19th century. The most famous Irish Catholic from the county was Abram Ryan. Baptized at St. Mary's Church in Hagerstown, Ryan became a Catholic priest and Chaplin in the Confederate army. Father Ryan became famous for his poetry of the Lost Cause. Because of his pieces, such as "The Conquered Banner" and "The Sword of Robert E. Lee," he was dubbed "The Poet Priest of the Confederacy."[18]

Not all of the region's inhabitants were of European descent. Black inhabitants had lived there since the colonial period. The 1820 Federal Census shows that 75 blacks, both slave and free, resided in the area. One misconception is that the German farmers did not own slaves. Sources indicate, however, that both "church" and "sect" people owned slaves, particularly in the 18th and early 19th centuries. A number of the farms on the battlefield also employed slave labor. For example, the Pry farm had a female slave named Georgianna. The Pipers also had a number of slaves before the war. One of them, Jeremiah Summers, received his freedom sometime prior to 1850. Summers was about 16 or 17 years old in 1862 and continued living and working on the farm. Records indicate that the Roulettes, Mummas, and Millers also owned slaves at one time or another. These slaves tended to be farm hands who worked alongside their owners in the fields.[19] In 1862, Samuel Mumma had a thriving farm of more than 186 acres with eight fenced fields. That year he had sixteen acres of corn, 60 acres of wheat, and 20-30 acres of pasture. Livestock included at least 200 chickens, about 15 hogs, 20 head of cattle, and an undetermined number of horses, sheep, turkeys and ducks. Just northeast of the barn was a small apple orchard.[20]

In September 1862 the Roulette farm was approximately 180 acres in size. Corn was its principal crop, while much of the rest of the farm was in pasture. In 1887, Roulette moved to Sharpsburg, leaving the farming operation to his son Benjamin. By the turn of the century, Benjamin was described as being "extensively engaged in feeding hogs for the market." Does this mean that the Roulette's had an "extensive" hog farm in 1862? Probably not. Farming in the mid-19th century was diversified and generally not so specialized. It is reasonable to assume, however, that the farm had its fair share of swine, poultry, and cattle. For instance, in the battle-damage claim that he submitted to the Federal government, Roulette cites the loss of "3 beef cattle."[21]

The Piper House was constructed of hewn logs, a shingled roof, and a stone chimney on the north side. A picket fence surrounded the house and yard in 1862. The building was altered in 1898, when weather boarding and a porch were added. A new chimney was built on the east side of the house, and in 1912 a second-story room was added above the kitchen. At the time of the battle, the farm consisted of 231 acres. Besides the house and barn, the property contained at least six other significant out-buildings. The field due north of the farm house, adjacent to the "Sunken Road," was planted in corn. Fields to the east were plowed and those to the south and west were either stubble or grass at the time of the battle. The original stone wall that borders the western edge of the farm remains. However, when Maryland Route 65 was widened in 1951, the wall was moved back approximately twenty feet. Between the farm house and the Piper Cornfield lay approximately 48,000 square feet of orchard. It was here that part of D. H. Hill's command rallied after falling back from the Sunken Road, and a number of Confederate batteries were posted there. The entire boundary of the orchard, except that along the Piper Lane and near the barn, was enclosed by about 820 yards of paling fence. The trees most likely were apple and perhaps some peach. It was not unusual to find orchards of this size on farms in 1862, although the large commercial orchards that are known today in that region did not come into prominence until the late 19th century.[22]

Cornfields obviously played an important role in some phases of the Battle of Antietam, but what did a cornfield look like in 1862? The corn of that period looked much different from what we see today. Both field and sweet corn of a non-hybrid variety were grown, but because this corn was non-hybrid, there was no consistency. Stalks varied in height between six and fifteen feet, and usually bore only one or two ears of corn. Prior to the use of chemical fertilizers and mechanized farm machinery, corn fields were planted in a "check row" pattern. The corn was planted at the intersection of these lines, resembling a checker-board with two to four stalks per intersection, with the intersections placed about a yard apart. This spacing allowed a single horse and cultivator to run in any direction. During this period it was not uncommon to see other crops planted amidst the corn stalks, typically pumpkins and pole beans.

Other crops also differed from their 20th century variety. Wheat was non-hybrid as well, long stemmed, and bearded. Plowed fields also looked different, with deeper furrows than modern "no till" operations. Both wheat and corn were among the crops taken to mills along the Antietam Creek to be ground into flour and meal. A common route used by the farmers was the old "Hog Trough" road which, eroded and sunken in many sections, gained notoriety as "Bloody Lane."[23]

In regional sentiment Sharpsburg followed the lead of the rest of the county and the western part of the state, which was decidedly Unionist. Two companies of the 1st Maryland Regiment, Potomac Home Brigade, were raised in Sharpsburg and the surrounding area. Roger E. Cook, a local citizen, became its commander. Numerous graves at the Mountain View Cemetery in Sharpsburg support the assumption that many local men served in other Maryland Union regiments as well.[24]

This is not to say that there were not any Confederates from the community or surrounding area. The most famous, Henry Kyd Douglas, grew up at Ferry Hill Plantation, just three miles west of Sharpsburg overlooking the Potomac River opposite Shepherdstown, West Virginia. Douglas is best known as the youngest member of "Stonewall" Jackson's staff and the author of *I Rode With*

Stonewall. His father, the Reverend Robert Douglas, was a Reform minister and pastor at the Reform Church in Sharpsburg for a time.

Two other Sharpsburg citizens gained a small measure of prominence in the Confederate army. Joseph McGraw started the war as a teamster and ended the war as a major commanding an artillery battalion in the Army of Northern Virginia. Franklin P. Turner was commander of Company E, 36th Virginia Infantry. One account states that he fought at Antietam, although his regiment was not in the battle. Later he attained the rank of major and is said to have served on the staff of Lt. Gen. Jubal Early. Others from the area served in humbler positions in the ranks. Hirem O. Clipp was born in nearby Jefferson County, (West) Virginia and moved to Sharpsburg in 1861 when he was 18 years old. In 1862, he joined the Confederate army but was soon discharged due to illness. During the Battle of Antietam, he fled with his family and other refugees to the caves along the Potomac River.[25]

Thus, war came to the little town of Sharpsburg and its 1,300 residents. Today we live in an age when the handling of large events, such as the Olympics, are taken for granted. Manifestations of logistics for massive exhibitions, whether they be military operations or rock concerts, include restroom facilities, emergency vehicles, and refreshment stands. Cleanup crews and benevolent organizations (such as the Red Cross) usually are available with the latest technology to deal with a multitude of disasters, whether they be oil spills, fires, earthquakes, or other calamities. In the Civil War, these luxuries did not exist. The people of Sharpsburg and its environs suffered at three distinct levels as a result of the battle. The first was the immediate and residual consequences of having thousands of men and animals come to town, and all the problems that entailed. The second level was the destruction wrought by the battle itself, which included burned buildings, a scarred landscape, and denuded fields. The last level was the impact of having the dead, dying, and wounded in the midst of the community for days, weeks, and months. All of these factors influenced the economy, ecology, health, and the collective psyche of the community.

The Battle of Antietam was fought between the Confederate Army of Northern Virginia, numbering about 40,000 men, and the Union Army of the Potomac, with approximately 86,000 men. Records show that McClellan had more than 120,000 troops in the area within two weeks after the battle. Of these, I and IX Corps were camped in the immediate vicinity of Sharpsburg, within about a five mile radius. These two corps numbered more than 50,000 men. Therefore, between September 16 and October 26, from 50,000 to more than 120,000 men were camped in the Sharpsburg area.[26]

The effects of all this humanity crammed into a relatively small area was telling. Napoleon said "an army marches on its stomach." The logistics of providing sustenance for this many men was mind boggling. A soldier in the Army of the Potomac received three pounds of rations per day. Twenty percent of this could be beef "on the hoof," which necessitated herds of cattle traveling with the army. Supply trains carried an average of one ton of forage or food per wagon. The Army of the Potomac alone used more than 3,000 wagons during the Maryland Campaign. This would bring extra stress to bear on roadways, as well as surrounding pastures. For example, the Hagerstown Pike was built around 1856, making it a relatively new highway at the time of the battle. It was nearly ruined by the armies going back and forth over it. Fortunately for the turnpike company that owned the road, damage compensation was received from the Federal government. Most private citizens were not so fortunate.[27]

Since the army required so much food and forage, and since it was so bulky and difficult to transport, as much of it as possible was requisitioned from the local populous. An editorial in the Hagerstown *Herald and Torchlight* dated September 24, 1862, reported that

> [t]he region of the county between Sharpsburg and Boonsboro has been eaten out of food of every description. The two armies. . .have swept over it and devoured everything within reach. At Sharpsburg, we understand that the Rebels sacked the town, and when they left many of the citizens had not a morsel to eat. . . .The amount of personal property—horses, cattle, hogs, sheep, corn, hay, and other provender—which was taken from the farmers, was enormous, the whole lower portion of our county has been stripped of every description of subsistence, and what our people in that section of the county will do to obtain food for man and beasts during the approaching winter, God alone knows.

Compelled by hunger, some soldiers risked their lives in their search for provender. Emory Smith and his family returned to their home and found two Confederates who had been killed by an exploding Union artillery shell. One died while drawing water at the nearby well. The other was lying in the kitchen "literally torn to pieces," a bunch of onions still in his hand. One Union soldier recalled seeing dead Confederates on a hill east of town: "One dead batteryman had his pockets full of apples and was eating them when killed by a cannon ball going thru his body, tearing away his left leg. His comrades had placed the torn-off member carefully under his head as a pillow."[28] As a result of these hungry soldiers trying to satisfy their appetites, civilians returning to their homes usually found that nothing was left to eat. According to one young resident,

> Many of the inhabitants. . .terror stricken fled from the town to the country, carrying with them a few articles of clothing. Many who left their houses, on their return after the battle found them ransacked and plundered of every thing of value by rebel stragglers and rogues who followed the army for the express purpose of pilfering.[29]

Sixteen-year old James Snyder helped secure all the valuables in his family's Sharpsburg home. He then went with his mother to the Parson Adams Farm on the Harpers Ferry Road about one and a half miles south of Sharpsburg, where a large number of civilian refugees had gathered. On September 18, young James wandered back into town against his mother's wishes. He was not prepared for the sight that awaited him at his home. All the doors and windows were open and Confederate soldiers were lounging both inside and outside the house. Bureau drawers and closets which had been locked were found pried open by bayonets. The drawers' contents either had been used for hospital bandages or appropriated by the Southerners, since heaps of ragged uniforms were seen lying on the floor. In a back bedroom Snyder found a naked Confederate soldier lying on the bed, his dirty, tattered uniform piled on the floor nearby. The bold youth indignantly asked, "What are you doing in that bed in that condition for?" The soldier replied, "Young man I am here because I am sick, and I didn't want to soil this clean bed with my dirty clothes so I took them off." Later, when James' father returned to Sharpsburg, he met a group of soldiers on the street and one of them tossed him a daguerreotype and said, "Here old man, you can have this. It is no good to us." The elder Snyder was astonished to find it was a photo of his own wife, which had been taken along with other valuables from his house.[30]

Damage rendered by Union troops seems to have been equal to or in excess of Southern depredations. John T. Trowbridge visited Sharpsburg in 1865 and inquired about plundering that had occurred during and after the battle. One woman had fled with her neighbors the day before the battle and did not return until three days later. "When we came back," she wrote, "all I could do was just to set right down and cry. . . .Them that stayed at home did not lose anything; but if the soldiers found a house deserted, that they robbed." When Trowbridge asked which side did the most damage she replied "[t]hat I can't say stranger. The Rebels took; but the Yankees took right smart."[31]

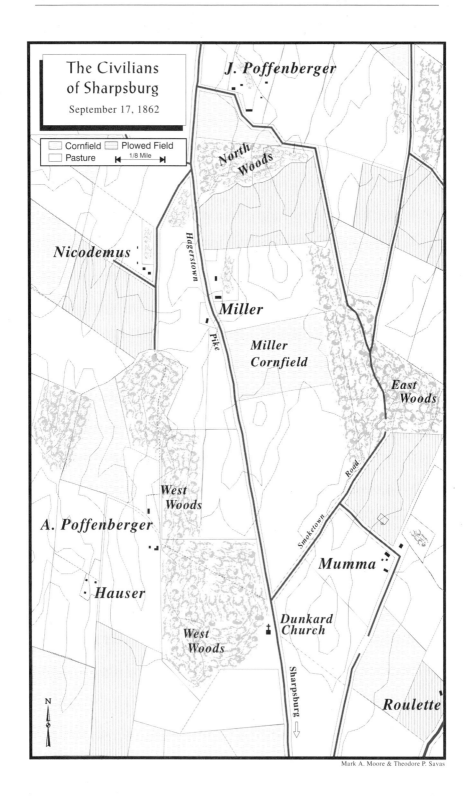

The Civilians
of Sharpsburg

September 17, 1862

Cornfield Plowed Field
Pasture   1/8 Mile

J. Poffenberger

North Woods

Nicodemus

Hagerstown

Miller

Pike

Miller Cornfield

East Woods

West Woods

A. Poffenberger

Smoketown Road

Mumma

Hauser

West Woods

Dunkard Church

Sharpsburg

N

Roulette

Mark A. Moore & Theodore P. Savas

The farms on the battlefield suffered the worst damage, probably more from plundering and vandalism than from combat. In his claim to the Federal government, Henry Piper asked for $25.00 in damages for both the house and barn. However, he claimed more than $2,000.00 in other damages. Ironically, most of the latter was attributable to Union troops during their post-battle foraging. The 3rd and 4th Pennsylvania Cavalry, and the 8th New York Cavalry, were camped on the Piper property after the battle. Union infantry also was camped in the area. Household property was damaged or stolen and all the livestock and harvested crops were taken. Claims records indicate the livestock the Pipers lost: one roan mare, eight milk cows, two steers, 14 other cattle, 40 hogs, 18 sheep, 200 chickens, 15 geese, and 24 turkeys. Crops and foodstuffs taken or damaged included 100 bushels of Irish potatoes, 30 bushels of sweet potatoes, 200 bushels of apples, 200 bushels of wheat, 800 pounds of bacon, 3,000 pounds of lard, and 20 acres of corn.[32]

Samuel Mumma suffered property damage amounting to around $10,000. This included 35 tons of hay and several hundred bushels of wheat, corn and rye taken. Most of this damage was done by Federals. Sadly, Mr. Mumma was never completely reimbursed for his losses, as the U.S. government blamed most of it on the Confederates. The Joseph Sherrick house suffered $8.00 damage from an artillery shell and $1,351 damage from occupying Federal troops.[33]

Even the presence of "friendly" troops and their commanding general was not a guarantee against theft and property damage. On September 15, Gen. George B. McClellan established his headquarters at the Philip Pry house, from which point he directed the battle. The entire II Corps camped there also. Indeed, the vista was excellent. Legend has it that part of the time the general viewed the battle with his telescope from an opening in the attic ceiling. He also apparently had telescopes strapped to fences on the high ground behind the house. After making battle arrangements on the 16th, the general went to bed at 10:00 p.m. and did not awake until 8:00 a.m. the next morning, several hours after the battle had begun. A history of the Cost family states that Philip Pry said years later that McClellan was the laziest man he had ever seen.

The commander of the Army of the Potomac kept his headquarters there until September 25, when he moved to a house on Mills Road about five miles south of Sharpsburg. On the morning of September 17 an ambulance brought Maj. Gen. Joseph Hooker to the Pry House for medical care (he had been wounded in the foot), and McClellan ordered another to carry Mrs. Pry and the children to Jacob Keedy's farm near Keedysville. Meanwhile, Philip Pry remained at the Pry House in a futile attempt to look after his property. In the afternoon Hooker was moved to Keedysville.

Another wounded general officer brought to the Pry House was Gen. Israel Richardson, who was mortally wounded in the Union attack on Sunken Road. Richardson was placed in the large upstairs bedroom of Philip Pry. Richardson's wife and sister stayed at the Pry house and nursed the general. President Lincoln visited him on October 2, and Mrs. Pry fixed breakfast for him. (Later, the president sent Mrs. Pry a thank-you note for her kindness.) General Richardson died on November 3, and for years afterward, the Pry's kept the large bedroom in which he died closed off. According to family tradition, the children were afraid to go into it so Mrs. Pry kept cakes and pies there.

The Union occupation of his farm ruined Philip Pry, whose damages exceeded $2,400. Losses included 900 bushels of wheat which were consumed by the horses of McClellan's cavalry escort, the 12th and 13th Pennsylvania Cavalry. He also lost 20 acres of ripe corn, 150 bushels of apples, 10 sheep, and 22 hogs. In addition, all of his fences were used for firewood by the Union troops. Pry went through a considerable amount of bureaucratic red tape to receive payment from the government. He was never fully compensated, so in 1873 he sold the farm and moved his family to Tennessee.[34]

Despite stringent regulations promulgated by the commanders of the opposing armies, depredations from either side sometimes took the form of bodily harm. One local story tells of "Confederate scouts" during the campaign making several attempts to find out where local farmer Henry F. Neikirk hid his eleven horses. At first they threatened to burn his barn. When that did not work they hung him up by a leather halter, but he still would not tell. The Confederates left him hanging, satisfied with finding several hundred dollars that his daughter Lizzie had concealed. Neikirk's son George is said to have cut his father down just in time to save his life.[35]

Being a Democrat and/or exhibiting luke warm support toward the Lincoln government was cause for harassment or arrest by the Union army in at least one case. Samuel Michael complained in a letter to his brother that after the battle, he was "arrested frequently" by the authorities, who presumably were aided by some of Sharpsburg's Unionist citizens:

> They held me once in Williamsport and in Martinsburg nine days. I was marched in the rain one whole day in water four feet deep and had to sleep in my wet clothes until they dried on me. And had to sleep on the floor in mud two or three inches deep. . . .The charges was for helping the Rebels to capture a cannon. All of them was false and forged against me. I have got enough of

the Negro War and think a great deal of the North. This you can interpret to suit yourself.[36]

The presence of thousands of soldiers obviously affected the ecology of the area, a fact often overlooked by modern visitors to Civil War battlefields, with their neatly mowed lawns and well-maintained tour roads. Also, it is often forgotten that besides thousands of soldiers, the armies needed animals to pull their equipment. On October 1, 1862, the Army of the Potomac had 22,493 horses and 10,392 mules. The number of Confederate animals can only be estimated. Lee wrote to President Jefferson Davis that his army was "feeble in transportation, the animals being much reduced." In fact, at Antietam the average Confederate artillery battery had four-horse teams, and in many cases wagons were being used in lieu of caissons. Roughly estimated, Lee's army utilized about 16,000 horses and mules during the Maryland Campaign.[37]

The stench of nearly 50,000 horses and mules not only was an inconvenience, but a tremendous health hazard. Each horse or mule produced an average of thirteen and one-half pounds of manure and two gallons of urine per day. This, along with the waste of thousands of soldiers and the thousands of dead and wounded men and animals, threatened the local water supply and attracted disease carrying insects, particularly flies.[38]

Disease, not bullets, was the major killer during the war. Incredibly, the rate of attrition in a Civil War regiment sometimes exceeded that of a bomber command in World War II. According to medical historian Paul Steiner, "The Civil War provided the last opportunity in the pre-microbiological era for the major pathogenic microbes to exhibit their maximum effects without effective deterrence." Dysentery, malaria, typhoid fever, and cholera were diseases common to both soldier and civilian prior to the twentieth century. According to Steiner, "Healthy, latent, or mildly ill carriers of the causative agents existed in every sizable group of Americans." Accordingly, if the Battle of Antietam was fought today, there would be much less of a public health threat from its aftermath. Many of the diseases are no longer prevalent in the industrialized world, and only diseases commonplace before a disaster are likely to be a threat after the event transpires.[39] Thus opposing armies brought with them a variety of illnesses during that fatal week of September 17, 1862, and exposed the civilian population to them by their mere presence in the region. The large amounts of both human and animal waste further enhanced the possibility for sickness.[40]

No definitive study has been undertaken to determine the extent of disease among the civilian population as a result of any Civil War battle. However, the conditions were ripe for sickness, and anecdotal evidence suggests that illness was a major problem in the civilian population as a result of the presence of the armies and the bloody battle. Nearly three months after the fight, Jacob Miller, a local farmer, prominent civic leader and relative to the family that owned the "Miller Cornfield," wrote in a letter of the sickness and death around him,

> Your Unkle [sic] Daniel Miller is no more. . . .He was not well when he left home the day before the big battle. . . .He came to town several times. After he got back he was taken with a diarear [sic] which was a very common complaint with the troops and citizens. Both armies were afflicted with the disease, however. Daniel took sick on Monday or Tuesday and continued getting worse with sick vomiting spells.

Miller's letter continued with a description of neighbors and friends who were afflicted by or had succumbed to sickness:

> Mrs. Adam Michael is no more she took her flite [sic] this day a weak [sic]. Her oldest daughter had just gon [sic] before her about eight or ten days. . . . Hellen and Janet had a severe attack of tayfoy fevour [sic—typhoid fever] but are both getting better. . . .Jacob and Annmary's children nearly all. . .had Scarlet fevour [sic] but are all geting [sic] well—Henry Mumma's wife is no more, she departed this life about two weaks [sic] since. She had the same fevour [sic]. [N]early all or quite all of [J]ohn Smith['s] family [are] wore down but are getting better. Many other citizens and hundreds of soldiers have been taken with the same, and many died. . . .[41]

The Michael family mentioned in Miller's letter was particularly hard hit. Adam Michael lost not only his wife but, as noted above, his "oldest daughter" Elizabeth as well. In addition, Michael's son Caleb and youngest daughter Catherine also fell sick, although they were lucky enough to have recovered. Another son, Samuel, penned a letter to his brother describing the tragedy. Samuel put the blame directly on the presence of a Union hospital established in their house. The hospital, he wrote,

> was continued in our parlor for several weeks. I do not know how many has died in it. They have left it now. It looks like a hog pen. . . .[T]he disease of the hospital has affected three of our family. . . .Mother died with this disease on the 25th day of November. Was buried today by Mr. Adams and Shufford. We could not have no funeral for neither of them had no place to preach. Mother complained but a short time was taken with three very severe hemorrhages of

the bowels—took place about 12 o' clock at night, the first one. She died the next day 10 minutes before two. She was a beautiful corpse.[42]

The village of Sharpsburg is in a small valley screened by a ridge to the east that runs north and south (Sharpsburg Ridge). Confederate artillery occupied the ridge during the battle and projectiles from Union counter-battery fire east of Antietam Creek frequently passed through or over the Confederate positions and into the town. Having lost their momentum, these shells fell in the streets or pierced the east walls or roofs of homes, businesses and churches. Eyewitness accounts by soldiers confirmed that "[f]ew were the houses that had not been pierced by solid shot or shell." About three years after the battle, it was noted that "[o]n the side of the town fronting the Federal line of battle every house bears its marks; indeed I do not know that any altogether escaped." One civilian observed that some barns were "burnt" along with "4 or 5 small houses, and stables in Sharpsburg."[43]

The regimental historian of the 118th Pennsylvania recalled that "One of the inhabitants said that he and his family were about to sit down at the dinner table, when a solid shot crashed through the wall, and, falling on the table, spoiled the dinner and the dishes, and, he added, quaintly, 'also our appetites.'"[44] Young John P. Smith with his "mother, two sisters and brother fled to the farm of Mr. Harry Reel. . .two miles west of Sharpsburg, where we remained from the 15th to the 17th," he remembered. "Shot and shell fired on the 17th fell in the yard where we were staying, so we were obliged in the midst of flying shot and shell to retreat to the farm of Mr. William Cox a mile further west where we remained until Friday morning the 19th, when we returned to our homes. . . ."[45]

About 100 people hid in the cellar of Mr. John Kretzer on Main Street— among them were a mother with a three-day old child. A shell exploded just outside the cellar wall, causing some panic among the people. Similarly, a piece of shell struck and removed part of the door sill of the Miller home in Sharpsburg. Miss Savilla Miller was standing in the doorway at the time but escaped unhurt.[46] Jacob McGraw had sought safety in the Kretzer cellar with scores of other citizens. In mid-afternoon he ventured outside and down the street several blocks. He was standing outside his brother's hotel when a shell stuck the brickwork above his head, showering him with fragments. McGraw immediately rushed back to the safety of the cellar.[47] The small, one and a half story log home of Aaron Good, was struck by a shell and caught fire. Four young ladies that had sought refuge in a nearby house saw the blaze and filled basins and buckets at the town spring and extinguished it.[48]

That the artillery rounds still had a punch when they landed in the town is evinced by the numerous anecdotal accounts of shells hitting homes. One, a two story brick structure on Main Street, had a shell land inside that had passed through the adjacent Masonic Temple. Another brick house was struck by a cannon ball which passed through the east gable, continued through four rafters, and exited out the other gable of the home and into the property next door.[49]

With all of this shelling one would think that there would have been numerous civilian casualties. At least two references mention the death of a young girl from the shelling. Stephen Sears, in his classic study on Antietam entitled *Landscape Turned Red,* and Union army surgeon Dr. Thomas T. Ellis in his diary mentions that at least one young girl was killed. In the fifteen years since the publication of Sears' book, historians have sought corroborative evidence, particularly in local records. To date, no such documentation has been found to support a Sharpsburg claim to having a "Jenny Wade" of Gettysburg fame.[50]

There is, however, abundant evidence that people were injured or killed after the battle by tampering with unexploded artillery projectiles. John Keplinger had cleared and "broke" about ninety-nine shells from fields around "Bloody Lane." He was not so fortunate with number one hundred, which exploded and "tore him up so badly that he died from it." George Reilly, a resident of nearby Keedysville, "put a round shell in some wood and set fire to it" along Antietam Creek. The explosion that resulted sent one large chunk of the shell flying between three citizens standing nearby, one of them being the Reverend Robert Douglas, father of noted Confederate Henry Kyd Douglas. The residual effects of these live rounds lingered for some time. In post-war years, a local youth placed a shell in the family cook stove, which resulted in an explosion that destroyed the stove and part of the house. Worse yet, the boy lost an eye, arm, and several fingers on his surviving limb.[51]

Due to the very nature of the fighting, the farms suffered the most immediate damage. Major General Joseph Hooker's report that "every stalk of corn" in the Miller corn field "was cut as closely as could have been done with a knife" from artillery fire is well known. Miller's adjacent stone wall bordering the Hagerstown Road was "pretty well knocked to pieces [by] balls and shells."[52] Similar damage occurred on every farm. Rail fences also suffered from artillery and small arms fire. Many were torn down to facilitate the movement of advancing troops, and the rails were later used as fire wood by the armies.

The barn of David Reel, located northwest of Sharpsburg, was gutted by fire from the direct hit of a stray Union artillery shell. At the time it was being used as a Confederate hospital and a number of the wounded soldiers perished in the flames. Samuel Mumma's house and barn were deliberately burned on the morning of September 17 when Confederate Brig. Gen. Roswell Ripley, who feared it would be used by Union sharpshooters, order some of his soldiers to torch it.[53]

On the west side of the Roulette farm house were bee hives, which were knocked over during the morning of the battle by artillery rounds. The upset hives spewed forth thousands of angry bees. When the 132nd Pennsylvania Infantry moved through the farm during its assault against the Sunken Road, the bees presented such a nuisance that the Pennsylvanians were forced to break ranks and reform beyond the house. During the battle, the Roulette Farm was directly in the path of the attack of William French's Federal division, which was also moving against the Sunken Road position. Prior to this, elements of the Confederate division of Maj. Gen. Daniel H. Hill occupied the farm as skirmishers. According to Thomas J. C. Williams' account of the action, "the buildings were struck by shot and shell, of which they still bear the marks. One shell pierced the southern end of the dwelling, went up through the parlor ceiling, and was found in the attic." While most citizens had fled the area when it was learned a battle would be fought there, the Roulettes sought refuge in the cellar of their farm house. Accounts suggest that the family shared their refuge with both Union and Confederate soldiers who either were wounded or just taking a respite from the fierce fighting outside. At one point, Mr. Roulette is said to have left the cellar to urge on a passing Union formation which had driven the Confederate skirmishers from the area.[54]

During the course of the battle, the Piper Farm was held by the Confederates and for much of the day was surrounded by Confederate artillery. After the Confederate line broke at the Sunken Road, remnants of the Southern units withdrew to the Piper Farm. Both Maj. Gen. James Longstreet and Maj. Gen. D. H. Hill are said to have used the farmhouse as a temporary headquarters. The Pipers, however, in anticipation of the approaching battle, had fled the property on Monday afternoon, September 15. Henry Piper took his family and horses to his brother's farm on the Potomac River, where they remained until Friday, September 19. Miraculously, the barn and house sustained very little battle damage because these structures were located in a hollow, which allowed artillery and small arms rounds to pass safely overhead.[55]

On Monday, September 15, the Confederates urged the Mumma family to leave the premises as a battle was pending. That afternoon, the large family evacuated their farm. The father, mother and younger children rode in a two-horse buggy, while the older children walked. Their destination was the Manor Church, about five miles to the north, a gathering place for many local civilians

Alfred R. Waud sketch, "Burning of Mr. Mumma's houses and barns at the fight of the 17th Sept."

Library of Congress

who found themselves refugees from their own homes. The next evening two of the Mumma boys, Samuel Jr. and Daniel, returned to the house to get some clothing. To their dismay, they discovered the Confederates had completely ransacked the place and taken everything of value. They then started for Sharpsburg and were detained for a time by D. H. Hill and his staff, who quizzed them about their family and the roads leading into the area. That night the young men slept in their own beds at home. Of the hundreds of local citizens that suffered property damage during the battle and occupation of the two armies, the Mummas lost the most. On the morning of the 17th, their home was burned, the only private structure deliberately destroyed during the battle. Throughout the engagement, the farm was the center of activity, either of combat or staging for combat. Two thirds of D. H. Hill's Division moved through the farm in support of Jackson on the north end of the field. Three Confederate attacks—Kershaw's, Manning's, and Cooke's—traversed the Mumma property. Hill's Division, augmented by Richard H. Anderson's Division, held the southern edge of the Mumma farm throughout the morning. At various times during the battle, the farm was also the target of Southern artillery.

Union occupation of the farm was even more extensive. Greene's division of the Union XII Corps held the place for much of the morning. French and Richardson launched their attacks on the Sunken Road from the Mumma property. Tompkin's Rhode Island Battery was posted at various points on the farm, and in the afternoon William Franklin's VI Corps held the area.[56]

Another impact of the battle was the dislocation of civilians. Besides seeking refuge in local cellars, many fled to neighboring communities and farms. Some sought shelter along the banks of the Potomac in the Killingsburg Caves and at other sites. Bud Shackleford was eighteen at the time of the fight. The day before the battle he went to Snyder's Landing on the Maryland side of the river, where he saw around 200 children staying at a farm house. The problem of feeding them was resolved when someone got two barrels of flour from a nearby warehouse, and before long the children were all eating short cakes.[57]

The bloody results of twelve hours of brutal combat rendered scenes that were never forgotten. Nearly 4,000 corpses were scattered over a three-mile front. Otho Nesbitt of Clear Spring, Maryland, kept a detailed diary of the Civil War years. He visited the field on September 18 and 19 and was appalled by what he witnessed. "The whole country around about is a hospital," he wrote. "Houses and barns full. . . .I saw a man with a hole in his belly about as big as a hat and about a quart of dark-looking maggots working away."[58] Colonel David Hunter Strother of McClellan's staff rode across the northern end of the battlefield on the 18th and observed that the bodies of dead Confederates were "already far advanced in putrification, hideously swollen, and many of them black as soot."[59] According to the historian of the 118th Pennsylvania, on the morning of the 18th

> [t]he unburied dead lay around. Many of the bodies, struck by the heavier missiles, were horribly torn and mangled. There was a leg, with its ragged, bloody edges, severed near the thigh, evidently by a solid shot; another, in its garment, separated from its unseen trunk, lying in a fence corner.[60]

The story was the same everywhere. Scenes of death dominated the landscape. In Sharpsburg, dead bodies, mostly Confederates, were found in gardens, alleys, and parlors. Dead horses could be seen lying in the streets for days after the battle. One local story tells of the Grice family returning home and being shocked to find three dead Confederates lying inside their dwelling and two more in the yard.[61]

Besides the dead soldiers, there also were a large number of dead horses and other animals. The army paid local farmers to collect and burn the carcasses of the poor brutes. Most were destroyed where they had fallen. Near the Hagerstown Pike, Otho Nesbitt saw a "white bull or steer lying on his back all swelled up and two sheep nearby all swelled up and ready to burst. . . .At another farm house I saw a steer dead in the yard and a horse dead at the end of the barn and 2 gray horses in the lane. . . ." In a letter to his wife, Capt. David Been of Company H, 14th Indiana, wrote that "hundreds of dead horses strew the fields in every direction."[62]

John P. Smith, a boy in the fall of 1862 and later the town historian, recalled that "[t]he stench arising from the battlefield was intolerable." Another citizen said "the stench was terrible. We had to close doors and windows to shut out the nauseating odor of decaying corpses." The odor was noticeable for miles away. Soldiers on burial details often drank whisky to kill the smell. Samuel Fletcher led a burial party of the 15th Massachusetts. "The weather was very hot," recalled Fletcher. "The bodies were getting soft and it was very unpleasant. . . .I tasted the odor for several days."[63]

After a battle it was important to dispose of the bodies as soon as possible. Diseases such as typhoid and cholera could be spread by contact with a corpse. The cadavers attracted clouds of flies which also spread disease. The burial of the Union dead began on September 19, while burial details started on the Confederates the following day. The whole process took until the 22nd, but even after that date farmers still found overlooked bodies lying under ledges and hidden in bushes. Many of the Antietam dead, particularly the Confederates, were buried in shallow graves which later were rooted up by hogs. At some places on the field the Confederate dead ended up in mass burial trenches. In his damage-claim affidavit, Roulette stated that 700 soldiers were buried on his property in this manner.[64]

For some civilians the battle proved to be a financial boon. The Dunker Church was converted into a temporary embalming station, where this relatively new science was being practiced by contractors for those families who could afford the service. Local farmers, meanwhile, made extra money hauling coffins with embalmed Union soldiers from the church to the railroad depot in Hagerstown.[65]

In addition to the 4,000 dead, about 19,000 others were wounded in the battle. Their care posed a logistical nightmare that encompassed an area of more than 40 miles and parts of three states. The 118th Pennsylvania's historian wrote that "everything had been absorbed for the moment in one universal hospital. Houses and out-buildings were filled, and lawns and gardens covered with the Confederate wounded." Indeed, practically every house, church, barn, and shed in and around Sharpsburg was used as some sort of hospital. The wounded also were taken to hospitals in nearby villages such as Keedysville, Boonsboro, and Bakersville. Frederick and Hagerstown grew into major hospital sites, and approximately 400 wounded soldiers were sent 40 miles northward to Chambersburg, Pennsylvania. The Confederates established hospitals in Shepherdstown, Charlestown, and Winchester, Virginia.[66]

By the time of the Vietnam War, medical evacuation of wounded personnel was usually undertaken in less than 30 minutes. During the Civil War, however, injured soldiers sometimes remained on the field for days, and Antietam was no exception. Some accounts tell of soldiers lying on the battlefield for two or three days.[67] Much has been written about the work of Clara Barton, "The Angel of the Battlefield." While her endeavors were commendable, local citizens also did their part to alleviate the suffering of these unfortunates. Among them was Mrs. Angela K. Davis of Funkstown, a village on the National Road about eight miles away. She and her husband directed both Union and Confederate sympathizers in their town to prepare food to take to the wounded. In her very vivid reminiscences, Mrs. Davis wrote, "we sat up most of the night, killing and cooking chickens etc. and the next morning our dining room, kitchen and wash house were all filled with jars or crocks of mashed potatoes, fried ham, chicken and beef sandwiches. . . .We distributed the sandwiches as best we could (which seemed like a drop in the bucket). . . ."[68]

As army surgeons and civilians did their part to ease the suffering of both Union and Confederate wounded around Sharpsburg, about five miles away similar efforts were rendered for many of Lee's wounded in the Potomac River community of Shepherdstown, (West) Virginia. Mary Bedinger Mitchell was a young Shepherdstown resident who volunteered to help. She recalled that

> [t]he wounded continued to arrive until the town was quite unable to hold all the disabled and suffering. They filled every building and overflowed into the country round, into farm-houses, barns, corn cribs, cabins,—wherever four walls and a roof were found together. Those able to travel were sent on to Winchester and other towns back from the river, but their departure seemed to make no appreciable difference. There were six churches, and they were all full; the Odd Fellows' Hall, the Freemason's, the little Town Council room, the barn-like place known as the Drill Room, all the private houses after their capacity, the shops and empty buildings, the school-houses,—every inch of space, and yet the cry was for room.[69]

Viewing the operations of a Civil War field hospital was an experience never forgotten by those that had the dubious opportunity to do so. John P. Smith was a boy at the time of the battle. He vividly recalled the gore present at a Confederate medical facility on the Harry Reel farm:

> I saw a number of wounded and dead Confederates brought into the yard. Some were having limbs amputated, others horribly mangled, were dying. One man in particular I shall never forget. His entire abdomen had been torn and mangled by a piece of exploded shell. He uttered piercing and heart rendering cries, and besought those who stood by for God's sake to kill him and thus end his sufferings. Death however came to his relief in a short time and he was hastily buried in a shallow grave. . . .[70]

One can only speculate what effect such scenes had upon the many local children who witnessed them.

Most eye witness accounts of hospital operations at Antietam feature one common denominator: the prevalence of severed limbs. According to one regimental historian, "[b]y a broken down frame building, that had been a field hospital, arms and legs, hurriedly amputated, were scattered here and there." One of the wounded, Sgt. Jonathan Stowe of the 15th Massachusetts, wrote, "The horrid smell from mortifying limbs is nearly as bad as the whole we have to contend." Another soldier noted that at a hospital in Keedysville, the limbs thrown into a pit "would amount to several hundred pounds." The thousands of severed human appendages, sometimes buried and often not, would have posed as much of a health threat as dead bodies. The Sharpsburg civilians received the full brunt of the residue of the hospital, the blood of the wounded forever staining the floors and walls of their homes.[71]

Although the Union army departed the Sharpsburg area in late October, some of the hospitals existed well into the following year. And for some residents, the scars of the event could not be visibly measured. Because of post-battle looting by Union soldiers which left the family destitute, Mrs. Jacob Houser "was taken suddenly ill from fright and could not be moved for weeks after the battle."[72]

Even finding spiritual solace was a challenge. The Lutheran and Episcopal churches suffered so much damage they had to be torn down. It was several years before new buildings were erected. The Methodist Church was used as a hospital and the pews were taken out and used to make coffins. It was not back in use until 1864. The Reform Church also was pressed into service as a hospital and did not hold religious services for some time. The Dunker congregation was not able to return to their house of worship until 1864.[73]

After the battle of the 17th, the Mumma family relocated to the Sherrick house on the southern end of the battlefield until their own home was rebuilt. They moved back in June 1863, just in time to see more Confederates marching toward Pennsylvania.[74] A Union soldier passing over the battlefield in the summer of 1864 wrote: ". . .at every stop the eye rests upon something to remind the traveler of that awful day of carnage." For years after the battle residents and visitors saw human bones scattered in gutters and fence corners. Erosion and the rooting of hogs had exposed many of the shallow graves, particularly those of the Confederates. It was not uncommon to see hogs with human limbs in their mouths.[75]

Travel-chronicler John T. Trowbridge toured the field and made one final stop in town before departing for points south during his 1865 tour. He wrote:

> Returning to the village, I visited the spot chosen as a national cemetery for the slain. The ground had been purchased, but work upon it had not yet commenced. In the Antietam cemetery it is understood that the Rebel dead are to be included. Many object to this; but I do not. Skeletons, rooted up by hogs and blanching in open fields, are not a sight becoming a country that calls itself Christian.[76]

Notes

1. Until the Battle of Antietam, most major Civil War actions took place in relatively sparsely populated areas. Among them are counted Shiloh, Pea Ridge, First and Second Manassas, and the engagements in Thomas J. "Stonewall" Jackson's Valley Campaign. During the Peninsula Campaign of 1862, for example, a number of organized communities were involved but not as adversely impacted as was Sharpsburg. Yorktown sustained some damage from Union shelling during the siege there in late April 1862. However, military casualties were minimal during this same period—less than 500— and most were incurred during a failed Union attempt to break through the Confederate lines on April 16. Yorktown and vicinity was affected by the presence of approximately 169,000 men in the opposing armies, more than were at Antietam. However, casualties and property damage came nowhere near the proportions seen at Sharpsburg. (Conversely, during the Revolutionary War siege of Yorktown, nearly 80% of the town was destroyed by artillery fire and some accounts refer to civilian casualties. Only about 1,000 military casualties were incurred during the same period and no more than 25,000

some troops were in the vicinity of Yorktown). The next major action of the Peninsula Campaign, the Battle of Williamsburg, May 5, 1862, was a relatively small affair and took place several miles outside of the town. Stephen W. Sears, *To the Gates of Richmond: The Peninsula Campaign* (New York, 1992), pp. 48, 56, 66, 70-83. Information also provided by Supervisory Park Ranger Mike Litterest, Colonial National Historical Park, February 23, 1997.

The Southern capital at Richmond was inundated with thousands of wounded from the battles on the Peninsula, but again did not suffer the immediate carnage of Sharpsburg. Constance Cary Harrison, "Richmond Scenes in 62," in Robert U. Johnson and Clarence C. Buel, eds., *Battles and Leaders of the Civil War*, 4 vols. (New York, 1884-1889), vol. 2, pp. 439-448. Winchester, Virginia is another community that can contend for the dubious distinction of having a battle impact it. The Battle of First Winchester took place on May 25, 1862, and involved approximately 25,000 men and 3,000 casualties—many of them prisoners. Some fighting actually took place in the town as "Stonewall" Jackson's Confederates chased Nathaniel Banks' retreating Federals through the streets. The fleeing soldiers tried unsuccessfully to burn part of the town before departing. At least one building, a foundry, was set ablaze but the fire was put out by the townspeople. Roger DeLauter, Jr., *Winchester in the Civil War* (Lynchburg, 1992), pp. 29-33. After Sharpsburg, other communities would feel the immediate concentrated effects of large land battles. Fredericksburg, Gettysburg, Vicksburg, Atlanta, and Petersburg are examples of population centers ravaged by combat.

2. Daniel Faust letter, October 7, 1862, Harrisburg Civil War Roundtable Collection, U.S. Army Military History Institute.

3. William H. Groninger, "Lincoln's Visit to Antietam Battlefield," *The National Tribune*, April 7, 1927, p. 5.

4. J. Thomas Scharf, *History of Western Maryland*, 2 vols. (Philadelphia 1882), vol. 1, pp. 13, 33, 35, 36; Thomas J. C. Williams, *A History of Washington County Maryland*, 2 vols. (Hagerstown, 1906), vol. 1, pp. 9, 17, 18, 21, 23, 24. Sharpsburg was considered as the county seat, but "lost" out to Hagerstown.

5. Ibid., pp. 23-24. Lee and Barbara Barron, *The History of Sharpsburg* (Sharpsburg, 1972), pp. 44-45, 63-67.

6. John T. Trowbridge, *The Desolate South, 1865-1866: A Picture of the Battlefields and of the Devastated Confederacy* (New York, 1956), p. 26.

7. Daniel Wunderlich Nead, *The Pennsylvania German in the Settlement of Maryland* (Lancaster, 1914), p. 61; Charles H. Glatfelter, *The Pennsylvania Germans: A Brief Account of Their Influence on Pennsylvania* (University Park, 1990), pp. iii, 1-3.

8. Ibid., pp. 1-3.

9. Miller Family (file, Antietam N.B.).

10. Glatfelter, *The Pennsylvania Germans*, pp. 3, 12-15.

11. Ibid., pp. 15-18. Scharf, *A History of Western Maryland*, 1, pp. 463-465, 476, 489-498, 507, 517-528; 2, pp. 937-938; Gary Scott, "The Philip Pry House, Historic

Structure Report" (unpublished, Antietam N.B., 1980), p. 16; John W. Schildt, *Drums Along the Antietam* (Chewsville, 1972), pp. 183-184.

12. George Siekkinen, Jr., "The Piper Barn, Historic Structure Report" (unpublished, Antietam N.B., 1982), pp .6-10. The following year as members of Hood's Texas Brigade marched through Franklin County, Pennsylvania, about 25 miles north of Sharpsburg, one soldier noted that the barns were "more substantially and carefully built and fitted out than any house. . .in. . .Texas." He went on to write "The barns were positively more tastily built than two thirds of the houses in Waco." Harold B. Simpson, *Hood's Texas Brigade: Lee's Grenadier Guard* (Waco, 1970), p. 256.

13. Siekkinen, "The Piper Barn," pp. 5, 8, 19-23.

14. Rev. A. Stapleton, *Memorials of the Huguenots in America: With Special Reference to their Emigration to Pennsylvania* (Carlisle, 1901), pp. iii, viii, 1-25, 33-37, 133-135; G. Elmore Reaman, *The Trail of the Huguenots in Europe, the United States, South Africa and Canada* (Baltimore, 1966), pp. 129-130.

15. Williams, *A History of Washington County,* 2, pp. 1239-1240. In September 1862, the names and ages of the Roulette children were as follows: Ann Elizabeth, 13; John Daniel, 11; Joseph Clinton, 10; Susan Rebecca, 6; Benjamin Franklin, 5; and Carrie May, age 2.

16. Stapleton, *Memorials of the Huguenots,* p. 135; Francis F. Wilshin, "Mumma Farm, Piper Farm, Sherrick Farm, Historic Structures Report" (unpublished, Antietam N. B. 1969), pp. 10-17; Julia Angeline Drake and James Ridgely Orndorff, *From Mill Wheel to Plowshare: The Story of the Contribution of the Christian Orndorff Family to the Social and Industrial History of the United States* (Cedar Rapids, 1938), pp. 91-93.

17. Williams, *A History of Washington County,* 1, pp. 341-342.

18. Ibid., p. 480.

19. Barron, *The History of Sharpsburg,* p. 44. References to the German "sect people" and slavery are in Nead, *The Pennsylvania German,* pp. 118-120. See also, Klaus Wust, *The Virginia Germans* (Charlottesville, 1969), pp.121-128, and Daniel R. Lehman, *Mennonites of the Washington County, Maryland and Franklin County, Pennsylvania Conference* (Litiz, 1990), pp. 10, 39. The Dunkers or German Baptist Brethren had banned slavery in the 1770s, but individual members sometimes owned slaves. For more on this, see J. Maurice Henry, *History of the Church of the Brethren in Maryland* (Elgin, 1936), pp. 364-368 and Carl F. Bowman, *Brethren Society: The Cultural Transformation of a "Peculiar People"* (Baltimore, 1995), pp. 81, 86. Information on Sharpsburg area farm families with slaves is in Wilshin, "Mumma Farm," pp. 116-117; Scott, "The Philip Pry House," p. 38; Drake and Orndorff, *From Mill Wheel to Plowshare,* p. 64. Antietam N.B. Seasonal Park Ranger Al Fiedler has conducted an oral-history project in the Sharpsburg area that has yielded some evidence of farm families owning slaves before the war. The balcony of the Christ Reformed Church in Sharpsburg served as the seating area for slaves. For more on slaves in the Sharpsburg area see Kathleen A. Ernst, "Broken hearts Can't be Photographed: The Social, Political, and Economic Impact of the 1862 Maryland Campaign on the Residents of Washington

County, Maryland", Masters Thesis, Antioch University, 1993, pp. 9-11. (The 1860 Federal Census reveals there were 1,435 slaves in Washington County.)

20. Wilshin, "Mumma Farm," pp. 41-44.

21. Williams, *A History of Washington County,* 2, p. 1240; William Roulette Civil War Claims File, Antietam National Battlefield.

22. Wilshin, "Mumma Farm," pp. 169-177. Piper Farm Historic Background File, Antietam National Battlefield. Williams, *A History of Washington County*, 1, pp. 375-376.

23. "Antietam: A Documentary Mini-Series," unpublished proposal to Superintendent, Antietam N.B. from Media Magic Productions, Inc. (Lansing, 1996), pp. 38-39.

24. Roger Keller, *Roster of Civil War Soldiers from Washington County, Maryland* (Baltimore, 1993), p. 40; Williams, *A History of Washington County*, 1, p. 308; *History and Roster of Maryland Volunteers, War of 1861-5*, 2 vols. (Baltimore, 1898), vol. 1, pp. 483-485, 510-515, 523-529.

25. Keller, *Roster*, pp. 37, 38, 40-42, 44- 45, 113-114; Williams, *A History of Washington County*, 2, pp. 1044, 1310; Robert K. Krick, *Lee's Colonels: A Biographical Register of the Field Officers of the Army of Northern Virginia* (Dayton, 1979), p. 234.

26. After the battle, the Army of the Potomac was spread out on a thirty mile front. Its left flank was at Harpers Ferry and the right at Williamsport. The I, V and IX Corps camped within a five mile radius of Sharpsburg. For strengths, see *The War of the Rebellion: The Official Records of the Union and Confederate Armies*, 128 vols. (Washington, D.C., 1890-1901), series I, vol. 19, pt. 2, pp. 336, 374, 410. Hereinafter cited as *OR*. All references are to series I unless otherwise noted.

27. Paul Chiles, "Logistics in the Army of the Potomac" (handout, Antietam N.B., 1997); Paul Chiles "Two American Armies: One Battle" (lecture given to Smithsonian Associates, Washington, D.C., March 16, 1997); Oliver T. Reilly, *The Battlefield of Antietam* (Sharpsburg, 1906) p. 21.

28. Reilly, *The Battlefield of Antietam*, p. 20; Groninger, "Lincoln's Visit," p. 5.

29. John P. Smith of Sharpsburg was a boy at the time of the battle. As an adult he became a leading local historian of the area. His "Recollections" were serialized in the *Antietam Valley Record*, a newspaper published in Keedysville, Md. This reference appeared in the September 19, 1895 issue. This account and others may be found in "Recollections of John P. Smith: The Battle of Antietam, The History of Antietam and the Hospitals of Antietam, 1895" (file, Antietam N.B.).

30. Fred Cross, "A Sharpsburg Boy at Antietam," *Hagerstown Daily Mail*, January 16, 1934, in "Stories of Sharpsburg by Fred Cross"(file, Antietam N.B.).

31. Trowbridge, *The Desolate South*, p. 27.

32. Piper Farm Federal Court Claims (file, Antietam N.B.).

33. Wilshin, "Mumma Farm," pp. 7-8, 37-58.

34. Scott, "The Philip Pry House," pp. 18-38, 45-47.

35. Reilly, *The Battlefield of Antietam*, p. 25.

36. Samuel Michael Letter, November 27, 1862 (file, Antietam N.B.).

37. Jay Luvaas and Harold W. Nelson, eds., *The U.S. Army War College Guide to the Battle of Antietam: The Maryland Campaign of 1862* (Carlisle, 1987) pp. 270-271; *O.R.,* 19, pt. 1, pp. 94-97; *O.R.*, 19, pt. 2, p. 590; Chiles, "Two American Armies."

38. Blake Magner, *Traveller and Company: The Horses of Gettysburg* (Gettysburg, 1995), pp. 47-48.

39. Paul E. Steiner, *Disease in the Civil War: Natural Biological Warfare in 1861-1865* (Springfield, 1968), pp. 14-25. Recent wars and population dislocation in Third World countries have caused diseases prevalent in the Civil War to be manifest. Today in the Industrialized World, the disposal of bodies after events such as natural disaster is more of a social problem than a disease threat. Information provided by Annemarie Wasley, Sc.D, Disaster Assessment and Epidemiology Section, National Center for Environmental Health, Centers for Disease Control and Prevention, Atlanta, Georgia, January 14, 1997. See also, Paul A. Blake, "Communicable Disease Control" in "The Public Health Consequences of Disasters 1989: CDC Monograph, U.S. Department of Health and Human Services (Atlanta, 1989), pp. 7-12; and J. Seaman, *Epidemiology of Natural Disasters* (London, 1984), p. 50.

40. Wasley, "Disaster Assessment"; Steiner, *Disease in the Civil War*, pp. 16, 148-149, provides data on illness that was rampant in the Army of the Potomac during the summer of 1862 on the Virginia Peninsula. New recruits were particularly susceptible to disease in both armies. For more information on sickness in the Army of Northern Virginia during the Maryland Campaign, see *OR* 19, pt. 2, pp. 651, 657, 679, 686.

41. Jacob Miller Letter, December 7, 1862 (file, Antietam N.B.).

42. Michael Letter, November 27, 1862.

43. J. L. Smith, *History of the Corn Exchange Regiment: 118th Pennsylvania* (Philadelphia, 1888), p. 52.

44. Smith, *118th Pennsylvania,* p. 52.

45. "History of the Antietam Fight" by John P. Smith (from his scrapbook) (file, Antietam N.B.), p. 5.

46. Ibid., pp. 4-8.

47. Fred W. Cross, "The Strong Stone House," *Hagerstown Daily Mail*, March 22, 1934 in "Stories of Sharpsburg" (file, Antietam, N.B.).

48. Antietam Relic Lists, Photo Lists, Bibliographies and Human Interest Stories, vol. 2. (Antietam, N.B.), p. 48.

49. Smith, "Recollections," pp. 4-5.

50. David Hunter Strother, in "Personal Recollections of the War by a Virginian," *Harpers New Monthly Magazine,* February, 1868, p. 287, wrote " I hear that a child was killed, but no other citizen injured."

51. Reilly, *The Battlefield of Antietam*, p. 28.

52. *OR* 19, pt. 1, p. 218. Miller Letter, December 7, 1862.

53. William A. Frassanito, *Antietam: The Photographic Legacy of America's Bloodiest Day* (New York, 1978), pp. 266-267. James F. Clark, Sergeant Major of the 3rd North Carolina, was in charge of the detail that burned the Mumma farm. In 1906 he

wrote a letter to the Postmaster of Sharpsburg requesting the name of the family of the farm he burned. Ironically, the postmaster was Samuel Mumma, Jr., son of the owner. Clark's letter and Mumma's reply are in Wilmer M. Mumma, ed., *Antietam: The Aftermath* (Sharpsburg, 1993), pp. 24-26.

54. Williams, *A History of Washington County*, 2, pp. 1239-1240.

55. Wilshin, "Mumma Farm," pp. 109-116.

56. Ibid. pp. 1-6.

57. Bud Shackelford Interview, January 24, 1934, in "Interviews with Local People" (file, Antietam N.B.).

58. Otho Nesbitt Diary entry for September 19, 1862, published in David Wiles, ed., *Windmills of Time* (Clear Spring, 1981), pp. 193-194.

59. Strother, "Personal Recollections," p. 285.

60. Smith, *118th Pennsylvania,* pp. 46-47.

61. "Stories Supplied by Hilda Mose" in Collection of Pat Holland, Sharpsburg, Maryland.

62. Nesbitt Diary, p. 195; Beem letter in Richard Skidmore, *The Alford Brothers: "We all Must Dye Sooner or Later"* (Hanover, Indiana, 1995), pp. 321-322.

63. Smith file; John Schildt, ed., *The Sharpsburg Echo,* (Hagerstown, 1970), p. 4; Origin G. Bingham letter, September 21, 1862, 137 Pennsylvania Infantry (file, Antietam N.B.); "Samuel J. Fletcher: A Short Account of My Army Life" in 15th Massachusetts Infantry (file, Antietam, N.B.).

64. Steven R. Stotelmyer, *The Bivouacs of the Dead: The Story of Those who Died at Antietam and South Mountain* (Baltimore, 1992), p. 6.

65. Ibid., pp. 12-13; Reilly, *The Battlefield of Antietam,* p. 23.

66. Smith, *118th Pennsylvania,* p. 52; Roger Keller, *Events of the Civil War in Washington County, Maryland* (Shippensburg, 1995), p. 91. In Frederick, Maryland, twenty hospitals cared for approximately 4,000 wounded. These hospitals included a number of hotels, schools, churches, and one convent converted for that purpose. T. J. C. Williams and Folger McKinsey, *History of Frederick County, Maryland*, 2 vols. (Baltimore, 1910), vol. 1, pp. 380-381; Jacob Hoke, *Historical Reminiscences of the War; In and About Chambersburg,* (Chambersburg, 1884), p. 27. For information on Confederate hospitals in the lower Shenandoah Valley after Antietam, see Edward H. Phillips, *The Lower Shenandoah Valley in the Civil War* (Lynchburg, 1993), pp. 98-99; and Roger U. Delauter, Jr., *Winchester in the Civil War* (Lynchburg, 1992), pp. 41-42.

67. The author was involved in helicopter support team (HST) operations with the 1st Marine Division in Vietnam 1969-1971. When casualties were incurred, "medevac" helicopters were frequently on the scene in 15 minutes or less.

68. "War Reminiscences," by Angela K. Davis (file, Antietam N.B.), pp. 43-45.

69. Mary Bedinger Mitchell, "A Woman's Recollections of Antietam," *Battles and Leaders*, 2, p. 687.

70. Smith, "History of Antietam." There probably is not enough evidence to develop a modern psychological study of how the battle impacted anyone, let alone chil-

dren. Accordingly, we may never know if manifestations such as alcoholism, domestic violence, crime, or an increase in the "lunatic" population were caused by the battle. Indeed, it is only since 1983 that Post Traumatic Stress, PTSD has been observed in children. Studies of disasters such as the Chowchilla school bus kidnaping, to the Cambodian children who survived the Pol Pot regime, to those exposed to the destruction of Hurricane Andrew, emphasize the high prevalence of emotional trauma caused by these events. Did Victorian mores serve as a bulwark against such emotional trauma? Were Victorians emotionally stronger than people in the industrialized nations of the late twentieth century? Information provided by Dr. John Carrill, Child Psychiatrist, Brook Lane Psychiatric Hospital, Hagerstown, MD, January, 1997.

71. Smith, *118th Pennsylvania*, pp. 46-47; Jonathan P. Stowe Diary, September 28, 1862, in 15th Massachusetts File (Antietam, N.B.); John Schildt, *Antietam Hospitals* (Chewsville, 1987), p. 27. Blood stains were a problem at the Reform Church and the Grove farm, where the famous photograph of Lincoln and McClellan was taken.

72. Reilly, *The Battlefield of Antietam*, p. 28.

73. Ibid., pp. 21, 25-26; Old Lutheran Church (file, Antietam N.B.); St. Paul's Episcopal Church (file, Antietam N.B.); Methodist Church (file, Antietam N.B.); Christ Reformed Church (file, Antietam N.B.). Contrary to popular belief, the Dunker Church was not used as a field hospital after the battle. It was used by the Confederates as a temporary medical aid station the evening following the battle and up to the time of the Confederate withdrawal from the field. Robert L. Lagemann, Historic Structure's Report for The Dunkard Church (unpublished report, Antietam N.B., May 25, 1960), pp. 49-50.

74. Samuel Mumma Family History (file, Antietam N.B.).

75. James H. Montgomery Diary, p. 23, Civil War Miscellaneous Collection, U. S. Army Military History Institute; Reilly, p. 25.

76. Trowbridge, *The Desolate South*, pp. 28-29. Confederates were not buried in the Antietam National Cemetery. Regional prejudice prevailed and only Union soldiers were afforded the privilege of burial there. The Antietam Confederate dead remained on the battlefield in shallow graves, in many cases their bones exposed by erosion or uprooted by animals. The situation became a national scandal. In 1872, the Confederate dead were finally reinterred in the newly established Washington Confederate Cemetery in Hagerstown, Md. Charles W. Snell and Sharon Brown, *Antietam National Battlefield and National Cemetery: An Administrative History* (Washington, 1986), pp. 1-20; Stotelmyer, *Bivouacs of the Dead*, pp. 33-38.

Yet even before all of the carnage was cleared, efforts were being made to memorialize the Union fallen. In the graveyard at the Smoketown Hospital, a wooden monument ten feet high with a cannon ball on top was erected. John Smith, "The Battle of Antietam: Hospitals," *Antietam Valley Record*, Keedysville, MD, October 31, 1895, in "Recollections of John P. Smith. The Battle of Antietam, the History of Antietam and the Hospitals of Antietam" (file, Antietam N.B.).

The Lost Order and the Press

Scott M. Sherlock

For years, historians have considered the matter of when Robert E. Lee discovered that his orders outlining Confederate troop deployments in Maryland had been found by Federal troops. A recent search of contemporary publications demonstrates conclusively that the contents of the "lost" order were published in at least two Northern newspapers prior to the battle of Antietam.

It is generally believed that the discovery of Lee's Special Orders 191 by Sgt. John M. Bloss and Cpl. Barton Mitchell of the 27th Indiana Infantry on Saturday, September 13, 1862, gave Maj. Gen. George McClellan the mettle to initiate the aggressive maneuverings that culminated in the Battle of Antietam. The lost order described, in detail, the location of, and instructions for, each of Lee's divided formations. The tactical draw at Antietam, follwed by Lee's retreat into Virginia, provided the victory President Abraham Lincoln needed to issue the Emancipation Proclamation. That proclamation, in turn, launched forces which changed the political and moral character of the war against the South.

As observed by historian Stephen Sears, "the lost order represented the opportunity of a lifetime." Indeed it did, for it provided McClellan with a complete understanding of the plans of his opponent. Sears quotes General McClellan as saying, "Here is a paper with which if I can not whip Bobbie Lee, I will be willing to go home."[1] Of some interest to historians has been the issue of exactly *when* General Robert E. Lee learned that a copy of Special Orders 191 was in the hands of the Federals. As Sears noted, "it is. . .hard to imagine. . . [General Lee] taking his defiant stand at Sharpsburg on September 15 and 16—daring enough as it was—with the knowledge that McClellan knew the exact dispositions of the still-scattered commands of the Army of Northern Virginia."[2]

Lee's biographer, Douglas Southall Freeman, believed his subject learned of the Federal discovery on the evening of September 13. Freeman related that a Marylander of Southern sympathy was at Army of the Potomac headquarters when the order was received by McClellan in the late morning of Saturday, September 13. The Marylander subsequently traveled through the porous Federal and Confederate lines to Maj. Gen. Jeb Stuart's headquarters and advised him of the intelligence catastrophe. Stuart, accordingly, directed a dispatch to Lee's headquarters advising him of the matter.[3]

Sears takes issue with Freeman's assertions that Lee actually knew the order was in the hands of the Federal commander on September 13—or at any time prior to the Battle of Antietam. And his arguments are persuasive. Sears observes that a copy of General Stuart's dispatch has never been located. He also cogently notes that the existence of the "lost" order was never mentioned at any time by the anyone in the Confederate high command prior to General Lee's drafting of his official report of the Maryland Campaign in August 1863. Moreover, Sears finds it simply unbelievable that General McClellan or one of his staff would be so careless as to reveal the details of such an incredible find to an unknown civilian from a border state who just happened to be visiting the headquarters of the Army of the Potomac. It is far more likely, contends Sears, that what the Marylander learned (and which subsequently was conveyed to General Stuart) was that McClellan had received some intelligence of unspecified sort that made him confident and offensive-minded.[4]

Wilbur D. Jones, Jr., in an article in this publication (*Civil War Regiments*, vol. 5, no. 3) noted that the first public discussion of the lost order may have been in June of 1863, when McClellan discussed the order in testimony before the Congressional Committee on the Conduct of the War. Jones also observed that earlier that year a Northern newspaper published a reference to a Confederate dispatch—possibly Orders 191—that was found prior to the Battle of Antietam.[5]

All of this leads to a paragraph printed on the second page in the *Washington Star* on Monday, September 15, 1862:

> A member of Colonel Colgrove's [sic] regiment found a paper purporting to be Rebel Order No. 119 [191], which conveyed the information that one portion of the army was to go to Hagerstown and hold that place; another portion proceed to Harper's Ferry and dislodge Miles; and the third proceed

against General White; and the force afterwards to concentrate at Hager-stown.[6]

On Tuesday, September 16, the *Baltimore Sun* published the same article verbatim. While Colonel Cosgrove's name was misspelled, and Order Number 191 is transposed as 119, the described dispatch was in fact Special Orders 191.

While newspapers in 1862 were a critical source of military intelligence, and the routes by which newspapers and correspondence crossed military lines are well documented, there is no indication that either of the articles were seen by Confederate intelligence sources prior to the September 17th Battle of Antietam. Since wartime copies of both the *Washington Star* and the *Baltimore Sun* frequently made their way to Richmond, it is fair to speculate that Confederate intelligence was aware of the lost order as early as the fall or winter of 1862.

Still, one is left to ponder these intriguing facts: on Saturday, September 13, the order was found and brought to the attention of General McClellan. Less than 48 hours later, on Monday, September 15, the essential facts of the find were described in detail in the *Washington Star*. Two days later, on September 17, the Battle of Antietam was fought. As Stephen Sears pointed out, if General Lee had been aware his orders were in the hands of the Federals, he never would have fought at Antietam.[7]

We are left with this obvious conclusion: the general newspaper-reading public of Washington and Baltimore knew critical information about a Federal intelligence coup profoundly pertinent to the Confederate military leadership that General Lee was not aware of as he prepared for battle in the small farming community of Sharpsburg, Maryland.

Notes

1. Stephen W. Sears, *George B. McClellan* (New York, 1988), p. 282; Sears, *Landscape Turned Red* (New Haven, 1983) p. 115.

2. Sears, *Landscape Turned Red,* p. 352.

3. Douglas Southall Freeman, *Lee's Lieutenants: A Study in Command*, 3 vols. (New York, 1942-44), vol. 2, p. 172; Shelby Foote, *The Civil War: A Narrative*, 3 vols. (New York, 1958), vol. 1, p. 676.

4. Sears, *Landscape Turned Red*, pp. 351-352.

5 Wilbur D. Jones, Jr., "Who Lost the Lost Order?" *Civil War Regiments*, vol. 5, no. 3 (1997), p. 12.

6. *Washington Star*, p. 2

7. Sears, *Landscape Turned Red*, p. 351.

BOOK REVIEWS

Civil War Generalship: The Art of Command, by W. J. Wood. (Greenwood Publishing Group, P.O. Box 5007, Westport, CT 06881-5007). Illustrations, maps, notes, biblio., index. 271pp. $59.95. Cloth

Wood, a retired U. S. Army lieutenant colonel born in 1917, has spent a good part of his life studying and analyzing the art of command. Here, he focuses on six Civil War commanders, organizing his book into five progressive parts. Part One defines the underlying problem with which opposing commanders were faced. Parts Two, Three, and Four present the campaigns and battles within which the commanders displayed their mastery (or relative lack thereof) of the art. Wood does not, however, attempt to present all, nor even in one instance the best known, of those campaigns and battles; indeed, he is highly selective, and possibly subjective as well. Part Five reviews the character of each of the six commanders.

Wood's six selected commanders are Thomas J. "Stonewall" Jackson, Nathaniel Banks, William S. Rosecrans, Braxton Bragg, John B. Hood, and George H. Thomas. This is justified enough, as far as Wood's aims go, but it reduces the scope of the study to a level below the most prominent echelons of command. The battles and campaigns follow naturally from the selected commanders. They are Cedar Mountain, Chickamauga, and Nashville. From Cedar Mountain—assuredly rather lesser-known and less-appreciated than the other two—one learns much about the modern concept of a "Meeting Engagement."

Wood rightly points out that the tendency of many historians to label the Civil War as the "first modern war" robs it of a true context, "so that we fail to see it in a meaningful perspective: as a war sandwiched between the end of the Napoleonic Wars and the wars of German Unification" (p. 6).

Perhaps the most significant insight that Wood offers is that sometimes a commander's keenest assets can be tinged with a dark side of inadequacy or distortion: e.g., sometimes a trait can be both a "main strength and a weakness." All the commanders had this to some extent, but Stonewall Jackson lifted it to a quintessential level. But, what a guy he was: "Stonewall Jackson was probably the only Confederate general who was ever cheered by Union prisoners when they caught sight of him in the field" (p. 37).

These people are all complex characters. Even the poorer commanders, such as Nathaniel P. Banks, "showed a number of redeeming qualities" (p. 48). Luck plays a role in how any commander fares, and sometimes a good one can influence, possibly even make, his own luck. Terrain and weather, for example, are always important factors—and they *will* have an impact, so if a commander cannot predict them, at least he can be cognizant and exploitative. Perhaps the most significant of the miscellaneous tidbits that Wood sprinkles here and there is a quotation from Sun Tzu, author of *The Art of War*: "He who knows when he can fight and when he cannot will be victorious" (p. 189).

Wood's last chapter, "Reflections," is the most valuable. There seems no doubt that he is a well-read, zestful student of his subject. He is not, alas, a great writer. It may be that a few discerning and thoughtful readers will be stimulated and instructed by his effort, but most will find the construction and syntax far beyond a commonly enjoyable level of reading.

Herman Hattaway   University of Missouri-Kansas City

Stonewall Jackson: The Man, The Soldier, The Legend, by James I. Robertson. Macmillan Publishing Co., 866 Third Ave., New York, NY 10022), 1997. Maps, biblio., notes, photos, 950pp. $40.00 Cloth

It took me two months to read this book. That was partly due to its length and size of print, and partly due to my hectic schedule. But it was worth it. One additional confession: although I have read the Henderson and Chambers biographies, and much else written on General T. J. Jackson as part of my work on Jedediah Hotchkiss, Stonewall's topographer, I cut my teeth on Frank Vandiver's *Mighty Stonewall*, which I had read just before becoming Frank's student at The Rice Institute (however much this admission may embarrass him now) in 1958; for forty years, my Gospels were Matthew, Mark, Luke, John—and Frank. After reading this book, I expand that roster to include "Bud" Robertson.

It is obvious from examining all the trappings of the academy that testify to Robertson's research that he has examined more material on Jackson than any previous biographer, and likely more than anyone ever will again. It also is obvious that he has pondered what he has read in the primary sources as well as the findings of predecessors. It is gratifying that he has preserved the religious dimensions and crusading nature of Jackson. Before the end even Robertson seems to weary of Jackson's incessant giving glory to God for every thing, but he allows this essential aspect of his subject to remain as paramount in his biography as it obviously was in Jackson's life.

Vandiver "humanized" Jackson a little more; he made us aware of and appreciate Jackson's love for his two wives. His handling of Jackson's death remains classic. Robertson's perspective does not differ much, although he is more definite about just which river Jackson intended to cross. He sticks more to the military story and does an excellent job of demonstrating how completely Jackson's image had gripped the Confederate nation while he yet lived. Robertson goes a little farther in an epilogue to tell readers what happened next, at least through Jackson's funeral and with sketches on the fate of his family.

I would recommend either book to any reader—beginner, buff, or scholar—but its freshness gives Robertson a considerable edge. Caution: do not undertake the reading of *Stonewall Jackson* without commitment. It required dedication, and as someone learned before us long ago, one gets out of a thing what one puts into it. Perhaps my reading a chapter or so at a time, over eight weeks, with time to think about it, was not so bad. There was never any question of abandoning it despite interruptions. I expect no book on the Civil War has been more anticipated, and probably none has lived up to that anticipation better.

I wish Bud Robertson well with this book. He has captured, amplified, and preserved the persona of Man, Soldier, and Legend with which we peripheral students of Jackson and his staff have become comfortable. He has, in words borrowed by a popular song of the recent past, pushed "it [our unending affair with the Jacksonian enigma] to the limit, one more time." And, I thank Robertson for giving Jedediah Hotchkiss the role so close to the center of Jackson's circle he always deserved but has received only recently.

Good book. One really isn't a Civil Warrior without reading it.

Archie P. McDonald   Stephen F. Austin State University

Lincoln's Generals, edited by Gabor S. Boritt (Oxford University Press, 200 Madison Ave., New York, NY 10016), 1996. Intro., photos, notes. 248pp. $11.95. Paper, $19.95 hardcover.

Lincoln's Generals is a collection of essays edited by Gabor S. Boritt. The book, in Boritt's own words, "takes a hard look at the interaction of five leading generals with their Civil War commander-in-chief (p. xv)." It offers five essays about Lincoln and his relationships with: McClellan, (Stephen Sears); Hooker (Mark Neely, Jr.); Meade, (Gabor Boritt); Sherman, (Michael Fellman); and Grant, (John Y. Simon).

The essays give great insights into the personalities of the generals and of Lincoln. McClellan was a capable leader but not an aggressive general. He ". . . failed the test the President was. . .applying to all his generals—did they know how to win on the battlefield (p. 39)." Hooker was an aggressive general, according to Neely, and he was almost reckless, but failed under the burden of overall command. Meade was capable of a great victory at Gettysburg, but disappointed and frustrated Lincoln by not being able to do any more. Sherman was practically insubordinate to Lincoln's policy of recruiting black troops, but Sherman knew how to win on the battlefield and therefore had Lincoln's support. "In general, Sherman and Lincoln shared only one goal, the defeat of the South and the preservation of the Union (p. 151)." Lincoln finally found his general in Grant, who was capable of providing the aggressive leadership necessary to win the war. Although theirs was far from a perfect relationship, "Grant and Lincoln forged an effective partnership in a turmoil of clashing authority (p. 198)."

Each of the authors are able to effectively condense their subjects into compact, informative essays. What emerges from the entire collection is a portrait of Lincoln's growth and development as Commander-in-Chief. Lincoln's ability to grasp and clearly understand what was needed to win the war was amazing.

The book is very informative and enjoyable to read. It is well documented with extensive footnotes and contains an excellent "for further reading" section. This is a good book for either the novice or avid student of the Civil War.

Frank Prater   El Cajon, CA

Herndon's Informants: Letters, Interviews, and Statements about Abraham Lincoln, Douglas L. Wilson & Rodney O. Davis, editors (University of Illinois Press, 1325 S. Oak St., Champaign, IL 61820), 1998. Register, index. 827pp. $49.95. Hardcover.

Scholars have long debated the impact William H. Herndon had on the life and political future of Abraham Lincoln, Herndon's Illinois law partner of nearly twenty years. There is little doubt, however, that Herndon considered his influence and advice to be a vital factor in guiding Lincoln to political success and the presidency. Following Lincoln's assassination on April 14, 1865, such thinking also motivated Herndon to believe that he was one of the few people who could write reliably about the life of the martyred president.

To this end, Herndon began to scour the country shortly after Lincoln's death for friends, relatives, or casual acquaintances of the president from various stages of his life, soliciting their knowledge of him through written recollections or by conducting oral interviews with his "informants." Herndon single-handedly undertook this amazing and far-reaching project until the mid-1880s, when Jesse W. Weik, a government employee living in Indiana, began to assist in the endeavor. The two men made extensive use of the material they gathered in their collaborative effort, *Herndon's Lincoln: The True Story of a Great Life*, published in 1889. After Herndon passed away in 1891, Weik retained possession of most of the documents, keeping them beyond the reach of many contemporary Lincoln historians and authors, and using them for his 1922 biography *The Real Lincoln.* Following Weik's death in 1929, the Lincoln accounts passed through numerous hands, with the majority of them eventually comprising the Herndon-Weik Collection at the Library of Congress, though portions of the papers remained scattered in archives from California to New York. Despite the fact that many of the hand-written texts were eventually reproduced as microforms, the immense treasure trove remained primarily for the benefit of serious scholars until the publishing of this book. Academics and casual purveyors of the study of the sixteenth president owe editors Douglas L. Wilson (Monticello's Saunders Director of the International Center for Jefferson Studies) and Rodney O. Davis (Szold Professor of History at Knox College) a large debt for undertaking this massive effort and making available this well-arranged compilation.

Herndon's Informants begins with a summation of the lives of Herndon and Weik, and explains how they went about obtaining information on Lincoln. This introduction also sets up Part 1, the largest section of the book, wherein the hundreds of documents provided by the "informants" are contained. The accounts are organized chronologically in the order in which they were gathered throughout the nineteenth century. Each entry is numbered, provided with a concise, clear heading explaining who supplied the material, whether Herndon or Weik collected the information, and whether one is perusing the text of a letter or a transcript of an oral interview. At the conclusion of each passage, Wilson and Davis indicate where the original document is archived, and if applicable, mention where typescript copies of the section in question may be found.   Readers of *Herndon's Informants* will also be grateful for the user-friendly footnotes that identify many of the people, places, and things mentioned in the accounts. The reminiscences of Lincoln are provided by the famous and the obscure, and run the gamut from the earthy to the urbane. They deal with his relationships with Mary Todd Lincoln, Ann Rutledge and other women, his views on religion, and a host of other personal information. Though much of the text deals with Lincoln's pre-presidential political career, several contributors comment on his actions relating to the Civil War.

Some of the entries are bound to raise a smile. Abner Y. Ellis, who worked with Joshua F. Speed, a Springfield associate of Lincoln, wrote a rustic letter to Herndon in 1866 in which he related how Lincoln compared the tentative Union general George B. McClellan to "Bap McNabbs Red Rooster." It seems Bap had a rooster that loved to crow and strut on its own "dung hill," but the fowl wilted and fled when placed in the cock-fighting ring. Such behavior caused McNabb to chastise his bird, "you damn little cuss, you are Great on a parade but you are not worth a Dam in a fight." "It is said," continued Ellis, "that Mr L remarked to a friend soon after McClelland's fizzle before Richmond that Little McClelland reminded him of Bap McNabbs Little Red Rooster" (pp. 190-191).

Other accounts reveal somber aspects of Lincoln's life. Elizabeth Todd Edwards, Mary Todd Lincoln's younger sister, expressed the opinion that "Mr. Lincoln" was "odd and wholly irregular" and "loved nothing," and recounted how she and her husband advised "Mary" not to wed the up and coming lawyer (p. 444). Often discussed is Lincoln's morose, fatalistic behavior. One of Herndon's interviewees remembered that Lincoln's first Springfield law office contained only a "small dirty bed, one buffalo robe, a chair and a bench," and that the lanky attorney so often remained *"abstracting"* and "glooming" in this environment many feared he would "Commit Suicide" (p. 251).

Some of the materials collected no longer exist in their original form, but only as material Herndon and Weik copied and synopsized for inclusion in *Herndon's Lincoln*. Such data is contained in Part 2. Part 3 includes information about Lincoln that Herndon gleaned from the accounts he received and conveyed in letters to Weik.

In regard to all the primary source information contained in *Herndon's Informants*, Wilson and Davis issue a caveat: their mission, they explain, is to "maximize access" to the collection (p. vii). In keeping with this philosophy, they have not established the veracity of the majority of the accounts, though they have corrected a few of the more glaring factual errors. The reader, then, should approach this material with the healthy skepticism they would any collection of primary documents, and tred cautiously through this forest of Lincolnalia. Of course, Herndon and Weik conducted their oral interviews without the aid of tape recorders, writing down the information as the informant spoke. In some cases, the men transcripted the sessions from memory some time after the interview had occurred. Both of the above factors might have caused Herndon and Weik to inadvertently record less than accurate versions of their interviews.

Furthermore, as a spate of recent books concerning memory as a historical source have observed, as time passes and participants or witnesses to an event or a persona age, the more likely it is that their remembrances of the same will be changed, shaped, and molded by more current events and prejudices. Some of the accounts of Lincoln were acquired twenty years or more after his death, a critical factor to keep in mind when examining their content. To help researchers stand more firmly on the slippery slope of reminiscence and memory, biographies of the over 260 people who contributed to Herndon's and Weik's study comprise Part 4, the final section of *Herndon's Informants*. These invaluable sketches, also researched and compiled by Wilson and Davis, generally at least indicate the background of a particular contributor and the circumstances and length of their association with Lincoln. Often, they also contain data regarding political affiliations, and sometimes mention whether a person enjoyed a pleasant or acrimonious relationship with Lincoln. Studying these entries allows one to begin to establish the reliability of the accounts contained in Part 1.

Readers will find *Herndon's Informants* a fascinating and well-edited collection of material on Lincoln's life and character that can be used as a serious research tool, or for enjoyable "quick reads." The information in this book, used in conjunction with other recent works on Lincoln's life and political achievements, helps to peel off the layers of enigma and myth that for so long have surrounded the tall, brooding politician. Editors Wilson and Davis are to be credited for this very worthy and valuable contribution to the study of Lincoln.

Dana B. Shoaf   Frederick, Maryland

They Rode with Forrest and Wheeler, John E. Fisher (McFarland & Co., Publishers, P. O. Box 611, Jefferson, NC 28640), 1995. Maps & Illustrations. Epilogue. Notes. Bibliography. Index. 310pp. $29.95. Hardcover.

John E. Fisher explains in his preface that he wrote *They Rode with Forrest and Wheeler* to fill gaps found in his grandfather, Thomas Burr Fisher's, Civil War memoirs. Thomas and his four brothers were members of the Fourth and Eleventh Tennessee Cavalry Regiments, which served intermittently under famed Confederate cavalry commanders Nathan Bedford Forrest and Joseph Wheeler. Fisher informs his readers that he desires to do more than simply recount what his family members did, and for that he is to be commended. Civil War history is overcrowded with narrowly focused, anecdotal accounts that add little to a critical understanding of the war's lasting meaning.

Unfortunately, Fisher has bitten off more than he can chew. He wants to recount his family's story and present a combination regimental history, biographical study of Forrest and Wheeler, narrative of the Western Theatre, and an overall assessment of why the South lost. He includes asides about the plight of the common soldier, race and class issues, thumbnail sketches of various officers and men, and a lengthy discussion of his grandfather's postwar theological views. The result is an unfocused, poorly written text that offers nothing particularly new or noteworthy about the war experience, cavalry operations, or the Western Theatre.

At times it is hard even to find the five brothers. The prose is wordy and awkward, and the author easily distracted. Fisher does not portray his family members as particularly distinctive or memorable personalities. Spotty regimental records and a paucity of personal papers make the cavalry soldiers almost ghostly figures who move in and out of the text, barely making an impression on the reader. Fisher must frequently speculates on the brothers' whereabouts. Near the end of his book, he confesses: "Little is known now of their personalities, skills, interests, and motivations" (p. 229).

The book's subtitle uses the word "chronicle" and in some ways this is an appropriate label. A chronicle records events in sequence with little attempt to analyze critically cause and effect. But Fisher does not always write in chronological order. His final five chapters overlap in time (and sometimes in space), when he describes actions in Tennessee, Georgia, and Alabama from the fall of 1863 to the end of the war. For example, Chapter Six traces the fall of Atlanta to Appomattox; the remaining four chapters in piecemeal fashion follow John B. Hood's demise in the West, followed by a chapter on James H. Wilson's Alabama raid. Fisher devotes little space to the brothers' whereabouts in these chapters; in fact, he does not know exactly where they were. Even photographs are out of order. Chapter six includes portraits of the five brothers after the war (p. 141), but the next four chapters backtrack to the war. These photographs would have been better placed in the epilogue, where the author attempts to piece together their postwar lives.

There are other serious problems. The book has no thesis or strong organizational idea, and transitional sentences and paragraphs are nearly nonexistent. One example will suffice: in his chapter entitled "Through the Chickamauga Holocaust," Fisher includes an anecdote about Thomas Fisher unknowingly curing a weak stomach by eating several green apples. Fisher ends the paragraph by stating: "Completing his consumption of the fruit, he went back for another until his delicate appetite was less fragile and sufficiently satiated" (p. 48). The next paragraph begins with this long-winded, rambling sentence:

> While Forrest had been away in pursuit of Colonel Streight in Alabama, Earl Van Dorn had been fatally shot on May 7 by a resident of the vicinity of Spring Hill, George B. Peters, 45, a farmer and physician, who fled to the enemy's lines after claiming he had acted because Van Dorn had violated the sanctity of his home by his attentions to Peter's wife, Jessie, 25, while Peters was away attending to his farming interests in Mississippi. (p. 48)

Fisher's understanding of the Confederate experience is also problematic. He seems genuinely baffled by the brothers' decision to enlist in the fall of 1862. Using 20/20 hindsight, Fisher writes: "Despite the overwhelming evidence that they were championing a lost cause, the Fisher brothers made their decision and obviously meant to adhere to it to the end" (p. 23). There is no proof that the brothers ignored "overwhelming evidence" that their cause was lost in 1862. Modern readers may find it amazing, but at the Confederacy's core there always remained a cadre of white Southerners wholly and religiously committed to the war, despite suffering, desertion, dissent, and defeat. Historians recognize that there were cracks and holes in the Confederate nation before its formal demise, but the Fisher brothers clearly remained committed until the bitter end.

The Depression-era Progressive school of historians, and Fisher's own Southern bias, affects his entire presentation of the war. He sharply attacks Northerners who "made a great deal of money from government contracts, federal debentures issued to finance the war, and the rising prices of manufactured goods" (p. 222). While Southerners fought for "home, hearth and heartland" (p. 221), Northerners fought for what Fisher dismissively calls "the lofty rhetorical purpose" of saving the Union (p. 222). He is silent about Southern blockade runners who also profited from the conflict, nor does he mention that by 1863, the fighting had indeed become a war to end slavery.

Fisher repeatedly lauds Nathan Bedford Forrest. Forrest, he declares, was the "most striking military leader produced in the Civil War." He also maintains "that the South might have had a better chance to win its fight for independence had it leaders given Forrest the larger role that his successes instantly indicated he could have handled" (p. 26). True, Forrest was a successful commander, especially late in the war when military prospects turned increasingly bleak for the Confederacy. But it is pure speculation to imply that one man alone could have changed the war's outcome. A careful and critical reading of participants' words and actions demonstrates that no one battle or person lost the war for the South. Instead, a complicated and interconnected number of military, economic, political, social, and cultural factors converged to bring Confederate defeat.

Finally, Fisher has neglected the last fifteen years of historical scholarship almost entirely. He relies mainly on a handful of dated books in his notes, although he lists a few newer studies in his bibliography. Fisher's original intention to round out his grandfather's personal memoirs is entirely admirable. The author attempts to use his family members' military service to say something larger about the war and its lasting significance. But holes in his family records, uneven scholarship, and the author's personal biases produces more questions than answers. Were the Fisher brothers' Civil War experiences in the Western cavalry typical, atypical, or a combination of both? After over 280 pages of text and notes, this reader is hard pressed to know the answer.

Lesley J. Gordon   University of Akron

Island No. 10, by Larry J. Daniel and Lynn N. Bock (The University of Alabama Press, P. O. Box 870380, Tuscaloosa, AL 35487-0380), 1996. Illustrations, maps, notes, biblio., appendices, index. 203pp. $24.95. Paperback.

Battle books and biographies abound in Civil War historiography: *Island No. 10* represents something of the best of both genre. It is a vivid, focused analysis of an important campaign, and an insightful, reasoned description and discussion of the men in command.

What makes *Island No. 10* even more valuable is the fact that it treats a campaign long neglected by the historical community. The authors make clear that the consistent disregard for the campaign derived in large part from the fact that the fall of Island No. 10 "was squeezed between two of the largest battles fought in the West—Fort Donelson and Shiloh" (p. ix). Alternatively, the authors note that some contemporary observers recognized the significance of the Union victory at Island No. 10. A cursory review of period literature confirms the authors' assessment. For instance, in his compendium, *The Rebellion Record 1866*, Robert A. Campbell gave almost as much space to the fall of Island No. 10 as he did to the battle of Shiloh. Campbell accorded too much significance to Island No. 10, but he was closer to the truth than many subsequent students of the war who ignored the campaign. As Bock and Daniel correctly note, the campaign early in 1862 that culminated in the capture of Island No. 10 represented the practical end to Confederate power on the upper Mississippi. Furthermore, the Confederate defeat at Island No. 10 closely foreshadowed the fall of Vicksburg. Island No. 10 was an event of true strategic significance.

The authors trace the contest for Island No. 10 from its origins to its conclusion in a concise, but thorough, manner. A close attention to important details is a hallmark of the book. Certainly, readers will take away a clear sense of the material imbalance between Confederate and Union forces. The *ad hoc* and inept distribution of meager resources also marred Confederate efforts to sustain a presence on the upper Mississippi. The Confederate officers immediately responsible for Island No. 10 were, largely, officers of modest ability; their modest abilities were *magnified* by their reliance on poorly equipped and poorly trained troops and by the inadequate logistical and technical resources.

The senior Confederate commander in the theatre, Albert Sidney Johnston, draws sharp criticism from Bock and Daniel. The much-admired Confederate general is chided by the authors for failing to concentrate his forces effectively early in the war, a failure with large strategic implications for the Confederate fortress on Island No. 10 and the war in the West generally.

Readers also will be interested in the authors' balanced treatment of John Pope and Andrew Foote, Union commanders whose careers have often been the subject of overly simplistic characterizations. Excellent maps, the judicious use of quotations from primary sources, a fine index, and the overall production values of the book all complement Bock and Daniel's skillful narrative.

Only a few minor criticisms of the book come to mind. Once or twice the authors make almost gratuitous asides on some important issues. The usual canard against Jefferson Davis for his failure to recognize the importance of the war in the West is restated with a lack of analysis that belies the usual perspicacity of the authors; though, in fairness, the authors tempered their disapproval of Davis with a thoughtful critique of Albert Sidney Johnston. Such flaws, however, do not diminish the importance of this small volume. Bock and Daniel have rescued an important campaign from obscurity and placed it properly in the landscape of Civil War historiography. Anyone interested in the Civil War will read this book with real benefit.

Kenneth M. Startup   Williams Baptist College

Rebel Georgia, by F. N. Boney (Mercer University Press, 6316 Peake Rd, Macon, GA 31210-3960), 1997. Photos, notes, biblio., index. 117pp. $15.95. Paperback.

F. N. Boney, professor emeritus at the University of Georgia, has joined a growing number of authors who have written brief overviews of Civil War topics. In barely over eighty pages of text, Boney surveys wartime Georgia. This is not Albert Castel's 1993 *The Atlanta Campaign* or Lee Kennett's more general *Marching Through Georgia: The Story of Soldiers and Civilians During Sherman's March* (1995). With only three chapters, Boney has aimed his text at the novice, for this small volume serves as an introduction to someone with no background in the Civil War.

In his first chapter, Boney looks at the state on the eve of war. In the presidential election of 1860, Southern Democrat John C. Breckinridge won with 51,893 votes, but compromise candidate John Bell earned a respectable 42,886. Clearly not all Georgians championed secession, including such prominent national figures as Alexander H. Stephens and Herschel V. Johnson. But the state's radical and pro-Southern governor, Joseph E. Brown, was a dominant figure, and he carefully maneuvered Georgia out of the Union. Still, there was opposition, for the formal election approving the secession ordinance, 208 to 89, indicated nearly one-third of the delegates questioned the course selected.

The second chapter looks at the people in the first three years of war. Boney describes better known personalities such as Robert Toombs, Howell and Thomas R. R. Cobb, and Stephens. Yet, the strength of this chapter is not the author's brief accounts of national figures but the story of how the war affected the homefront. Governor Brown continually clashed with the government in

Richmond, but his popularity at home won him re-election throughout the war. The state worked to provide for its citizens, and distributed millions of tax dollars to needy families. When Brown supported the Confederate effort to encourage the cultivation of corn instead of cotton, he even tried to reduce the amount of corn distilled into whiskey. Yet Brown argued with Richmond more than he cooperated, and as the war progressed he gained allies, such as Stephens and Toombs. In the first years of the fighting Georgia was free of any major military threat, although there were minor incursions on its borders. Even industry performed relatively well into the fourth year. White women and black slaves struggled to keep life as normal as possible, although slaves—forty-four percent of the population—often were requisitioned by the Confederate army or pressed into service in various industries. Nonetheless, before the war ended, over 3,500 black Georgians had joined Union armies.

The final chapter deals with William T. Sherman's campaigns in 1864. Continuing his overview pattern, Boney omits any detailed description of battles and dispatches the entire Atlanta Campaign in just over six pages, the March to the Sea in nine. Boney describes Joseph E. Johnston as an "able-but-not-brilliant Virginian" who fought "a skillful but cautious defensive campaign" (p. 63) to the outskirts of Atlanta. President Davis, who became frustrated with Johnston, replaced him with John Bell Hood. In one of the many analogies that dot the text, Boney concludes of Hood: "In football terminology he was a fine linebacker or fullback but a poor quarterback—or as Lee put it, he was all lion and no fox" (p. 65). Indeed, Hood lost Atlanta at the first of September and Boney's description of the explosions that rocked the city as the retreating rebels blew up the railroad depot is another example of his use of comparisons. The area, decided Boney, looked "like downtown Hiroshima at the end of World War II" (p. 67). The author frequently compares the Civil War with the Second World War, as when he says Sherman destroyed the state's rail line "much as Allied strategic bombers went after Nazi Germany's essential and vulnerable railroads and synthetic oil facilities late in World War II" (p. 69). Again, using modern comparisons, Boney characterizes Andersonville and other southern prisons. They were "not Gulags or Buchenwalds," he notes, "they were inadequate nineteenth-century American prisons, not twentieth-century Eurasian death factories" (p. 71).

While this book will be useful to a person with little or no knowledge of Georgia's role in the war, it will not appeal to someone who possesses meaningful background. It is written for the general public, although Boney's references to World War II require the reader to have a more sophisticated understanding of modern warfare. Moreover, his frequent use of clichés may bother some readers. Still, it is a modest brief survey that highlights Georgia's Confederate history.

Anne J. Bailey   Georgia College & State University

Blue Lightning: Wilder's Mounted Infantry Brigade in the Battle of Chickamauga, by Richard A. Baumgartner (Blue Acorn Press, P. O. Box 2684, Huntington WV 25726), 1997. Illustrations, appendix, notes, biblio., index. 245pp. $30.00. Hardcover.

Many Civil War fighting units became famous for their battlefield exploits. Recent publishing trends reveal a resurgence in newly-written and reprinted regimental histories. Few brigades receive similar attention—the Iron Brigade and Stonewall Brigade being exceptions to the rule. Besides these two famous brigades, perhaps only the Confederacy's Orphan Brigade and the Union's Irish Brigade hold similar name recognition. In *Blue Lightning: Wilder's Mounted Infantry Brigade in the Battle of Chickamauga*, Richard A. Baumgartner attempts to show that Col. John T. Wilder's "Lightning Brigade" deserves the same lofty reputation as the units mentioned above.

The Lightning Brigade, named for its speedy capture of Hoover's Gap during the Tullahoma Campaign, began to take shape in the fall of 1862 when Wilder commanded the 17th, 72nd, and 75th Indiana, 98th Illinois, and 18th Indiana Battery. The brigade served in Maj. General Joseph J. Reynolds's 4th Division of the XIV Corps of the Army of the Cumberland. After participating in a grueling and unsuccessful campaign to end John Hunt Morgan's second raid into Kentucky in December 1862, Wilder began thinking of ways to increase his brigade's mobility and firepower. He decided to equip his regiments as mounted infantry—troops who would travel on horses but fight on foot. His men voted on this change of status, and only the 75th Indiana balked at the idea; the 123rd Illinois replaced them.

Wilder did not obtain his new mounts through government channels, but instead raided the Tennessee countryside for horses and mules. One six-day expedition netted about 1,500 animals. Wilder's means of acquiring more effective weapons was equally bold and even more creative. He settled on seven-shot Spencer repeating rifles as his weapon of choice, but realized that he would need more than 2,000 guns to arm the brigade properly. Each man in the brigade signed a promissory note agreeing to buy his own rifle at $35. Wilder then sought funds from friends in Greensburg, Indiana, offering to mortgage his own home and iron foundry as collateral. On the condition that Wilder co-sign each soldier's promissory note, local bankers approved the loan. The Spencer instilled great self-confidence in Wilder's troops. Corporal Benjamin Magee happily remembered, "It never got out of repair. . . .It could be taken all to pieces to clean, and hence was little trouble to keep in order—quite an item to lazy soldiers" (p. 34)

Wilder's men had their confidence tested in the campaign to oust Braxton Bragg's Army of Tennessee from the vicinity of Chattanooga. The brigade served on detached duty, participating in Maj. Gen. William S. Rosecrans' demonstration against the city from the north while the bulk of the Federal army moved southeast of Chattanooga to flank the Confederates. The Lightning Brigade played a crucial role in deceiving the Confederates into thinking that a large force approached Chattanooga from the north. "Details were made nearly every night to build fires indicating large camps," recalled Wilder, "and by throwing boards upon others and hammering on barrels and sawing up boards and throwing the pieces in streams that would float them into the river, we made them believe we were preparing to cross with boats" (p. 81). After the defenders abandoned the city, the 92nd Illinois held the disputed honor of being the first Federal unit to enter Chattanooga.

Rosecrans believed that the Confederates had commenced a headlong retreat and would offer little resistance to the pursuing Union columns (which were becoming progressively isolated from one another as they pursued the enemy). The Lightning Brigade's skirmish at Leet's Tanyard on September 12 offered Rosecrans an opportunity to discern that he had not entirely routed the Confederates: just before the fight, one of Wilder's scouts captured some Rebel mail that suggested that troops from Mississippi and Virginia were reinforcing Bragg. However, the Federal high command placed little confidence in this information. The two-hour skirmish increased the brigade's rising confidence in their own fighting prowess and that of their weapons. "Had it not been for our men being armed with the Spencer Rifle," Cpl. William Records claimed, "there is no doubt but that the entire battalion would have been gobbled up" (p. 100).

On September 18, the brigade defended Alexander's Bridge across Chickamauga Creek for almost three hours with only a few casualties. Wilder's defense foiled Confederate plans to cross the creek and sweep into Maj. Gen. Thomas L. Crittenden's flank. The following day Wilder's brigade anchored the Federal line on the west end of Viniard Field. The men stood their ground despite the confusion of multiple Confederate attacks and Federal counterattacks in the area, using its Spencers to great advantage. Major Connolly remembered,

"We think our Spencers saved us, and our men adore them as the heathen do their idols" (p. 147). As the rest of Wilder's men were fighting, the 92nd Illinois served on detached duty near Rosecrans's headquarters and again offered the commander important information. Colonel Smith Atkins presented Rosecrans with a young prisoner from Lt. Gen. James Longstreet's Corps as proof that the Virginians had reinforced Bragg, but again Rosecrans dismissed the information out of hand.

The men of the brigade spent a sleepless night among the wounded and, save for the 92nd Illinois, moved to the far Federal right on the morning of September 20. Longstreet's successful assault on the Union center cut Wilder off from George H. Thomas, who was attempting to make a stand near Snodgrass Hill with the left wing of the Federal army. Wilder determined to cut through Longstreet's attacking columns by striking their flank and relying on the Spencers' increased firepower to reach Thomas and disrupt the Confederate attack. Whether or not Wilder's attack plan moved beyond the idea stage remained a point of contention into the postwar years. Before Wilder could attack, a disheveled Assistant Secretary of War Charles A. Dana approached and either ordered or strongly suggested the brigade retreat to Chattanooga. Wilder, unsure of the extent of Dana's authority, compromised by calling off his attack but remained on the battlefield, where he covered the retreat toward Chattanooga. He later claimed that if he had been allowed to attack, "it would have been fatal to Bragg's army" (p. 183). Recalling the night of September 20 many years after the battle, Wilder noted that his troops "slept in hunger, but ready to spring to arms at a moment's notice notwithstanding they had been for three days in almost constant battle, had expended over two hundred rounds of cartridges per man. . .We had repulsed every attack, and had not been driven a single rod" (p. 185).

Baumgartner claims his study features "likely the largest assemblage of Wilder's brigade portraiture ever gathered" (p. 2) and the reader will not be disappointed with the result. The book is profusely illustrated, even including an occasional photograph in the notes section. Baumgartner effectively places portraits within the text, matching eyewitness accounts with a photograph of the witness. The photographic vignettes sometimes offer unusual stories that strengthen the work. In one instance, a photo of Pvt. Thomas M. Rider accompanies the text of a letter from his father Daniel to Indiana Governor Oliver P. Morton, trying to secure for his son "some post of honor, as well as profit" (p. 45). Another pictorial focuses on the bureaucratic misunderstanding over Capt. John J. Waller of the 17th Indiana, who returned to his regiment after sick leave unaware that he had been dismissed from the army for being absent without leave. Most of the photographs feature members of the Lightning Brigade; only a few relate to the other "major players" in the Chickamauga campaign.

The author uses a wide range of published and manuscript primary sources in his study to present a detailed account of the Lightning Brigade's exploits in the Chickamauga campaign. At times Baumgartner's enthusiasm for the sources hampers his presentation. Often he presents long quotations and passages from soldiers that would be more effective if paraphrased or shortened. The fact that many of the block quotations come from unpublished sources mitigates this weakness somewhat, but their overall effect is to weaken the focus of the work.

A lack of succinct analysis also hampers Baumgartner's book. He suggests that his study will show why Wilder's brigade was one of the Civil War's premier fighting units by telling the story of its "integral role" at Chickamauga. The detailed account he provides suggests the brigade's effectiveness and importance to the battle, but apart from a few sentences in the preface, Baumgartner rarely moves beyond the narrative to give an assessment of the brigade's performance during the battle. Such analysis is important to any argument about the effectiveness of Wilder's brigade, but the study does not provide the reader any real criteria to judge how important the brigade was to the Federal effort. Instead of discussing Wilder's postwar career and the construction of the brigade's monument at Chickamauga, Baumgartner might better serve the reader by offering such an analysis.

Blue Lightning effectively provides a detailed account of Wilder's brigade during the Chickamauga *Campaign*, however, and the photographs alone make it an appealing book for those interested in the Lightning Brigade. Baumgartner has written an informative and attractive book, but by failing to provide a more succinct analysis he misses a good opportunity to strengthen his case for the Lightning Brigade's status as one of the Civil War's premier fighting units.

Jonathan M. Berkey   Pennsylvania State University

Weep Not For me, Dear Mother, Elizabeth Whitley Roberson (Pelican Publishing Company, P. O. Box 3110, Gretna, LA 70054), 1996. Maps, illus., index. 168pp. $19.95. Paperback.

Weep Not For Me, Dear Mother, a biography of Eli Pinson Landers, focuses on the years from his enlistment in Company H (Flint Hill Grays), 16th

Georgia Infantry, from late summer of 1861 until his death in 1863. The author tells Pinson's story with lengthy passages from letters written to his family or they to him, connecting these with a narrative that helps to explain events and flesh out the story. The youthful private soldier's personal concerns are the core of the letters and, consequently, are the focus of the author and the resulting story. Those concerns primarily involve Landers' efforts at coping with the new society and the military life in which he found himself.

In 1861, Landers was a nineteen-year old a farm boy from Yellow River, Gwinnett County, Georgia. His family owned a small parcel of land on which they grew wheat, cotton and corn; they did not keep slaves. When the war came, his father was already dead and his mother and sisters depended upon him to support the family. Nonetheless, Landers joined the army and was sent almost immediately to the Virginia theatre, where his unit became a part of James Longstreet's First Corps.

The issues that concerned Landers were typical of those that interested thousands of other young men swept up in the war. His letters explain why he joined the army, offer observations on camp life, and try to explain the meaning of battle. There are no insights into the general state of military affairs, an absence hardly unexpected in the writings of a man of Lander's rank. Neither does he offer opinions of the leadership of his regiment's commanders, James G. Barrow and Howell Cobb.

Landers expended considerable time explaining why he had joined the army. He saw the war as an effort by the North to subjugate the South and, as a result, believed his liberty was threatened. He usually referred to his purpose in fighting as securing independence and liberty. The revolutionary ideology of almost eighty years before was firmly fixed in his vocabulary. Within this ideological framework he had little choice but to fight; his honor required it. His letters repeatedly expressed his need to do his duty and come home with honor or to die. For Landers, not to fight would be to disgrace himself and his relations.

Joining the army to fight for freedom, Landers quickly discovered, as did many other soldiers, that military life presented its own challenge to personal independence, and this theme became a major one in his letters. At Richmond in 1861, he noted that it was "hard for a white man to tote a written pass like a Negro!" (p. 27) Later he would write, "We are like birds in a cage but I have given myself up to Providence and I hope I will be present both soul and body" (p. 30). On the whole, Landers' early impressions of military life were that the army was dreadful; it is clear that only his belief that he was doing the right thing held him to his duty. Increasingly, his letters shifted from descriptions of events he was experiencing to a devotion to affairs at home and appeals for more news so he would not lose contact with local events.

Some of the best letters are Landers' descriptions of battles. He was engaged with his unit in most of its battles, beginning at Lee's Mill on April 16 1862, through the Seven Days' Battles, Crampton's Gap, Sharpsburg, Fredericksburg, Chancellorsville, Gettysburg, and Chickamauga. His description of his first battle at Lee's Mill indicated that even after almost a year of training, the 16th Georgia was not prepared for a fight. In a charge on Federal units that had driven Confederate forces from their trenches, Landers and his friends drove forward without forming a line, shot whenever they had a chance, and took cover behind trees. Landers noted that some never fired a shot, while others "lay behind logs as close to the ground as young rabbits till the battle was over" (p. 72); still more headed back to camp.

Landers also provided insights into the meaning of battle for the participant. During his first confrontation with the enemy, "when the bullets would whistle around my head I felt sort of ticklish" (p. 73). While not frightened, battle quickly destroyed any heroic illusions he may have possessed. The horrors of battle and particularly its dangers became a pervasive theme in his correspondence. At Crampton's Gap, all of his mess mates were killed, wounded, or captured. Only five of the men of his company were present at Sharpsburg three days later. His letters home on September 25, 1862, demonstrated that he had acquired a fatalism not previously revealed when he wrote: "Goodby my good old Mother if I never see you again" (p. 89). Afterwards his letters increasingly were preoccupied with his own death and preparing for it. Despite his premonitions, death in battle was not his fate. Like so many other soldiers, Landers perished in Rome, Georgia, from typhoid fever on October 27, 1863, while his unit was participating in the Knoxville Campaign.

This biography will not offer the specialist or scholar new insights into the life of the common soldier. The author does not go beyond the generalizations offered in studies such as Bell I. Wiley's *The Life of Johnny Reb* (1943), Gerald F. Linderman's *Embattled Courage* (1987), Reid Mitchell's *Civil War Soldiers* (1988), or James I. Robertson, Jr.'s *Soldiers, Blue and Gray* (1988). Still, Landers' story is an engaging one and well worth reading, in part because his letters are so informative and well-written.

Carl H. Moneyhon   University of Arkansas at Little Rock

INDEX

WHEN the DEVIL CAME DOWN to DIXIE

Ben Butler in New Orleans

Chester G. Hearn

"A lucid, balanced account of Butler's New Orleans days. . . . For well over a century the story of Ben Butler has been read in New Orleans and much of the South as a horror tale. Read today it comes much closer to comedy. . . . The spectacle of the giddily venal Butler sacking the arrogant banks and corrupt civic coffers of New Orleans is genuinely delicious. . . . Though Hearn is no comedian, he provides the raw material, and the reader can do the rest."—Jonathan Yardley, *Washington Post Book World*

Illustrated · $26.95

The Pride of the Confederate Artillery

The Washington Artillery in the Army of Tennessee

Nathaniel Cheairs Hughes, Jr.

"One of the finest southern unit histories in decades. Deeply researched and superbly written, [it] never loses its focus."—Peter Cozzens, author of *The Civil War in the West*

"Civil War history at its best . . . a finely crafted book detailing the sweat and grit that made the Fifth Company, Washington Artillery an outstanding example of the heart and soul of the southern war effort."—Wiley Sword, author of *Embrace an Angry Wind*

A History Book Club Selection

Illustrated · $29.95

new in paperback

Wearing of the Gray

Being Personal Portraits, Scenes, and Adventures of the War

John Esten Cooke

With a New Introduction by Emory M. Thomas

"One of the finest, most charming of Confederate reminiscences. Cooke's accounts of life in the Army of Northern Virginia ring with the truth of intimate association. . . . A combination of validity and vitality almost unmatched in the literature of the Civil War."—*Civil War History*

$19.95 paper

Liddell's Record

St. John Richardson Liddell

Edited by Nathaniel Cheairs Hughes, Jr.

Liddell, a prosperous planter, served under P.G.T. Beauregard, William J. Hardee, and Albert Sidney Johnston, and associated with the upper circles of the Confederate military and political high command. Here is his judgment on why the South failed, an unusually harsh criticism of its leadership and soldiers rarely found in personal accounts.

$11.95 paper

New Civil War Titles

Lee's Last Major General:
Bryan Grimes of North Carolina

T. Harell Allen

The first biography of the last major general appointed by Lee. Grimes fought in most of the Army of Northern Virginia's battles and was prominent in the 1864-65 campaigns. Based on previously unpublished Grimes family letters, with a Foreword by historian Robert E. L. Krick. Oriiginal maps, photos, notes, biblio., index, d.j., 346pp. Cloth. ISBN 1-882810-23-6. $24.95

Triumph & Defeat:
The Vicksburg Campaign

Terrence J. Winschel

Foreword by noted historian EDWIN C. BEARSS!

Ten fascinating chapters on this complex and decisive campaign. Terry Winschel, chief historian at Vicksburg National Military Park, weaves a lifetime of scholarship into this collection. Topics include the battles of Port Gibson and Champion Hill, siege warfare, the river war, Grierson's Raid, Walker's Texas Division, civilian life, and much more. *Triumph & Defeat* sheds new light on this important campaign that sealed the fate of the Confederacy. Maps, photos, notes, biblio., index, d.j., 248pp. Cloth. ISBN: 1-882810-31-7. $24.95.

Savas Publishing Company
202 First Street S.E., Suite 103A, Mason City, IA 50401

Distributed by Stackpole Books, 5067 Ritter Road, Mechanicsburg, PA 17055. 1-800-732-3669.

"Groundbreaking"

Union and Confederate Submarine Warfare in the Civil War

Mark K. Ragan

If you think submarine warfare in the Civil War began and ended with the *CSS Hunley*, this groundbreaking study by underwater expert Mark Ragan will surprise you. In reality, both sides designed, constructed, and launched numerous operational submarines. Ragan's work examines in-depth how and where these vessels were constructed, who built them, what they looked like, and what role they played. Details submarine attacks in Hampton Roads, Mobile Bay, Charleston, and more, including information on·the little-known Triton Group, a clandestine Southern operation, and the Singer Submarine Corps.

Union and Confederate Submarine Warfare in the Civil War is based on previously undiscovered Confederate Secret Service documents, letters, factory records, diagrams, and blueprints! This book will forever change the way you look at the Civil War. Map, photos & drawings, notes, biblio., index, d.j., 336pp., cloth. ISBN: 1-882810-32-5. $29.95

Foreword by best-selling author CLIVE CUSSLER!

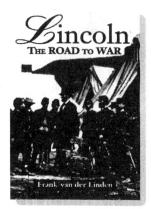
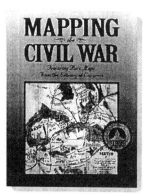